Visual Studio 2013 Cookbook

Over 50 simple but incredibly effective recipes to get you up and running with the powerful features of Visual Studio 2013

Jeff Martin

Richard Banks

PUBLISHING

professional expertise distilled

BIRMINGHAM - MUMBAI

Visual Studio 2013 Cookbook

First published: September 2012

Second Edition: March 2014

Production Reference: 1100314

Published by Packt Publishing Ltd.
Livery Place
35 Livery Street
Birmingham B3 2PB, UK.

ISBN 978-1-78217-196-6

www.packtpub.com

Cover Image by Dan Martin (www.danfm.net)

Credits

About the Authors

Jeff Martin is a long-time technology enthusiast and has been a contributing writer for InfoQ (www.infoq.com) for over two years, focusing on .NET and Microsoft-based platforms. Having experience in writing, testing, and designing software, he enjoys learning about new technologies and explaining them to a broader audience.

Readers are encouraged to follow @VSDevTips on Twitter to receive updates on the book as well as news for getting the most out of Visual Studio.

I would like to thank my lovely wife Carolyn for her love and understanding during my frequent late-night writing sessions. Your support for these projects means more to me than I can express.

I would also like to thank my brother Dan Martin for providing a great photo for the cover of this book.

Finally, thank you to my entire production team at Packt Publishing for their effort and assistance in producing this book.

Richard Banks has developed software for the last 20 years for a wide range of industries and development platforms. Over the years he has played many roles including that of a developer, team lead, project manager, and CIO/CTO. He is a Professional Scrum Trainer, runs the Sydney ALT.NET user group and the Talking Shop Down Under podcast. He owns and contributes to a few open source projects, and has spoken at Microsoft TechEd and a number of other events and user groups around Australia. For some strange reason, he gets a real kick out of helping development teams to improve and produce great software. If you want to get in touch, he tweets at `@rbanks54` and blogs at `http://www.richard-banks.org/`. He currently works as a Principal Consultant for Readify and is a Microsoft Visual Studio ALM MVP.

It might have my name on the front cover but a book is never the work of just one person.

I would firstly like to thank my fantastic wife, Anne, and my two wonderful children, Hannah and Leisel, for giving me the time and space to work on this book. Their support throughout the process has been invaluable, and without that I would never have undertaken this book in the first place.

I'd also like to thank the staff and Packt Publishing for the opportunity and help in bringing this together, and my tech reviewers who gave up their spare time reading my scribble and checking if what I wrote actually made sense instead of being just a delirium-fuelled pile of nonsense.

Thank you all!

About the Reviewers

Hulot has been working in the IT industry for more than 20 years in different capabilities, from software development, project management to IT marketing product development and management. He has worked for multinational companies such as Royal Philips Electronics, PricewaterhouseCoopers, and Microsoft. Currently, He has been working as an independent IT consultant. He is a Computer Science lecturer at two Brazilian universities. He holds a Ph.D. in Computer Science and Electronics from the University of Southampton, UK and a B.Sc. in Physics from University of São Paulo, Brazil.

> I would like to thank my wife Mylene Melly for her continuous support. I would also like to thank my many colleagues over the years who have made it possible to learn what I now know about software development and the computer industry.

Darren Kopp is a father, husband, software engineer, and gamer. Darren started programming when making a website for his clan in the game Tribes using ASP and then moved on to ASP.NET when .NET 1.1 was released.

Darren started professional development work in the golf industry, developing systems ranging from e-commerce solutions for golf shops to systems tracking swing profiles of golfers. He then moved on to the construction industry where he developed software that integrated payroll, human resources, service management, and project management.

Darren currently works for DevResults that provides web-based solutions to the international development and humanitarian community.

When Darren isn't coding or spending time with family, you can find him tweeting jokes and playing Team Fortress 2 and Battlefield 4.

Anand Narayanaswamy works as an editor with InfoQ based in Trivandrum, Kerala, India. He is an ASPInsider and was a Microsoft Most Valuable Professional (MVP) from 2002 to 2011.

Anand also worked as a chief technical editor for ASPAlliance.com and contributed several articles and reviews for DevPro, c-sharpcorner.com, developer.com, codeguru.com, and various other community sites.

Anand also worked as a technical editor for several popular publishers such as Sams, Addison-Wesley Professional, Wrox, Deitel, Packt Publishing, and Manning.

He blogs at www.learnxpress.com and can be reached at www.facebook.com/anandn. His twitter handle is @visualanand.

Sergiy Suchok graduated in 2004 with honors from the Faculty of Cybernetics, Taras Shevchenko National University of Kyiv (Ukraine) and has since then been keen on information technology. He is currently working in the banking sector and has a Ph.D. in Economics. Sergiy is the co-author of more than 45 articles and participated in more than 20 scientific and practical conferences devoted to the economic and mathematical modeling. He is a member of the *New Atlantis* Youth Public Organization (newatlantida.org.ua) and devotes his leisure time to environmental protection issues, historical and patriotic development, and popularization of a grateful attitude towards the Earth. He also writes poetry and short stories and makes macramé.

> I would like to thank my wife and my young daughter for their patience and understanding while I reviewed this book.

David Thibault has been a .NET developer since Version 1.1. He has worked on a wide variety of software solutions in various domains such as e-commerce, retailing, social networking, and business management. Besides .NET, he has recently acquired an interest for other technologies such as NodeJS and AngularJS. David currently works for Sigmund, a young agency focusing on bringing businesses to the digital age. He lives in Quebec City, Canada, and he loves Scotch whisky.

Ken Tucker is a Microsoft MVP who enjoys working on Windows Phone and Windows Store apps.

www.PacktPub.com

Support files, eBooks, discount offers, and more

You might want to visit www.PacktPub.com for support files and downloads related to your book.

Did you know that Packt offers eBook versions of every book published, with PDF and ePub files available? You can upgrade to the eBook version at www.PacktPub.com and as a print book customer, you are entitled to a discount on the eBook copy. Get in touch with us at service@packtpub.com for more details.

At www.PacktPub.com, you can also read a collection of free technical articles, sign up for a range of free newsletters, and receive exclusive discounts and offers on Packt books and eBooks.

http://PacktLib.PacktPub.com

Do you need instant solutions to your IT questions? PacktLib is Packt's online digital book library. Here, you can access, read, and search across Packt's entire library of books.

Why Subscribe?

- ▸ Fully searchable across every book published by Packt
- ▸ Copy and paste, print, and bookmark content
- ▸ On demand and accessible via web browser

Free Access for Packt account holders

If you have an account with Packt at www.PacktPub.com, you can use this to access PacktLib today and view nine entirely free books. Simply use your login credentials for immediate access.

Instant Updates on New Packt Books

Get notified! Find out when new books are published by following @PacktEnterprise on Twitter, or the *Packt Enterprise* Facebook page.

Table of Contents

Preface

The *Visual Studio 2013 Cookbook* has been written to provide you with an informative tour around **Visual Studio 2013** (**VS2013**). Topics have been broken down into quick-to-access segments called recipes, allowing you to easily find the material that interests you.

Some recipes will directly apply to your regular tasks while others are intended to shed some light on overlooked corners of Visual Studio. Given its long pedigree, extensive functionality has been added over the years, which is easy to overlook. The goal is that by reading this book, you will become more proficient with the tool that you use most as a Windows developer.

This second edition has been revised and expanded to cover the new features of VS2013 so that regardless of whether you are upgrading from VS2012 or are making a bigger step from an earlier version, there will be helpful tips and discussion of this new version. For those of you who purchased the first edition, welcome back, and to our new readers thank you for joining us. Let's get started!

While you were gone

Since the launch of VS2012, Microsoft has released four updates referred to as 2012.1, 2012.2, and so on. Each have added functionality to the original program, and each installed package is cumulative, meaning that only the newest one has to be installed to provide the benefits of all previous updates.

VS2012 Update 1

First and foremost is the ability VS2012.1 provides for C++ developers to target Windows XP clients while using the VS2012 compiler. This is a key ability if you desire to continue compiling applications that run on Windows XP and Vista as well as Windows 7 and 8. JavaScript programmers will appreciate the inclusion of memory profiling and memory analysis tools. SharePoint developers will gain load testing support and the use of SharePoint emulators. Full details are available at `http://support.microsoft.com/kb/2797915`.

VS2012 Update 2

This update includes ASP.NET and Web Tools 2012.2, unit testing support for Windows Phone, and broader unit testing capabilities for Windows Store apps. 2012.2 includes a host of bug fixes and stability improvements that benefit all areas of the program, right from the debugger to memory leaks in C++ based solutions, and several use cases that would cause the IDE to crash. Full details are available at `http://support.microsoft.com/kb/2797912`.

VS2012 Update 3

2012.3 primarily provides bug patches and performance improvements. Notable for those using VS2012 and VS2013 concurrently is 2012.3's improved compatibility with VS2013 projects. Several stability fixes were made that among other things prevent crashes in web projects, fix a conflict between VS2012 and VS2010, and correct slowdowns when developing mixed-mode C++ applications. Installing Update 3 provides the ability to install the Microsoft Visual Studio Tools for Git, a popular open source version control system. Full details are available at `http://support.microsoft.com/kb/2835600`.

VS2012 Update 4

Similar to 2012.3, this update is focused in bug fixes and stability enhancements. As this release coincides with the production release of VS2013, it provides some improved compatibility for sharing projects/solutions between VS2012 and VS2013. Full details are available at `http://support.microsoft.com/kb/2872520`.

 At the time of this writing, there is no reason to avoid installing the latest update available for VS2012 whether using an Express edition or one of the premium editions. Several meaningful improvements have been made to the product since its original release date that benefit all users. Microsoft provides both a web-based installer and a complete standalone ISO at `http://go.microsoft.com/fwlink/?LinkId=301713`.

Choosing a version of Visual Studio 2013

Visual Studio comes in several different versions, each with different capabilities and target audiences. In all cases, the minimum supported operating system is Microsoft Windows 7 SP1 on the desktop or Windows Server 2008 R2 SP1 on the server. The two biggest differences of the Visual Studio line-up are between the Express and non-Express (premium) versions. Express editions are offered by Microsoft free of charge, and target a specific type of application development:

> ▸ **Visual Studio Express 2013 for Web**: As the name implies, this is appropriate for those seeking to build web-based applications using technologies that include HTML5, CSS, and JavaScript.

- **Visual Studio Express 2013 for Windows**: Probably better titled "...for Windows Store apps", this edition targets Windows Store apps exclusively. HTML5/JavaScript, C#, C++, and Visual Basic are all acceptable choices for app development. An emulator is bundled for testing apps across various devices.

- **Visual Studio Express 2013 for Windows Desktop**: Traditional Windows desktop applications can be created with this edition using C#, C++, or Visual Basic.

 Multiple Express editions can be installed side by side, so you feel free to install any/all of the preceding editions as needed for your work.

The non-Express editions run from Visual Studio Professional 2013 to Visual Studio Ultimate 2013. Ultimate has the entire available functionality, whereas Professional is limited to **Peek Definition**. One advantage all non-Express editions share is that all possible development types (web, apps, and desktop) are available in a single installation. The non-Express editions are as follows:

- **Visual Studio Professional 2013**: This supports development of all application types and includes the Peek Definition feature.

- **Visual Studio Premium 2013**: In addition to the preceding edition, notable features include project management functionality, coded UI testing for XAML Windows Store 8.1 apps, and C++ Profile Guided Optimization.

- **Visual Studio Ultimate 2013**: In addition to the two preceding editions, notable features include CodeLens, IntelliTrace, Memory Dump Analyzer, and cloud-based load testing.

- **Visual Studio Test Professional 2013**: As its name implies, this edition primarily focuses on testing.

Visual Studio 2013 will make certain options available to you based on the underlying version of Windows that you are running. If you are running Windows 8.1, you will only be able to create new Windows Store applications for Windows 8.1. You will be able to open existing Windows 8 app solutions in VS2013, but not create new ones. You are able to create new Windows 8 apps only with VS2012, but this should be considered a special case given the arrival of Windows 8.1. Windows Store applications cannot be developed with any version of Visual Studio on Windows 7, Windows Server (any version), or previous versions of Windows.

Picking a version

If you are an independent developer, you will most likely want to download the Express edition(s) that apply to the type of program that you are developing. Express editions can be installed side by side, so there is no need to limit yourself to just one. Among the paid versions, choose which one meets the requirements of your work. If you are not price-limited, picking the Ultimate version is the simplest route. A full comparison of the various versions is available at `http://www.visualstudio.com/products/compare-visual-studio-products-vs`.

Visual Studio 2013 Update 1 has been released and primarily consists of stability patches and bug fixes. It should be applied to your system regardless of the edition of VS2013 that you have selected. More information about Update 1 is available at `http://support.microsoft.com/kb/2911573`. As this book goes to print, a preview of Update 2 has been announced. This release will be delivering new features as well bug fixes. Follow this book's Twitter feed for more news as this becomes available (`@VSDevTips`) or `https://twitter.com/vsdevtips`.

What this book covers

Chapter 1, Discovering Visual Studio 2013, starts us off by taking a tour of the new features found in the editor itself and covers all VS2013's key refinements, from logging in to project navigation.

Chapter 2, Getting Started with Windows Store Applications, examines the development process for Windows Store apps for Windows 8.1. The full process of obtaining a developer license to building, testing, and publishing an app is covered.

Chapter 3, Web Development – ASP.NET, HTML5, CSS, and JavaScript, covers several areas of web development and how VS2013 can assist you. Here, the multi-browser preview is covered as well as editor enhancements that can benefit HTML5, CSS, and JavaScript programmers.

Chapter 4, .NET Framework 4.5.1 Development, focuses on developing applications that run on .NET. Desktop application development is still a key market and shows ways VS2013 can help.

Chapter 5, Debugging Your .NET Application, profiles the various ways to debug your .NET-based code. Code isn't always available on your development environment and this profile shows ways to deal with separate machines, whether they are tables or in production.

Chapter 6, Asynchrony in .NET, deals with the use of asynchronous code to provide more responsive output and how it may benefit your applications.

Chapter 7, *Unwrapping C++ Development*, tackles the elder statesman of languages severed by VS2013. Several recipes are provided, which will benefit your C++ usage; some of the areas covered include unit testing, XAML, and DirectX.

Chapter 8, *Working with Team Foundation Server 2013*, describes how Team Foundation Server can benefit your productivity. Whether you are an independent developer or part of a large corporate effort, you'll see how modern source control can help.

Chapter 9, *Languages*, takes a moment to look at some useful languages that are new to Visual Studio: TypeScript and Python. Python has a long and successful history, and now it is a first-class citizen on Visual Studio. We'll take a look at how Python can help .NET developers.

Appendix, *Visual Studio Medley*, the assortment of preceding topics doesn't cover everything that VS2013 can do. We'll cover some ways to extend Visual Studio's abilities and how to get your app ready for consumption by end users.

What you need for this book

To follow the recipes in this book, you will need a copy of Visual Studio 2013. Some of the features covered in the recipes may only be available in specific editions of Visual Studio. Whenever possible, any specific version requirements will be noted.

If you wish to follow one of these recipes and you do not have the right edition, trial versions of the premium versions can be downloaded from the Microsoft website enabling you to see if a particular feature would benefit your project.

For any of the recipes that deal with Windows Store applications, you will need to be using Windows 8.1 as your operating system.

Who this book is for

If you already know your way around previous versions of Visual Studio, if you are familiar with Microsoft development, and if you're looking to quickly get up to speed with the latest improvements in the 2013 incarnation of Microsoft's number one development tool, then this book is for you.

If you are an experienced developer who has used Eclipse or Xcode, you should also be able to find this book useful for exploring the differences between your tools and the latest that Microsoft has to offer.

Conventions

In this book, you will find a number of styles of text that distinguish between different kinds of information. Here are some examples of these styles, and an explanation of their meaning.

Code words in text, database table names, folder names, filenames, file extensions, pathnames, dummy URLs, user input, and Twitter handles are shown as follows: "Open the `VS2012_Web` solution and run the application."

A block of code is set as follows:

```
<appSettings>
  <add key="vs:enableBrowserLink" value="true"/>
</appSettings>
```

When we wish to draw your attention to a particular part of a code block, the relevant lines or items are set in bold:

```
<system.webServer>
  <modules runAllManagedModulesForAllRequests="true" />
</system.webServer>
```

Any command-line input or output is written as follows:

```
Get-Command *intelli*
```

New terms and **important words** are shown in bold. Words that you see on the screen, in menus or dialog boxes for example, appear in the text like this: "The **Preview Selected Items** button is a toggle button."

Keyboard shortcuts such as *Ctrl* or *F4* are formatted as shown.

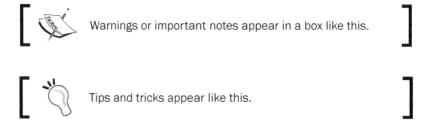

Warnings or important notes appear in a box like this.

Tips and tricks appear like this.

Reader feedback

Feedback from our readers is always welcome. Let us know what you think about this book—what you liked or may have disliked. Reader feedback is important for us to develop titles that you really get the most out of.

To send us general feedback, simply send an e-mail to `feedback@packtpub.com`, and mention the book title through the subject of your message.

If there is a topic that you have expertise in and you are interested in either writing or contributing to a book, see our author guide on `www.packtpub.com/authors`.

Customer support

Now that you are the proud owner of a Packt book, we have a number of things to help you to get the most from your purchase.

Downloading the example code

You can download the example code files for all Packt books you have purchased from your account at `http://www.packtpub.com`. If you purchased this book elsewhere, you can visit `http://www.packtpub.com/support` and register to have the files e-mailed directly to you.

Downloading the color images of this book

We also provide you a PDF file that has color images of the screenshots/diagrams used in this book. The color images will help you better understand the changes in the output. You can download this file from `https://www.packtpub.com/sites/default/files/downloads/1966EN_ColoredImages.pdf`.

Errata

Although we have taken every care to ensure the accuracy of our content, mistakes do happen. If you find a mistake in one of our books—maybe a mistake in the text or the code—we would be grateful if you would report this to us. By doing so, you can save other readers from frustration and help us improve subsequent versions of this book. If you find any errata, please report them by visiting `http://www.packtpub.com/support`, selecting your book, clicking on the errata submission form link, and entering the details of your errata. Once your errata are verified, your submission will be accepted and the errata will be uploaded to our website, or added to any list of existing errata, under the **Errata** section of that title.

Piracy

Piracy of copyright material on the Internet is an ongoing problem across all media. At Packt, we take the protection of our copyright and licenses very seriously. If you come across any illegal copies of our works, in any form, on the Internet, please provide us with the location address or website name immediately so that we can pursue a remedy.

Please contact us at `copyright@packtpub.com` with a link to the suspected pirated material.

We appreciate your help in protecting our authors, and our ability to bring you valuable content.

Questions

You can contact us at `questions@packtpub.com` if you are having a problem with any aspect of the book, and we will do our best to address it.

1
Discovering Visual Studio 2013

In this chapter, we will cover:

- ▸ Synchronizing settings
- ▸ Touring the VS2013 IDE
- ▸ Project round-tripping
- ▸ Managing the editor windows
- ▸ Finding Visual Studio commands
- ▸ Searching and navigating
- ▸ Navigating in depth

Introduction

The arrival of **Visual Studio 2013** (**VS2013**) marks the continuation of Microsoft's desire to produce more frequent updates to the Visual Studio platform. If you are coming to VS2013 from VS2012, you will find a more familiar appearance. Users upgrading to VS2013 from VS2010 will find greater differences and need to spend a bit more time learning the new interface. This chapter will provide a walk-through of the major changes and explain how VS2013's IDE will benefit you, regardless of the languages you are programming with.

VS2013 has focused a great deal on improving the usability and the power of the editor and surrounding windows that you use every day in your work. Before exploring specific features that apply only to certain areas, this chapter examines how the IDE can benefit your work regardless of whether you write C++ console applications or use JavaScript to write Windows Store apps.

The goal of this chapter is to provide you with an overview of the IDE-related features of VS2013. The chapter will begin by describing the integration of Microsoft accounts with the IDE and the value that this can provide. Next comes a review of the IDE, with a focus on the new features found in VS2013. Realizing that in the real world, circumstances can require supporting pre-VS2013 projects, we'll look at how Visual Studio utilizes project round-tripping to enable working with these older project types. The chapter will then wrap up with a couple of recipes on day-to-day editing and navigation tips designed to increase your productivity. Like any set of complex tools, an initial investment in learning the nuances can provide lasting dividends.

Synchronizing settings

One of the first things that you will notice upon opening VS2013 is the request to log in with a Microsoft account. You can use any existing Microsoft account that you have, including Outlook/Hotmail, OneDrive (formerly known as SkyDrive), and Xbox Live. If you have an MSDN account, Microsoft recommends that you use it to log in to Visual Studio. If you don't, or if you would prefer to use a new account, you can create one at `https://login.live.com/`. Microsoft groups the settings by product type, so there is one set of roaming settings linked to all editions of Visual Studio Professional, Premium, and Ultimate. A separate set of settings is synched across the Express editions of Visual Studio. The result is that the settings saved for VS Express 2013 for Windows will not sync when you log in to VS2013 Professional.

In this recipe, we will look at how this synchronization works and what it will coordinate on your behalf.

Getting ready

To explore, launch your copy of Visual Studio 2013.

How to do it...

If you are not prompted to sign in at startup, you can always sign in from within Visual Studio. The arrow in the following screenshot indicates where the **Sign in** option is located:

Currently, VS2013 will sync options from the following categories:

- **Environment** : This section consists of several subitems:
  - ❏ **Fonts and Colors**: This includes preferences for the text used throughout the editor
  - ❏ **Color theme of IDE**: This provides built-in themes including light/dark/blue
  - ❏ **Keyboard**: This includes user-defined keyboard shortcuts and the selected keyboard-mapping scheme
  - ❏ **Startup**: This indicates what should display when VS2013 opens

- **Text Editor**: A multitude of settings including tabs versus spaces, word wrap, scroll bar placement, and so on

- **Environment Aliases**: (Not shown, applies to premium versions only) Commands defined in the command window (*Ctrl + Alt + A*)

  The following screenshot highlights the synchronized categories:

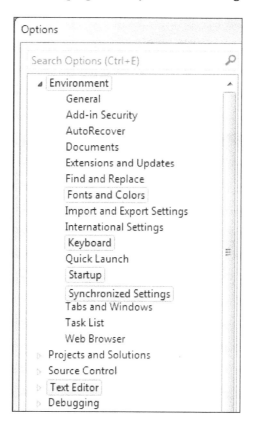

The **Options** dialog box in VS2013 has a couple of usability enhancements. First, it has its own integrated search box (once **Options** is opened, the hotkey is *Ctrl + E*) for specifically searching within the **Options** dialog box. Second, the dialog is now resizable, making it much more useful for viewing settings that have lengthy configuration options.

How it works...

Microsoft stores a copy of your settings on their servers. A constant Internet connection is not required to use Visual Studio, but your settings will not synchronize until you are reconnected. If a connection is not available, you cannot login until Internet access is restored, but Visual Studio will still be usable. Taking it one step further, VS2013 remembers if you were logged in the last time when you closed the program, so your last known settings will be available as they are stored locally.

There's more...

All synchronization options are configurable by navigating to **Options** | **Environment** | **Synchronized Settings**, and you may opt to have any combination of the preceding categories synched. This configuration of settings is specific to each machine and does not transfer. By default, VS2013 will attempt to synchronize all settings if you are logged in with a Microsoft account.

Touring the VS2013 IDE

The user interface in VS2013's IDE has several differences from VS2012 and the previous versions of Visual Studio. Let's take a look at what is available in this recipe.

Getting ready

All you will need for this recipe is a copy of VS2013 so that you can follow along with where different options are located. The following screenshot provides an overview of what will be covered:

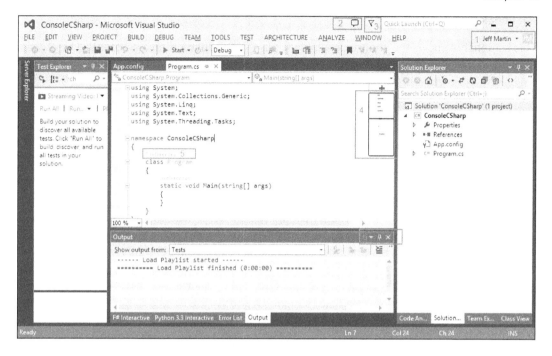

The legend for the highlighted items in the preceding screenshot is as follows:

- ▸ The user's account entry/selection is indicated with **1**
- ▸ The notification center is indicated with **2**
- ▸ The **Feedback** menu is indicated with **3**
- ▸ The scrollbar thumbnail is indicated with **4**
- ▸ CodeLens (Ultimate only) is indicated with **5**
- ▸ The editor window controls are indicated with **6**

How to do it...

Over the next few pages, we are going to take a firsthand look at the new areas of the Visual Studio IDE. You may follow along with your own project or use the sample project where indicated.

Feedback

This screenshot shows the choices available when the **Feedback** menu is accessed by clicking on the chat balloon (far left icon):

Indicated by a chat balloon, the feedback icon provides an immediate way to send feedback to Microsoft from within VS2013. When the chat balloon is clicked, a drop-down list appears, allowing you to select from either **Send a Smile** (indicating a positive commentary) or **Send a Frown** (indicating negative commentary). Functionally, there is no difference in the dialog box that appears, but the choice of a smile or frown allows you to provide context for your remarks so that there is no ambiguity in your message. Each option allows you to include an e-mail address so Microsoft has a way to respond, and the frown option has an additional checkbox to indicate whether or not your comments are describing a bug.

The menu also provides the ability to report a bug and access the MSDN forums within Visual Studio. Both options provide a quick way to accomplish these tasks so that you make a report or seek help and get back to coding with minimal distractions.

Notifications

Between the **Feedback** icon and the **Quick Launch** field is the flag icon representing notifications:

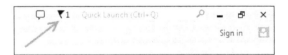

In the preceding screenshot, you can see that one update is pending. The notification flag is designed to provide an unobtrusive alert when updates to VS2013 and the installed packages are available. Notifications listed in the sidebar are color-coded with yellow and red, which are used to indicate medium and high priorities respectively. Examples of notifications that could appear include notices about updates to Visual Studio, updates to installed extensions or samples, or notices alerting that the trial period is ending. Notifications may be dismissed en masse, and once they are dismissed they do not reappear.

User account

If you have signed in to VS2013 with a Microsoft account (see the *Synchronizing settings* recipe), this area displays the graphical avatar along with your account's display name. The following screenshot shows the difference in the display that occurs when you log in:

It also provides a way to sign in if you have not done so, or if you wish to change the active account being used. In the preceding screenshot, the left-hand side has the text **Sign in**, and a grey icon indicates that the user has yet to login. On the right-hand side, you can see the difference when the user has logged in, as the username has replaced the **Sign in** text, and the gray icon has changed to reflect the user's avatar (which in this case is a green icon overlaid with the white initials of the user's name).

Scroll bar thumbnail

The scroll bar has expanded its usefulness in VS2013. You can now customize it to show your overall position in a source file, and provide a tool tip that lets you examine code elsewhere in your current file without changing your current location. The new option is called **map mode**, as opposed to the historical behavior that is called **bar mode** (which is the traditional scrollbar appearance and behavior). All aspects of the map mode are customizable, including whether it appears at all, its width (narrow, medium, or wide), and the ability to show the preview tool tip.

The following screenshot shows these features in action:

```
Program.cs  ⊉ ✕
  ⚙ BuildNeuralNetworkDemo.NeuralNetwork              ▾  ⦿ NeuralNetwork(int numInput, int numHidden, int num( ▾
                                                                                                      ╬
        // back-prop momentum specific arrays (could be local to method Train)
        private double[][] ihPrevWeightsDelta;   // for momentum with back-propagat
        private double[] hPrevBiasesDelta;
        private double[][] hoPrevWeightsDelta;
        private double[] oPrevBiasesDelta;
                                                                  1
                         2
        public NeuralNetwork(int numInput, int numHidden, int numOutput)
        {
            rnd = new Random(0); // for InitializeWeights() and Shuffle()

            this.numInput = numInput;
            this.numHidden = numHidden;        public void SetWeights(double[] weight
            this.numOutput = numOutput;        {
                                                   // copy weights and biases in weig
            this.inputs = new double[num]         int numWeights = (numInput * numHi
                                                   if (weights.Length != numWeights)
            this.ihWeights = MakeMatrix(r             throw new Exception("Bad weigh
            this.hBiases = new double[num
            this.hOutputs = new double[numHidden];
```

The preceding screenshot shows the scroll bar configured to be in map mode. The first arrow (marked as **1**) indicates that what is being displayed in the editor is located relative to the overall source file. The second arrow (marked as **2**) is pointing to the preview tool tip that appears when your mouse cursor hovers over the scroll bar.

The scroll bar's pull down feature remains. When it's used to split the main window, it allows for two independent viewing panes of the same file, and each can have their own independent vertical scroll bar. In the split view mode, both vertical scroll bars share the same options (width, bar mode versus map mode, and so on).

The following screenshot lists all of the options available for configuring the scroll bar's functionality. It can be accessed directly by right-clicking on the vertical scroll bar and selecting **Scroll Bar Options...**. Alternatively, it is accessible in VS2013's main **Options** dialog box by navigating to **Tools | Options**, with the scroll bar settings listed under **Text Editor | All Languages | Scroll Bars**. For additional customizations, you may set the language (C++, C#, and so on) settings for the scroll bar in the **Options** dialog box if desired:

Peek Definition

Visual Studio has had the **Go To Definition** (*F12*) option for several versions now. When we right-click on a method, or move the cursor to it, selecting the **Go To Definition** option will automatically bring you directly to the file with the corresponding definition. While you can easily navigate back and forth with (*Ctrl + -*) and (*Ctrl + Shift + -*), sometimes changing the open file is not what you would like to do. Enter **Peek Definition** (*Alt + F12*). This allows you to select a method and look it up, but instead of switching to the appropriate file, VS2013 will create a mini-window within your current editor. The following screenshot shows the results of using the **Peek Definition** option on the `ConfigureAuth()` method:

```
Startup.cs  ⊕  ✕
⚙ ASP_Net_Web.Startup                                    ▾  ⚙ Configuration(IAppBuilder app)              ▾
  ⊟ using Microsoft.Owin;
    using Owin;

    [assembly: OwinStartupAttribute(typeof(ASP_Net_Web.Startup))]
  ⊟ namespace ASP_Net_Web
    {
        1 reference
        public partial class Startup {
            2 references
            public void Configuration(IAppBuilder app) {
                ConfigureAuth(app);
                                                              Startup.Auth.cs  ✕
                // For more information on configuring authentication, please visit http://go.microsoft.com/fwlink/
                public void ConfigureAuth(IAppBuilder app)
                {
                    // Enable the application to use a cookie to store information for the signed in user
                    // and also store information about a user logging in with a third party login provider.
                    // This is required if your application allows users to login
                    app.UseCookieAuthentication(new CookieAuthenticationOptions
```

Sequential peeks can be performed, each opening via a tabbed interface. Navigation between these tabs (represented by circles) can be done via the mouse or keyboard: peek forward (*Ctrl + Alt + =*) and peek backward (*Ctrl + Alt + -*). The **Peek Definition** window uses the same scroll bar behavior as that of the parent editing window, and this behavior can be changed in either window by right-clicking on the scroll bar and selecting **Scroll Bar Options...**.

CodeLens (Visual Studio Ultimate Only)

CodeLens, also known as code information indicators, is a feature specific to VS2013 Ultimate. Activated by default, CodeLens provides real-time meta-information about the file you open in your main editor window:

```
6 references
public class HomeController : Controller
{
    1 reference | 1/1 passing
    public ActionResult Index()
    {
        return View();
    }
}
```

As illustrated in the preceding screenshot, shown inline with your code will be light colored term **references**, and the results of executed tests for each method/function as marked by the **passing** term. The **references** term indicates the number of places a method is used, and can also display a pop-up window on a mouse over that shows where it has been used. Likewise, the passing term relays the unit test results inline. While working with projects checked out from **Team Foundation Server** (**TFS**), CodeLens will also display the most recent author of the method in question. Clicking on that name will pop up a details window listing the change history.

If you would prefer to keep your hands on the keyboard, holding down *Alt* will bring up hotkeys that can be used to select among the features discussed earlier. The following screenshot illustrates these options, with *Alt + 2* opening a pop-up dialog box listing references for the selected method and *Alt + 3* listing details about unit tests. The display options for CodeLens are labelled as **Code Information Indicators** in the **Options** dialog box and can be found under **Text Editor | All Languages | Code Information Indicators**:

```
 2       3
1 reference | 1/1 passing
public ActionResult About()
{
    ViewBag.Message = "Your application description page.";
```

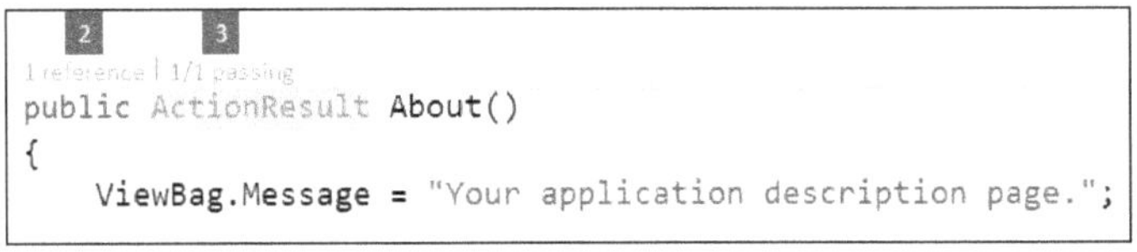

Code Maps (Visual Studio Ultimate Only)

VS2013 Ultimate continues the use of a code visualization tool that Microsoft calls Code Maps to provide a representation of the open project. The following screenshot shows Code Maps in action:

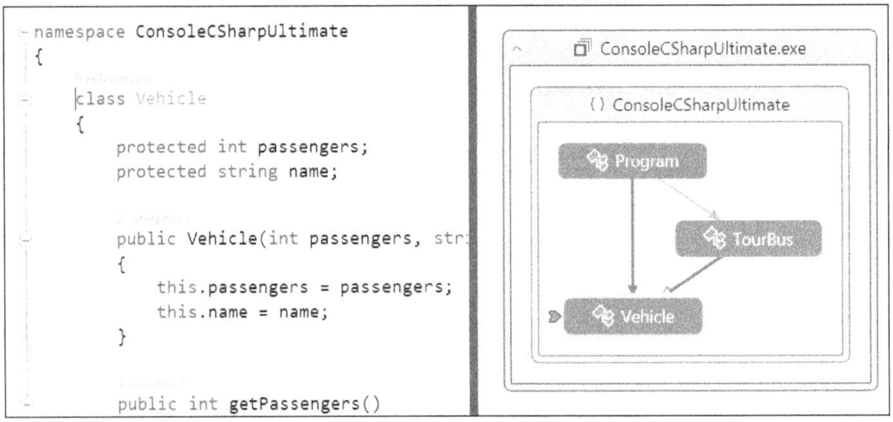

Code Maps can be created and used in VS2013 Ultimate, but VS2013 Premium and VS2013 Professional can only consume them. However, users of Premium and Professional can interact with the maps and add comments/flags as they are reviewed. Code Maps can be activated in an editor window via *Ctrl +* `, which is *Ctrl* plus the backquote key (typically found sharing a key with tilde). It can also be called by right-clicking in the editor window on a particular method or class that you want to map.

Once generated, the map may be manipulated in several ways, including zooming and the ability to expand to show related elements. Individual elements may be double-clicked so that they are brought up in the code editor for closer analysis. An element may also be right-clicked when in the **Code Map** for further navigation options (**Go To Definition**, **Show Base Types**, and so on) or to be commented on. This is particularly helpful for large or complex code bases where a map can assist in comprehension by visualizing the relationships and adding commentary external to the source code.

The Code Map indicates your position from the active editor window on the map with a green arrow icon. In the preceding example's screenshot, the editor is in the `Vehicle` class, which is pointed to on the Code Map by the green arrow.

See also

> ▸ The *Choosing a version of Visual Studio 2013* section in the *Preface*
>
> ▸ For an exhaustive list of differences between VS2012 and VS2013, refer to the MSDN article at `http://msdn.microsoft.com/en-us/library/bb386063.aspx`.

Project round-tripping

If you would like your .NET-based projects to be compatible with the previous versions of Visual Studio, be sure to choose a version of the .NET Framework that they support. For example, if you would like your project to support VS2010, be sure to target .NET 4.0, as .NET 4.5 is not compatible. Round-tripping is useful for situations where not all members of a development team have VS2013, as well as for situations when you wish to tread lightly on older projects.

> As a friendly reminder, be sure that both versions of Visual Studio are up-to-date while sharing projects between VS2012 and VS2013. As noted in the *While you were gone* section of the *Preface*, this means Update 4 should be applied to VS2012.

In this recipe, we will discuss how projects can be shared across Visual Studio versions and a few details about how projects are handled.

Getting ready

The default .NET Framework in VS2013 is 4.5, so it is very easy to create a project that cannot open in VS2010. If you are not using any features specific to 4.5+, it is merely a matter of changing the project's properties to target 4.0. Keep in mind that some features will not be supported outright, but will be gracefully ignored.

Round-tripping is useful for a number of reasons. While supporting legacy projects, it is usually preferred to alter the existing code as little as possible. The support for older projects means that you can use VS2013 to edit them without keeping a copy of VS2012 installed. It also provides a way for users of VS2013 to work with fellow developers who are yet to upgrade from VS2012.

How to do it...

The best practice is to test upgrading on a backup of your legacy project. This way, you have an easy way to return to the status quo in the event of a failure or complication. Most projects will simply open without any complaint, especially those from VS2012 and, to a lesser extent, VS2010. If Visual Studio doesn't object, it is simply a manner of opening your old project in VS2013 and getting to work. Upon making edits and checking your code (if necessary), fellow developers running VS2010/VS2012 will have no difficulty making their own contributions.

How it works...

Visual Studio uses solution files to store details about the projects and solutions you create. Ending with the `.sln` extension, these files help Visual Studio manage your project. For example, a solution created in VS2012 has the following header at the beginning of its SLN file:

```
Microsoft Visual Studio Solution File, Format Version 12.00
# Visual Studio 2012
```

By comparison, a solution created in VS2013 has this header as follows:

```
Microsoft Visual Studio Solution File, Format Version 12.00
# Visual Studio 2013
VisualStudioVersion = 12.0.20623.1 VSUPREVIEW
MinimumVisualStudioVersion = 10.0.40219.1
```

 The initial blank line is intentional for both examples.

The third line (prefaced with #) indicates the "human-readable" version of Visual Studio used to create the project. VS2013 projects add two additional lines to this header as shown in the preceding code snippet. The fourth line shows `VisualStudioVersion`, which specifies the full build version of Visual Studio used, while the fifth line lists the value `MinimumVisualStudioVersion`, which indicates the minimum version of Visual Studio that can be used to open the project.

There's more...

Not every project type supports round-tripping, as some require specific changes to be made in order to run under VS2013. Some notable project types and their exceptions are as follows.

Windows Store applications

Windows Store apps have some special requirements. Apps targeting Windows 8.1 require VS2013 and the underlying OS to be Windows 8.1. VS2013 can work with existing Windows 8 store apps if they were created by VS2012. As previously noted, Windows 8.1 will quickly replace Windows 8, so all new apps should target that platform.

The Model-View-Controller (MVC) framework

Visual Studio 2013 brings support for MVC 5 in addition to supporting MVC 4, while Visual Studio 2012 only supports MVC 3 and MVC 4. Visual Studio 2010 SP1 only supports MVC 2 and MVC 3. These limitations dictate whether or not your project will upgrade. However, there are tools and guidance on how to migrate your application to a newer version of MVC. Upgrading an MVC 2-based application to MVC 3 can be done with the standalone upgrade from CodePlex at `http://aspnet.codeplex.com/releases/view/59008`. Once this is completed, Microsoft provides guidance on upgrading the application from MVC 3 to MVC 4 at `http://www.asp.net/whitepapers/mvc4-release-notes#_Toc303253806`. Unfortunately, the upgrade from MVC 3 to MVC 4 is a manual process.

MSI setup (.vdproj)

This project type refers to Visual Studio Installer projects, which are not supported in VS2013.

Upgrading an existing project

Depending on the nature of the solution or project you are working on, Visual Studio may require you to convert your project. You will be prompted to make a conversion decision, as shown in the following screenshot:

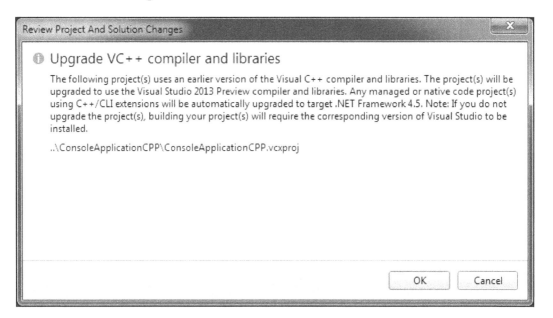

 If you decide not to upgrade the project, you may do so later via **Project | Upgrade Solution**. As you may expect, the best practice is to perform a trial conversion on a copy of your solution in the event of something going wrong.

Creating a new project

Starting a new project in VS2013 remains unchanged from previous versions, but some of the available choices have changed. If you have not previously updated VS2012, one of the changes to notice is that VS2013 offers .NET Framework 4.5.1 as a framework that can be targeted. Some other new choices include templates to create apps for SharePoint and Office, as well as Python-based projects. See the *Project round-tripping* recipe for important considerations while creating projects that are destined to be edited in different editions of Visual Studio.

Managing the editor windows

One of the advantages of using a graphical IDE is the ability to have multiple windows open, and learning how to customize their size and layout in Visual Studio is important for maximizing their productivity. Given the multitude of windows (editors, debugger output, and so on) Visual Studio has open, it can be helpful to learn how to place them where you want so that you can focus on your work without being slowed down by clutter.

Tab pinning allows you to mark individual windows so they stay open while you navigate through the editor. Previewing documents is a useful way to navigate across several files without cluttering your tabs with several open documents. This recipe will explore both options.

Getting ready

Open either the VS2010_Web sample solution or use a solution of your choice. Ensure that the **Solution Explorer** window is open.

How to do it...

The following steps will show how the position of open windows can be positioned to your liking. Let's get started:

1. In the **Solution Explorer** window, locate the Default.aspx.cs file in the VS2010_Web project and double-click on it. The source file will open in the main window area as in the previous versions of Visual Studio. However, you will now notice that the document tab features a pin icon next to the tab name, as you can see in the following screenshot. You'll use that pin in just a few steps:

2. Using the **Solution Explorer** window, open both the About.aspx.cs and Global.asax.cs files by double-clicking on them. You should now have three documents open with their tabs showing in the tab well (this refers to the row of tabs for each open document in the editor), as shown in the following screenshot:

3. Click on the `Default.aspx.cs` tab to select it and then click on the pin. The pin will change to point downwards indicating that the document is now pinned. Visual Studio 2013 will always keep pinned tabs visible in the tab well. These pinned tabs will remain visible even when Visual Studio needs to start hiding unpinned tabs to save screen display space. The pinned document tab will be moved to the left next to any other pinned documents you may have open, as shown in the following screenshot:

4. Right-click on the `Global.asax.cs` document tab and click on the **Close All But This** option to close all open documents except for the one currently selected. This will include closing any pinned documents, which are shown in the following screenshot:

 There is a related option: **Close All But Pinned**. This is useful when you would like to only keep pinned files open.

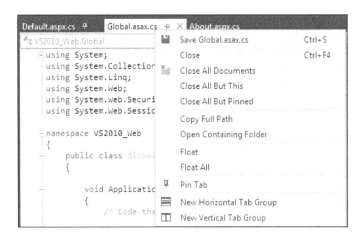

5. Reopen both the `Default.aspx.cs` and `About.aspx.cs` files that you closed by double-clicking on them in **Solution Explorer**.

6. One of the usability problems with document tabs in Visual Studio 2010 was that you could accidentally float documents by double-clicking on a document tab.

7. In Visual Studio 2013, this behavior has changed. Double-click on a document tab of your choice and notice how Visual Studio sets the focus to this tab instead of floating it. (This is the same behavior as single-clicking on a document tab.)

8. Press *Ctrl + Shift + F* to open the **Find in Files** dialog box. Enter the class in the **Find what** field and ensure **Look in** is set to **Solution**, then click on the **Find All** button.

9. In the **Find Results 1** window, select a result from the `ChangePassword.aspx` file.

10. The file will open in the preview tab, located on the right-hand side of the tab well.

11. The preview tab shows the contents of the currently selected document if it is not already open. In the **Find Results 1** window, select a result from the `Login.aspx` file. It will now be opened automatically in the preview tab, and the `ChangePassword.aspx` document will be closed.

12. Assume you now want to keep the `Login.aspx` file open for a while. Either click on the **Keep Open** icon on the tab or change the contents of the file. Any document in the preview tab that is changed is automatically promoted to a normal tab.

Visual Studio will move the document from the preview tab area into the main tab area. The color of the tab will also be changed from purple to blue indicating that the tab is now a normal document tab.

How it works...

Pinning documents works much like pinning does in any other part of Visual Studio, and is very handy for keeping the documents that you are working on regularly within easy reach, especially when you have many documents open at once.

The preview document tab is a great way to prevent tab clutter and becomes very useful while debugging deeply nested code. You may recall that **Go To Definition** as one function that uses the preview document tab. For example, multiple source files may be opened as you trace a program's operation across methods and classes. The preview document tab helps you cycle quickly through these files while preventing the tab well from filling up with documents that aren't needed for more than a few moments.

There's more...

As always, there are ways to customize the behavior of the document tabs in Visual Studio.

Single-click preview in Solution Explorer

The preview tab isn't restricted to just the **Find Results** window. It can also be used from within the **Solution Explorer**. If you activate the **Preview Selected Items** button in the **Solution Explorer** toolbar, then every item you click on will automatically be opened in the preview tab. The **Preview Selected Items** button is a toggle button (shown in the following screenshot). If you want to disable the behavior, you only need to click on the button to deselect it and the preview behavior will be turned off:

Customizing tab and window behavior

Navigating to **Tools** | **Options** in Visual Studio will show the following dialog box:

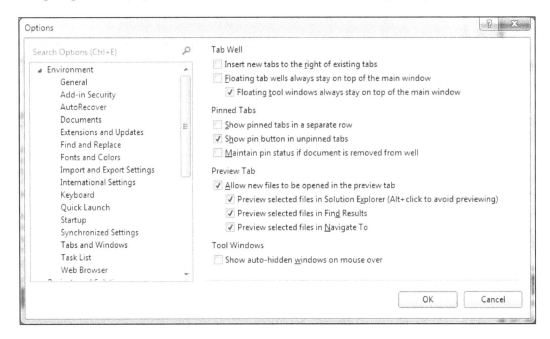

There are a number of options here that let you control how the tabs behave. With Visual Studio 2010 Productivity Power Tools, many developers found different ways to configure their tab well to get the experience they wanted, and while not everything from the power tools came across to the final Visual Studio 2012 product, a number of features most certainly did. Feel free to experiment with the **Tabs and Windows** settings to get Visual Studio working the way you like it most.

Finding Visual Studio commands

The goal of the **Quick Launch** box is to provide a keyboard-friendly way of accessing the extended features of Visual Studio without needing to clutter the central interface. Keyboard shortcuts are a great way to speed up tasks, but it can be difficult to learn and remember while first starting out, or while exploring a new area of Visual Studio. The **Quick Launch** option addresses this by providing a way to locate different areas of the program, learn keyboard shortcuts, and provide a keyboard-centric way to access commands.

Getting ready

Simply start Visual Studio 2013.

How to do it...

To try it out, start by pressing *Ctrl + Q*, then begin typing the topic/subject that you are looking for, as shown in the following screenshot:

What is important to notice is that **Quick Launch** can do even more than what may be obvious at first glance. In this example, notice that open was the term entered as a search term. **Quick Launch** produces a list of results to this query, grouped by the following categories: **Menus**, **Options**, and **NuGet Packages**. As you can see, this list of results is more than just commands, it also includes various areas in the **Options** dialog as well as **NuGet Packages**.

You can immediately navigate through the search results with the arrow keys on the keyboard if the desired result is immediately available. You can access a command directly from this list, and where available, the accompanying keyboard hotkey for a command will be listed. In this way, you can learn new shortcuts while doing your daily work.

In the next example, jquery was entered into **Quick Launch**, producing a list of results that includes context-specific **File** menu commands (**Save** and **Save As**), the option to switch to an open editor window with jquery in the file name (jquery.ui.autocomplete.min.css), or to search NuGet for packages using jquery as the search term.

The following screenshot is showing the availability of these various options:

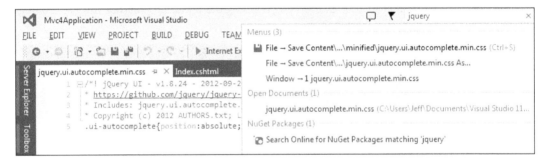

There's more...

The **Quick Launch** option can go further. Let's return to the results of the open term. Note that at the bottom, the **Quick Launch** option indicates that *Ctrl + Q* can index through additional views. Additional presses of *Ctrl + Q* will toggle the list of results to show only results from an individual category, in this case **Menus**, **Options**, or **NuGet Packages**. A final press of *Ctrl + Q* will return to displaying all of the available results. The ability to toggle through categories is particularly useful when your **Quick Launch** list is lengthy and you would like to ignore unnecessary categories that are cluttering the list of results. Pressing *Esc* once will clear the search results in **Quick Launch**, and pressing *Esc* again will return you to the open file in your editor.

Using the Command Window / Command Aliases

The **Command Window** (accessible via *Ctrl +Alt +A* and available on premium editions of VS2013) allows you to keep your hands on the keyboard while quickly accessing commands via an integrated command prompt window. As Microsoft ships Visual Studio preloaded with command definitions, entering an alias will display all of the currently defined commands, and the `alias` cmd action (where cmd is the desired name of your alias and action defines what should happen) will allow you to define your own. You can see from the following screenshot that typing `bl` is much faster than typing `Debug. Breakpoints`. Note that by default, command aliases are stored as part of your synchronized profile:

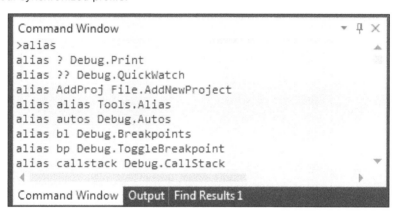

Searching and navigating

Visual Studio provides many ways to make maneuvering through your code easier and more efficient.

Getting ready

To best see this in action, open a project that has multiple files available for editing. This can be the sample project or one of your own choice. Once it is open, simply open a couple of source files.

How to do it...

Pressing *Ctrl + Tab* provides easy access to a couple of different ways to navigate around Visual Studio. If *Ctrl + Tab* is pressed and immediately released, Visual Studio will alternate between the two most recent files that you have opened in the editor window. This provides a quick way to move back and forth. If *Ctrl + Tab* is pressed and *Tab* is released, a pop-up window will appear. Continue to hold down *Ctrl* when it appears, and then arrow keys can be used to maneuver around the list of all active files and windows. To make a selection, either release *Ctrl* while highlighting the desired target, or while holding *Ctrl*, press *Enter*. This is shown in the following example's screenshot, where active files currently open in Visual Studio are shown in the right-hand side column, while open tool windows are shown in the left-hand side column:

There's more...

If you would rather take a hybrid (mouse + keyboard) approach, the window *Ctrl + Tab* produces also supports selection by mouse. Start in the same manner as done earlier in this recipe, holding down *Ctrl + Tab* to bring up the window. Release *Tab* while holding down the *Ctrl* key and then use your mouse to left-click directly on the file you would like to switch to.

Quickly searching your code

Searching a project file to find specific strings of text is a common daily task performed by developers. Visual Studio tries to make this easy by offering specific tools to find and replace text at various levels of your code base. Several options are available under **Edit | Find and Replace**, including **Quick Find**, **Quick Replace**, **Find In Files**, and **Replace In Files**.

The **Incremental Search** option (*Ctrl + I*) is a quick way to search within the file you are currently editing. When activated, a **Find** dialog box appears in your active editor window, allowing you to enter search terms.

The **Quick Find** (*Ctrl + F*) and **Quick Replace** (*Ctrl + H*) options share a common dialog box. Both provide the ability to search the current code block, the current project, all open documents, or the entire solution. If your search options include the file that's currently open, the vertical scroll bar will highlight any matches found. This provides quick visual feedback on the frequency of a search item:

Another feature that **Quick Find** and **Quick Replace** share is the ability to set the following search options: match case, match whole word, and whether or not regular expressions can be used. The use of regular expressions allows for more complex queries to be used, allowing users to extract more detailed information from their searches.

The **Find In Files** (*Ctrl + Shift + F*) and **Replace In Files** (*Ctrl + Shift + H*) options provide a more advanced method of conducting searches across a code base. They expand on the functionality offered by the quick tools by allowing you to specify certain file types that should be searched (for example, all HTML and JavaScript files) and provide the ability to display the results of an operation in a separate window.

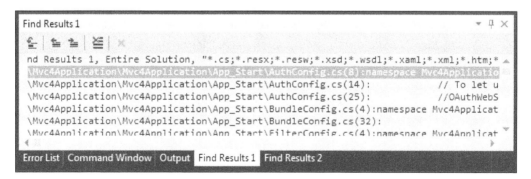

In the preceding example's screenshot, a simple regular expression was used to search the entire solution using the specified file mask. The results were outputted to **Find Results 1**, which is a live window. This means that you can click on a line with a particular search result and you will go directly to that file where the match was made.

Navigating in depth

The **Solution Explorer** window that we were accustomed to in Visual Studio 2010 was good for being able to understand how files were organized into the various projects of a solution, but it didn't do much more than that. With Visual Studio 2013, Microsoft has revisited **Solution Explorer** and given it an overhaul. It still contains all of the functionalities you know from the old **Solution Explorer**, and it adds to that a range of new features intended to make navigating and searching within your solution a more powerful yet simpler experience.

Getting ready

Open the same VS2010_Web solution that we have been using for the other recipes in this chapter or choose a solution of your own.

How to do it...

1. We'll begin by navigating through our solution. Locate the Default.aspx page in the VS2010_Web project and click on the arrow next to it so that its contents are displayed. As you would expect, there is a code-behind file and a designer file:

    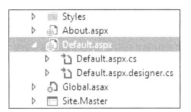

2. Look at the Default.aspx.cs file. You can see that there is a small arrow next to it just as there was for the Default.aspx page. Click on the arrow:

    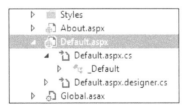

3. Visual Studio 2013 expands the file to show its contents, and in the case of a code-behind file, these contents are the class definitions it contains. Classes have methods and properties in them, so click on the arrow next to the _Default class to see the methods inside it. Since the VS2010_Web project is just a shell, there is only an empty Page_Load() method, as shown in the following screenshot:

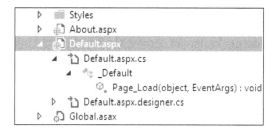

4. Now select the `IService1.cs` file from the `VS2010_Web.Services` project and expand it to see its contents. You will see that there is both an interface definition in this file (`IService1`) and a class definition (`CompositeType`), as shown in the following screenshot:

5. Right-click on the `IService1` interface and click on the **Derived Types** option to see what classes implement this interface:

6. The **Solution Explorer** window will change views to show you the types that either implement this interface or inherit from it, as shown in the following screenshot. Click on the back button (showing the blue background) to return to the standard **Solution Explorer** view:

7. Right-click on the `IService1` interface and choose the **Is Used By** option to see where the interface is currently being used. As with the **Derived Types** option, you will see **Solution Explorer** change its context to only show the interface and where that interface is used in the solution, including line and column numbers:

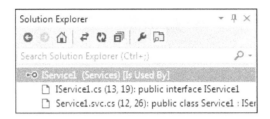

8. Return to the regular **Solution Explorer** view by clicking on the home button, shown in the following screenshot:

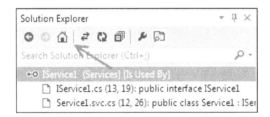

9. At this point, you know how to navigate using **Solution Explorer**, and you have already used the existing **Navigate To** feature in the *Finding Visual Studio commands* recipe while opening a file. With the enhancements to **Solution Explorer**, you can locate files in much the same way as with the **Navigate To** command, albeit with a slightly different user experience. Click on the **Search Solution Explorer** textbox at the top of the **Solution Explorer** window, or use the default shortcut key of *Ctrl + ;* (*Ctrl* + semicolon).

10. Enter `serv` in the textbox and wait a moment for the search results to display. The results should look similar to the following screenshot. You can not only see the filenames that match the search term but also any matching references, classes, and methods:

How it works...

The **Navigate To** feature from Visual Studio 2010 was a fantastic addition to Visual Studio. It had problems in large projects with many search matches as the location of a match was embedded in the result itself, making it hard to locate the specific match you were after. The new **Solution Explorer** search tool provides similar results to the **Navigate To** feature, but having the location of a match represented in the tree view makes it very easy to quickly identify the specific match you are interested in.

There's more...

It's worth mentioning a few other things about searching within your solution.

Navigation behavior

Assuming you have the **Preview Tab** enabled for **Solution Explorer**, as you navigate using **Solution Explorer** to various classes and methods, you may have noticed that the document preview tab was updating and showing exactly where the selected class, method, or property was declared. This makes it easy to see what the code is doing without the need to specifically open the file or scroll through a source file to see what code is actually inside a method, class, or property.

CSS, HTML, and JavaScript files

Even though it's possible to extract the structure from CSS, HTML, and JavaScript files, **Solution Explorer** doesn't show the internal structure of these files. You can navigate to the source file, but not to any of its contents.

2
Getting Started with Windows Store Applications

In this chapter, we will cover:

- ▶ Getting a Windows Store app developer license
- ▶ Creating a Windows Store app
- ▶ Adding a Windows Store item template to your app
- ▶ Using the Windows Store app simulator
- ▶ Defining capabilities and contracts
- ▶ Analyzing your App's performance
- ▶ Packaging your Windows Store app
- ▶ Validating your Windows Store app

Introduction

The appearance of the **Windows Runtime** (**WinRT**) brought forth a lot of attention when it was introduced as part of the shift in focus to Windows 8. Since the general availability of Windows 8-based systems and the OS itself, there is an opportunity to see first hand what the runtime meant. Essentially, Microsoft felt the need to advance the state of Windows application development by providing a new platform that recognized the rise of non-PC-based devices, touch interfaces, and to combine that with a method to obtain safe and secure Windows applications. WinRT abstracts away the underlying hardware, minimizes security risks, and prevents developers from making insecure or poorly performing calls via the traditional Windows API.

What WinRT offers developers familiar with Windows-based tools is the ability to easily create secure apps that run on Windows 8-based systems. Your users benefit from a straightforward shopping, purchasing, and installation process. As a developer, you will benefit from easier access to new customers and the ability to focus on building and maintaining great apps, not payment processing. Windows Store apps can be written using several different languages, including C#/VB, JavaScript, and C++.

> Don't confuse Windows Runtime with the Windows-based operating system named Windows RT that runs on ARM-powered Windows 8 devices. While they are related in the sense that Windows Store apps can be built to be consumed on WinRT devices, they are separate concepts. Windows Store apps run on any Windows 8-based device. Of course this is subject to minimum version requirements, for example, apps designed for Windows 8.1 would not work on Windows 8.0.

Windows 8 marks a shift in the historical presentation of Windows-based programs that used a desktop metaphor to a tile-based interface that features bold colors and sans-serif fonts. Programs targeting this new style are typically referred to as Windows Store apps, or apps in short, and programs designed for the historical interface are called desktop applications. Traditional Windows desktop application development is no way impeded by the arrival of Windows Store apps; as a developer, store apps merely provide you with another way to serve the needs of your users. In fact, with some types of programs such as Visual Studio, it makes more sense to continue using the desktop style.

Whether they run on Windows 8 or Windows RT, modern Windows apps are designed to be full screen, highly responsive, immersive, touch- and cloud-enabled applications. These apps can expect to be deployed to a wide variety of different form factors, including laptops, desktops, tablets, and anything else that hardware manufacturers may create in the future. They are a radical departure from the way we have thought of applications in the past and will require fresh thinking from developers and designers alike. Windows Store apps should follow modern design principles of minimalism, focusing the users' attention on the information they are interested in, and removing the distractions and visual noise that has traditionally been associated with Windows applications.

> What's in a name? Microsoft originally intended to call applications designed for the Windows Store "Metro apps". For legal reasons Metro has been discontinued with no solid replacement available. Generally speaking Windows Store apps, Windows 8, and Windows RT are all terms used to refer to apps that are running on the Windows Runtime. Programs historically called Windows applications still exist and are supported on Windows 8/8.1—just not Windows RT.

With Windows Store apps, Microsoft is also ensuring that touch-enabled devices work just as well as the standard mouse- and keyboard-based desktops and laptops. You can see this for yourself when running Windows 8 on a traditional desktop PC as a mouse can be used to manipulate touch-based controls. Likewise, installing the desktop-based Mozilla Firefox on your touch-enabled device such as a Surface Pro will work equally well.

As discussed earlier, the user experience is greatly improved for Windows Store apps. A user will no longer have to install separate utilities nor will administrator access be required in order to use an app. Downloading programs from the Internet will no longer involve uncertainty regarding their safety or security. The threat of malware or a messy installation process is removed. Instead, people will purchase Windows Store apps from the Windows Store, which can then be downloaded and run on whatever device they happen to be using at the time. Since Microsoft verifies all apps listed in the Windows Store for safety and to ensure they meet standard app guidelines, the users' only concern will be whether or not they like the app and not if it will ruin their Windows installation.

It's one thing to have an app that you can download onto any device you're using but genuine portability requires that the data be portable as well—especially when portable devices typically have limited storage abilities. Replicating data so that it is available where and when you want it can also be a chore. Microsoft has solved this problem by providing all Windows 8 users with SkyDrive storage space that Windows Store apps can use, making data available anywhere, anytime. Windows 8.1 brings even tighter integration between the OS and SkyDrive, giving users new ways to make their data accessible across their Windows-based devices while minimizing the local storage requirements on each device. SkyDrive clients are available for all Microsoft-based devices, including Windows, Windows Phone, and Xbox. Apple iOS-based devices as well as those running Android are also supported via native apps for their respective platforms. Finally, nearly all popular web browsers (Internet Explorer, Google Chrome, Apple Safari, and Mozilla Firefox) support access to SkyDrive over the Web. What does this mean to you as a developer? Simply that your users have an ever-growing amount of easily accessible data available for your apps to manipulate.

For legal reasons Microsoft will soon be renaming SkyDrive to OneDrive. Since the official switch has not occurred as of publication we will continue to use the term SkyDrive in this book. Expect this name change to occur at some point in 2014 but underlying functionality should remain the same.

Now at this point, since you're a developer, what you are most likely interested in is not what's different with the user interface but what has been changed under the hood. So, we'll begin by getting an app developer license and then explore the creation of a Windows Store app from start (picking an app type) to finish (getting your app published).

Getting a Windows Store app developer license

In order for your local Windows apps to be run on your local developer machine, you will need a developer license. Note that this license is free and different from a developer account. The license allows you to develop and test Windows Store apps on your local developer machine. The account is used in conjunction with distributing your app through the Windows Store. There is no cost to obtain a license; it is merely used by Microsoft to track who is developing Windows Store apps. Conversely, a fee is charged by Microsoft to obtain a developer account.

A developer license is required because there would be security implications if a malicious Store app was distributed independent of Microsoft's ability to verify its safety. Consequently, each machine or device that you intend to test your app on must have its own developer license.

In this recipe, we will cover obtaining the developer license needed so that you can get started with writing Windows apps. The *Submitting apps to the Windows Store* recipe in the *Appendix, Visual Studio Medley*, will address obtaining a developer account.

Getting ready

To develop Windows Store apps for Windows 8.1, you will need Windows 8.1 and either Visual Studio Express 2013 for Windows or Visual Studio 2013 Professional, Premium, or Ultimate. (Any of those projects can open existing Windows Store apps for Windows 8.0, but new apps for Windows 8.0 cannot be created).

How to do it...

Obtaining a license is easy to do with either version, and there is only a slight variation in Visual Studio's menus between versions. A screen similar to the following screenshot will appear whenever a developer license must be acquired or renewed:

On the non-Express editions of Visual Studio 2013, look for the **Project** menu, then navigate to **Store | Acquire Developer License....** This will cause Visual Studio to contact Microsoft's servers and retrieve a developer license. If you already have a license, it will renew it with a reset expiration date (30 or 90 days, depending on the account type). Note that in some cases the **Project** menu will not be visible; in this case, start or open a Windows App store project for it to appear.

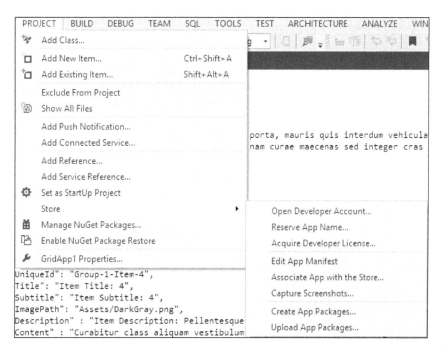

For Visual Studio Express 2013, click on **STORE | Acquire Developer License...:**

How it works...

There is no limit to the number of licenses that you may obtain, thus making it easy to acquire one for each development environment that you are working with. Licenses associated with a Windows Store developer account will be valid for 90 days. Those associated with a regular Microsoft account (Outlook, SkyDrive, and so on) are valid for 30 days.

There's more...

You may also obtain or renew a developer license at the Windows PowerShell command line. To do this, open a PowerShell terminal.

Opening a PowerShell terminal in Windows 8.1 can be done from your **Start** screen. Just start typing PowerShell and it will appear as an option. Click on it to run with normal permissions. To run with Administrator permissions, right-click on the icon and choose **Run as administrator** as shown in the following screenshot:

Type `Get-WindowsDeveloperLicense` at the command prompt to show whether or not a license is installed. PowerShell will display the expiration date/timestamp of the current license and whether it is valid or not. If, however, a license is not installed, PowerShell will throw an error stating, `There is no developer license on this computer`. This command does not require elevated permissions. The next two commands do, and to try them, you should open a PowerShell with Administrator permissions.

Despite its name, `Show-WindowsDeveloperLicenseRegistration` is actually used to acquire or renew a developer license. When executed, it will open a GUI-based dialog box similar to what is shown in Visual Studio and a prompt for your Microsoft account. Depending on whether you currently have a developer license, one will be acquired or renewed as appropriate.

In the event that you would like to remove your current developer license, this may be done with `Unregister-WindowsDeveloperLicense`. PowerShell will prompt for a confirmation before removing the license, as once it is removed, Windows Store apps under development will no longer be executable until a new license is obtained.

Developers without constant Internet access or who want a license that doesn't expire have the ability to obtain a nonexpiring license. This approach requires Windows 8.1 Enterprise or Windows 8.1 Pro and that this machine be connected to a Windows domain. For more information on this process, visit `http://msdn.microsoft.com/en-us/library/windows/apps/hh974578.aspx#NoInternet`.

Choosing the right development technology

Developing apps for WinRT offers several choices when it comes to picking a programming language. The .NET-based languages C# and Visual Basic, modern C++, as well as HTML5 with JavaScript are all first-class options for app development. Making the best decision involves reviewing the skill set and preferences of you and your team in conjunction with the project you are undertaking.

If you are already a .NET veteran, continue to build on that investment by using C# or VB. C# is also a good choice for developers with Java programming experience. Another benefit of the .NET approach is the availability of **Portable Class Libraries**, as they promote code re-use across multiple platforms. These will be discussed in *Chapter 4, .NET Framework 4.5.1 Development*.

If you have a C++ background or wish to utilize DirectX, C++ is the best choice. Web developers, especially those with little knowledge of C++ or .NET, will love the fact that they can build desktop apps with JavaScript and HTML5. These developers will find that the Windows Runtime APIs are exposed via the Microsoft-provided WinJS libraries.

Creating a Windows Store app

We'll begin by creating a basic Windows Store app that uses JavaScript/HTML. For this example, we will use the Hub app template.

Getting ready

Ensure that you are running Windows 8.1 in order to have the ability to create a new Windows Store app. You may use Visual Studio Express 2013 for Windows or one of the premium versions of VS2013 (Professional/Premium/Ultimate).

How to do it...

There are several types of app templates available, but we will start with the **Hub** style as follows:

1. From Visual Studio's **File** menu, navigate to **New | Project...**.

2. A dialog of available project templates will appear. From the **Installed** templates category, navigate to the **JavaScript | Windows Store | Hub App** template. A preview of the app layout will appear in the details pane as shown in the following screenshot:

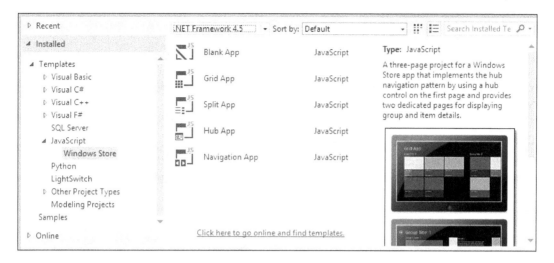

3. Leave the name as the default and click on **OK** to create the app.

4. The project will appear in Solution Explorer and the `default.js` file will be open in the document area.

5. Press *F5* to run the application in the debug mode. Visual Studio will package and launch the app for you and you should see the app appear displaying multiple items around a hub-based pattern. Explore manipulating the app, and how it can process inputs via touch or the mouse.

6. When you have finished exploring the app *Shift + F5* is the direct command to stop debugging, although you may find the best approach is to use *Alt + Tab* to switch back to Visual Studio and stop debugging from there.

How it works...

The packaged project templates in Visual Studio make it easy to quickly start working on new apps with the language that you prefer, while at the same time provide well-commented code. This makes customization easier and provides insight into what Microsoft considers important when writing Windows Store apps.

Regardless of the language used, the process described previously can be followed to create a new project.

There's more...

There's a lot to consider when starting your first Windows Store apps. Fortunately, Microsoft has made it fairly easy to choose the right starting point for the type of app you want to build. If you are making your first app, it makes sense before you begin to explore the various project types available to see which layout best fits your design.

Choosing the right project type

Each of the Windows Store project types, regardless of language, is described briefly here so that you can determine which template would make a good starting point for your development efforts.

Blank App

The **Blank App** template is exactly what you would expect. It is an empty shell ready for you to start coding with.

Grid App

The **Grid App** template is designed to show a summarized view of a data source in a grid layout. The project template includes a sample data source so that you can quickly get a feel of how the app works. Running the app without changes shows the grid summary page as shown in the following screenshot:

Note how the data is grouped into collections and how the individual items in each collection are shown with a placeholder for an image thumbnail and a few lines of text to describe the item. Selecting one of the items will navigate to the detail view of that item as shown in the following screenshot:

The template also includes a collection level summary page, shown when the back button next to the collection name is clicked or touched. This view is shown in the following screenshot:

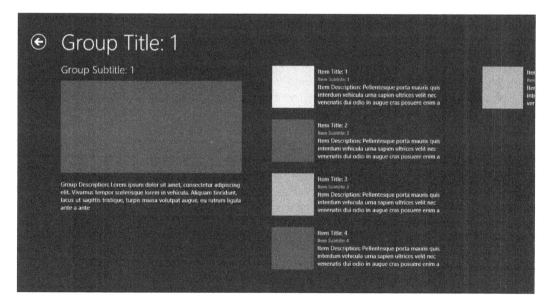

Split App

The **Split App** template is an alternative to the Grid App template, though it is still based around the concept of consuming data grouped into collections.

Just like the Grid App template, the Split App template provides a ready to run app so that you can see how it functions.

Launching the app shows a home page very similar to the Grid App template, but it has a very different group level page where the items in the collection are displayed in a column on the left side of the screen, and the details of the selected item are shown on the right, as shown in the following screenshot:

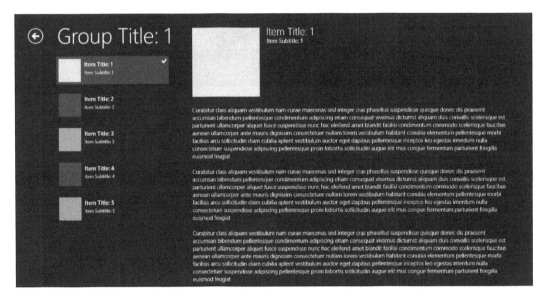

Fixed Layout App

The **Fixed Layout** App template is only available when using JavaScript and provides a basic app featuring a minimal splash screen and a skeleton HTML file, with all the necessary WinJS references ready for you to start building your app. Note that this layout type has been removed from VS2013 and is no longer available for new apps, so this will only be encountered when working with legacy Windows 8.0 apps.

Navigation App

The **Navigation App** template is a minimalist template that initially includes only one page for data. Additional pages can be added and be laid out as you see fit; Grid and Split layouts are also available. This template includes `navigator.js`, which provides the navigation model used by the app.

Hub App

As you noticed in the recipe earlier in the chapter, the **Hub App** template initially provides three pages and uses horizontal scrolling to navigate. As shown in the following screenshot, an angle bracket is used on the header for **Section 2** to indicate that more information than can be displayed is available. Clicking on the **Section 2** header will drill down to show more items.

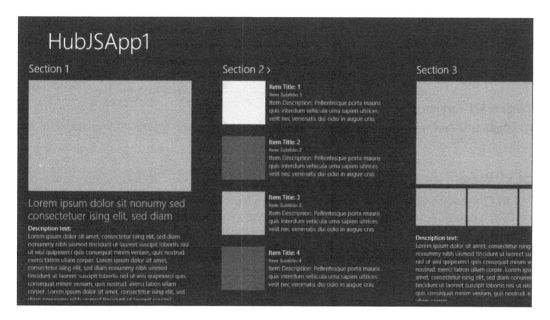

Class Library

The **Class Library** project creates a managed assembly for your app logic that is automatically set to use the .NET Framework 4.5 Windows Store profile.

Portable Class Library

Similar to a Class Library, targeting a Portable Class Library allows your code to be contained in a DLL (Dynamic link library) file, but with the added benefit that the resulting code can be used unchanged across multiple platforms such as Windows 7/8, Silverlight, Windows Phone, and Xbox 360. The functions available for each platform vary, but PCLs provide the opportunity to easily share common logic and maximize re-use. For more information, see the *Sharing class libraries across runtimes* recipe in *Chapter 4, .NET Framework 4.5.1 Development*.

Xamarin offers products to add support to VS2013 for the iOS and Android platforms. This includes support for writing PCLs. For more information on the integration, visit `http://blog.xamarin.com/pcl-projects-and-vs2013/`, and for information on PCLs, visit `http://docs.xamarin.com/guides/cross-platform/application_fundamentals/pcl/`.

Unit Test Library

The Unit Test Library project template creates a **Unit Test Framework** or a test assembly based on **CppUnit** for unit testing your code.

Coded UI Testing

The **Coded UI Testing** project template allows you to test your app via the GUI rather than underneath the hood as in the **Unit Test Library**.

DLL (Windows Store apps)

The **DLL** (**Windows Store apps**) template is a C++ project template for creating a DLL in which you can write your app logic. It contains all the include files you would expect for building a DLL for a Windows Store app as well as a skeleton DllMain function ready for you to implement. The resulting DLL can be used by an app directly or by a Windows Runtime Component.

Static Library (Windows Store apps)

The **Static Library** template is a simple skeleton project with the include files you need for building a static library in a C++ Windows Store app. This can be used as an app directly or by a Windows Runtime Component.

Windows Runtime Component

The **Windows Runtime Component** is a project template for creating code in one language that can be shared or consumed in other languages. C#/VB/C++ can both create and consume these components for Windows apps. JavaScript can only consume these components. Components let you take advantage of the features of each language. For example, code requiring high performance can be written into a C++ component and consumed by a JavaScript app.

DirectX App (XAML) and DirectX App

The **DirectX App (XAML)** and **DirectX App** templates are for C++ apps using the DirectX runtime for high performance graphics and audio processing. Typically, this will be for Windows Store game development, though they could also be used for many business apps such as medical imaging and audio processing. At this stage, DirectX is the only choice for Windows Store game development. XNA is not supported for Windows Store apps and XNA applications on Windows 8 will only run as Windows desktop applications.

Technology choice impacts available project templates

Given that there are a lot of project templates available and there is also more choice in development technologies, it is important to be clear about which project templates are available for which technology.

The following table indicates which Windows 8.1 app types are available for each language type:

	JavaScript	.NET	C++
Blank App	✓		
Grid App	✓		
Split App	✓		
Navigation App	✓		
Class Library		✓	
Unit Test Library		✓	✓
Windows Runtime Component		✓	✓
DLL			✓
Static Library			✓
DirectX App/DirectX App (XAML)			✓
Hub App	✓	✓	✓
Portable Class Library		✓	
Coded UI Test Project		✓	

.NET projects and the Windows Store apps profile

When developing projects in Visual Basic or C#, you will be working with .NET Framework 4.5 using the Windows Store profile. You will not have access to all of the .NET Framework methods and libraries that you are used to when building traditional Windows desktop or web applications, and if you look in your project references instead of the usual references, you will see a reference to .NET for Windows Store apps.

This change is largely because much of the functionality .NET historically provided has now been incorporated directly into Windows Runtime. .NET is now just a supplement to the Windows Runtime when used for Windows apps. Additionally, the .NET Windows Store profile removes classes and methods that aren't applicable for Windows Store apps, which results in a dramatically smaller application footprint. This removal is one of the reasons WinRT can offer more stability and security—it places limits on what apps can do.

Language interoperability

JavaScript Windows Store apps can call a function written in either C++ or .NET when that function is contained in libraries or DLLs that expose **Windows Metadata** (**WinMD**). Unfortunately, the reverse is not the case; .NET and C++ apps cannot call a function contained in JavaScript libraries. C++ Windows Store apps can, however, call a function in .NET WinMD files (that is created using the Windows Runtime Component project type), and .NET code can call C++.

The good news here is that there is no longer a need to use **COM Interop** for any of these cross-language calls, making language interoperability much, much simpler when developing Windows Store apps than it is for Windows desktop applications.

Adding a Windows Store item template to your app

Unless you're building a "Hello World" app, you're probably going to want to add more code files and assets to your project than are provided with the standard project templates. Since Microsoft wants Windows Store apps to not only offer great functionality, but to also meet the Windows Store design principles, it has provided a number of ready-made item templates for you to use as part of your development effort.

User interface item templates come with a common look and feel and subtle animations, so your app behaves like other Windows Store apps. Contract templates provide you with the boiler plate code and UI for building Windows 8 Contract support into your app.

In this recipe, you'll see how to use an item template to add functionality to a Windows Store app.

Getting ready

Create a new blank Windows Store app using C# by following the steps in the previous recipe, *Creating a Windows Store app*.

How to do it...

In order to use an item template to add functionality to a Windows Store app, perform the following steps:

1. Right-click on your project and navigate to **Add** | **New Item...** (The keyboard shortcut for this is *Ctrl + Shift + A*).

2. Select **Windows Store** from the left-hand panel and choose the **Items Page** template as shown in the following screenshot:

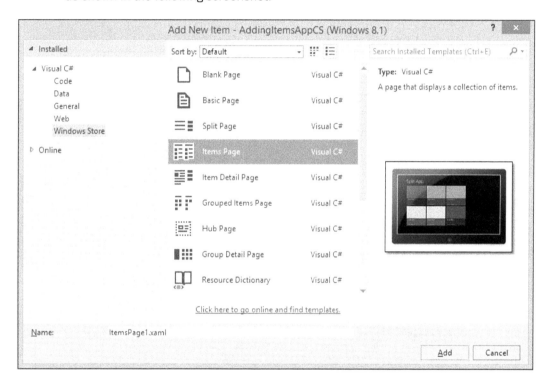

3. Leave the name of the item as the default and click on the **Add** button. The new item will be added to your project ready for you to start working on.

4. You may be prompted to add files to your project to resolve dependencies on the `Common` namespace. Click on **Yes** in the dialog box to continue, as shown in the following screenshot:

5. When the item page appears, the XAML will be displayed but the designer may indicate errors since the project has not yet been compiled. Build the project to ensure that the designer can display correctly.

6. Add a new class to the project named `DataClass` and define it as follows:

```
namespace InsertItemAppCS
{
    class DataClass
    {
        public string Title { get; set; }
        public string Subtitle { get; set; }
    }
}
```

7. Navigate to `ItemPage1.xaml.cs` and change the body of the `LoadState()` method to the following:

```
private void navigationHelper_LoadState(object sender, LoadStateEventArgs e)
{
    // TODO: Assign a bindable collection of items to this.DefaultViewModel["Items"]
    var list = new List<DataClass>() {
        new DataClass(){Title = "Fish", Subtitle="First Item"},
        new DataClass(){Title = "Lion", Subtitle="Second Item"},
        new DataClass(){Title = "Zebra", Subtitle="Third Item"}
    };

    this.defaultViewModel["Items"] = list;
}
```

8. In the `App.xaml.cs` file, locate the `OnLaunched()` method and the section where `rootFrame` is defined (line 58). Change the type used in the `Navigate` method from `MainPage` to `ItemsPage1` as shown in the following screenshot:

```
if (rootFrame.Content == null)
{
    // When the navigation stack isn't restored navigate to the first page,
    // configuring the new page by passing required information as a navigation
    // parameter
    rootFrame.Navigate(typeof(ItemsPage1), e.Arguments);
}
// Ensure the current window is active
Window.Current.Activate();
```

9. Press *F5* to debug and run the application. Your item list should now appear as shown in the following screenshot:

How it works...

Using an item template to add functionality to an app is generally the same as in previous versions of Visual Studio. The additional dialog to generate the Common namespaces only appears for the first item template you add to your project.

Legacy store apps written in C++/VB/C# for Windows 8.0 saw `DataTemplate` definitions for each item they displayed located in the `Common\StandardStyles.xaml` file, which is where the property names of the item-specific data bindings were found.

This has changed with Windows 8.1 as the number of support styles has increased, and now `DataTemplate` definitions are located directly in the XAML file for each page. For the UI item templates, support is provided for the various views that Windows Store apps need to support, specifically the Full, Fill, Snapped, and Portrait states.

There's more...

Of course, you aren't limited to just the **Items Page** template. You can use any of the other available templates to add functionality to your app.

Additional Windows Store item templates

The following list describes what will be added for each of the new Windows Store item templates.

Blank Page

The **Blank Page** item template gives you an empty blank page, which is desirable when you would like to customize every facet.

Basic Page

The **Basic Page** item template is the Blank Page item template with added layout awareness, a title, and a back button to give you a starting point for creating your own layouts.

Split Page

The **Split Page** item template displays a vertical list of items on the left and the details of the selected item on the right.

Items Page

The **Items Page** item template displays a flat view of an object collection.

Item Detail Page

The **Item Detail Page** item template shows a detailed view of a single item using a **FlipView** control. It also provides navigation options for moving to the next or previous item in the collection.

Grouped Items Page

The **Grouped Items Page** item template adds a summarized view of items arranged into groups.

Hub Page

The **Hub Page** displays items in sections using various presentation styles for each of those sections.

Group Detail Page

The **Group Detail Page** item template provides a panel for displaying the items from a single group in a collection, and summary views of the items in the group.

Resource Directory

Resource Directory is a dictionary-based collection used to store XAML resources, which is retrievable with a key. XAML elements that may be stored include subclasses of `Style`, `ControlTemplate`, and `Brush`. By defining them in one place, they can be re-used throughout the app to easily provide a consistent behavior and appearance.

Templated Control

Templated Control provides a blank control using the default styling that is ready to be customized for your app.

User Control

User Control is a completely blank user control.

File Open Picker Contract

The **File Open Picker Contract** item template is used to expose files in your app to outside apps. The code behind the item template includes the `Activate()` method; with the `FileOpenPickerActivatedEventArgs` parameter, you can query to determine what to show. You will also need to populate the `FileOpenPickerUI` property of this parameter to return selections to the calling app.

Search Results Page

The **Search Results Page** template provides a page to be customized for your app so that a user's search query of your app is handled in a meaningful way.

Share Target Contract

The **Share Target Contract** indicates that your app supports receiving items shared by other apps.

Settings Flyout

A **Flyout** is Windows 8 GUI element that is accessed when swiping from the edge of a window. The **Settings Flyout** template provides a blank flyout that can be customized to provide settings for your app.

Resources File

The **Resources File** is available for C++ based projects; this provides strings and conditional resources.

Page Control

Page Control is a JavaScript-specific template that provides a blank page complete with supporting HTML and CSS files.

Language impacts item template options

Just like the project templates you saw in the *Creating a Windows Store app* recipe, the development technology you choose limits the Windows Store item templates available for use. The following table indicates which items are available for each technology choice in the Windows Store item category:

	JavaScript	.NET	C++
Blank Page		✓	✓
Basic Page		✓	✓
Split Page		✓	✓
Items Page		✓	✓
Item Detail Page		✓	✓
Grouped Items Page		✓	✓
Hub Page		✓	✓
Group Detail Page		✓	✓
Resource Dictionary		✓	✓
Templated Control		✓	✓
User Control		✓	✓
File Open Picker Contract	✓	✓	✓
Search Results Page	✓	✓	✓
Share Target Contract	✓	✓	✓
Settings Flyout		✓	✓
Resources File			✓
Page Control	✓		

See also

▸ The *Creating a Windows Store app* recipe

Using the Windows Store app simulator

You may recall that one of the design goals of Windows Store apps was that they should run equally well on a multitude of devices, including tablets and other touch-enabled devices and they should also support a number of different views such as the Snapped and Full views.

As most developers use powerful desktops or high-end laptops for developing software, these machines exceed the capabilities of many portable devices. They also typically lack some of the other features found in portable devices such as GPS, or gyroscopes. To handle the differences between developer machines and the target devices, Microsoft includes a **Windows Store app Simulator** with Visual Studio that can be used to test your Windows Store apps without the need of a second physical machine to deploy to.

This recipe will show how to use the simulator to assist in developing your own apps.

Getting ready

Create a new C# based Windows Store project using the **Split App (XAML)** template and name it `SplitApp`. You can use the information from the *Creating a Windows Store app* recipe if you need a refresher on how to do this.

How to do it...

The steps for using Windows Store app simulator are as follows:

1. Go to the properties page of the `SplitApp` project (The properties page is available under the **Project** menu).
2. Select the **Debug** tab and change the target machine to **Simulator** as shown in the following screenshot:

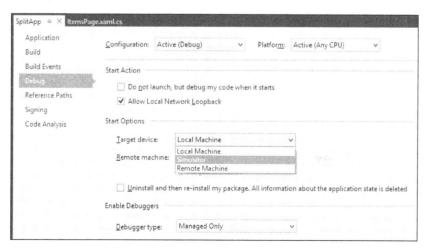

3. Start debugging the app by either pressing *F5* or navigating to the **Debug** | **Start Debugging** menu option.

4. Visual Studio will start the Windows 8 Simulator and launch the app for you as shown in the following screenshot:

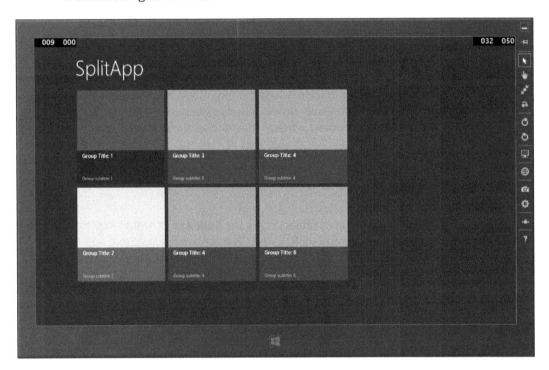

5. On the right-hand side of the simulator are a number of icons that control the simulator's behavior. By default, the simulator starts in mouse mode so that you can navigate within the app using the keyboard and mouse.

For reference, the toolbar icon functions are, from top to bottom: Minimize, Always on top, Mouse mode, Basic touch mode, Pinch/ Zoom touch mode, Rotation touch mode, Rotate clockwise, Rotate counterclockwise, Change resolution, Set location, Copy screenshot, Screenshot settings, Change network properties, and Help.

6. Click on the **Group Title: 3** group and then the **Item Title: 3** item from the list on the left and move the mouse over the detail section on the right. You should see the contents of the details panel change and a scroll bar should appear as shown in the following screenshot:

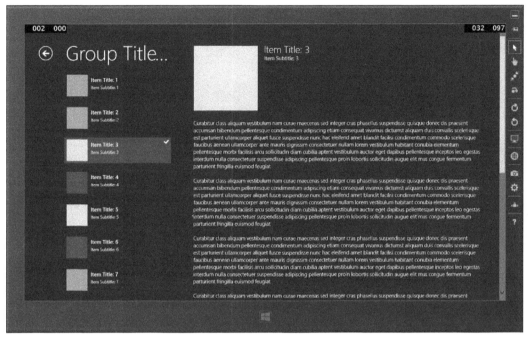

The Windows Logo works and will toggle the desktop

7. Switch to **Basic touch mode** by selecting the icon on the simulator toolbar.

8. As you move your mouse over the simulator, you will see that the cursor has now changed to be a small crosshair in a circle icon. Click on the second item in the collection to select it.

9. Move the mouse over the details pane and simulate an upward swipe by left-clicking and dragging upward with your mouse to scroll the details pane.

10. As you do, you should see the pointer change to a partially filled-in circle indicating that you are touching the screen, and the contents of the pane should scroll as you move the mouse. This is illustrated in the following screenshot:

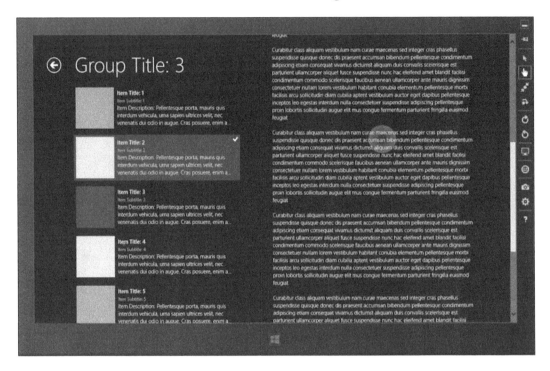

11. So far so good. Now it's time to flip the simulator to the portrait mode. Click on the **Rotate clockwise (90 degrees)** icon.

12. The simulator should now look as it does in the following screenshot with the layout of the content adapting as the device is rotated:

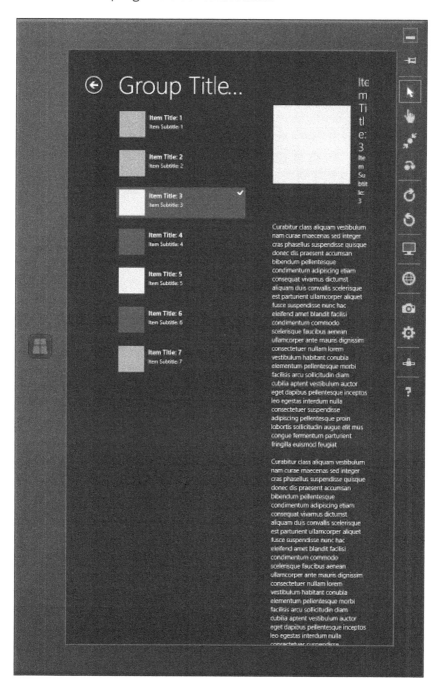

13. When the simulator has focus, it will capture the keyboard and handle key combinations such as *Alt + Tab* or *Alt + F4*. Close the simulator using *Ctrl + Alt + F4*.

14. Back in Visual Studio, open the `SplitPage.xaml.cs` file and locate the `ItemListView_SelectionChanged()` method.

15. Set a breakpoint in the `ItemListView_SelectionChanged()` method by either pressing *F9* or clicking in the gutter to the left of the code. This method may be found easiest by searching for it's name in the the quick find. Once located, set a breakpoint where shown in the following screenshot:

```
private void ItemListView_SelectionChanged(object sender, SelectionChangedEventArgs e)
{
    // Invalidate the view state when logical page navigation is in effect, as a change
    // in selection may cause a corresponding change in the current logical page.  When
    // an item is selected this has the effect of changing from displaying the item list
    // to showing the selected item's details.  When the selection is cleared this has the
    // opposite effect.
    if (this.UsingLogicalPageNavigation()) this.InvalidateVisualState();
}
```

16. Start debugging the app again by pressing *F5*.

17. When the application starts, select a group to display. The breakpoint will be hit and you could at this point step through the code to understand how it works.

How it works...

The Windows Store app simulator is actually connecting to your local machine via a remote desktop connection, and this is why the **Start** screen in the simulator looks the same as the Start screen on your Windows 8 development machine and why you are signed in automatically.

Because it's a remote desktop connection running on the local machine, the debugger is simply connecting to a local process running in a different session. If you open the **Attach to Process** window via the **Debug | Attach to Process** menu, you can see the details of the process Visual Studio has connected to. The following screenshot highlights the details of the running `SplitApp.exe` executable and shows that it is in session **3**, which is the Windows Store app Simulator session:

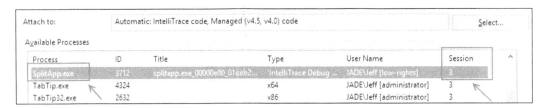

There's more...

There are a few more things to note about the simulator that we didn't touch on in the recipe.

Resolution and resizing

You can adjust the resolution the simulator is running at, allowing you to experience your app at different predefined resolutions and device sizes, shown as follows:

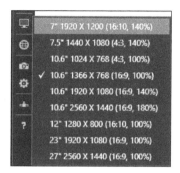

Along with changing the resolution, you can also change the onscreen display size of the simulator by dragging the bottom-right corner of the simulator just like a normal desktop window. This can help if you are simulating a device on a high-resolution desktop and you have the screen real estate to spare. It also may point out areas that are just too small for the end user and require a rework.

Remote debugging

You may have noticed that when you set the debug option for using the simulator that there was also an option to use a **Remote Machine** as the target device. Remote debugging is much simpler under Visual Studio 2013 developing Windows Store apps than has previously been the case for Windows desktop apps. For the Remote Machine option to work, you need to have the Remote Debugging Monitor running on the remote machine; the firewall needs to allow connections and you need a reasonable network connection between the two machines.

On your development machine, you simply specify the machine name of the remote machine you are targeting and start debugging. Visual Studio connects to the remote machine, prompts for credentials if required, deploys the app, and connects the remote debugging monitor for you.

From that point forward, the debug experience is almost the same as if it were a local process. As long as you have a stable network connection, you should find the experience very straightforward.

Location settings

The simulator lets you enter a simulated location that incorporates not only latitude and longitude but also the altitude and an error radius so that you can test location-aware apps on hardware that doesn't support GPS or location awareness.

If you have a location-aware device, then you can turn off the simulated values and use the values of the device itself if desired.

Taking screenshots

When you want to take screenshots of your Windows Store apps for creating your store listing, for example, then you can do so via the simulator. Simply click on the copy screenshot button on the toolbar (represented by a camera icon) and the screenshot will be placed on the clipboard and optionally in a file on your hard drive. You can control this behavior using the screenshot settings button (represented by a gear icon below the camera icon) on the toolbar.

See also

▶   The *Creating a Windows Store app* recipe

Defining capabilities and contracts

Windows 8 provides Windows Store apps with the ability to communicate with any other app on the computer without prior knowledge of what those apps might be through a concept called **Contracts**. A Contract is an operating system level interface that consumers or providers of information implement. The operating system then keeps track of which apps support which contracts and coordinates the information between apps using those contracts.

Window 8, as part of its focus on improving the trust level in the apps it runs, expects Windows Store apps to communicate the capabilities they need. A **Capability** is a permission or access right that a Windows Store app requires for it to run correctly, for example, an app that requires Internet access or local network permissions. There is a range of capabilities that the operating system can provide to Windows Store apps. An app that doesn't request capabilities from the operating system will be provided minimum level access, meaning that it will run in its isolated process space with no access to any external resources at all.

Similarly, an app may have one or more **Declarations**. A Declaration is an attribute of the app that provides extra information that the operating system can use to further integrate the app into the standard operating system experience. For instance, an app declaring the file picker contract is telling the operating system that it can be a source of files when the user is using a file picker.

In this recipe, you will add a contract declaration and adjust the capabilities of a Windows Store app.

Getting ready

Open the SplitApp project you created in the previous *Using the Windows Store app simulator* recipe.

How to do it...

In order to add a contract declaration and adjust the capabilities of a Windows Store app, perform the following steps:

1. Open the Package.appxmanifest file from **Solution Explorer**. The manifest file will open up in the main document window as shown in the following screenshot:

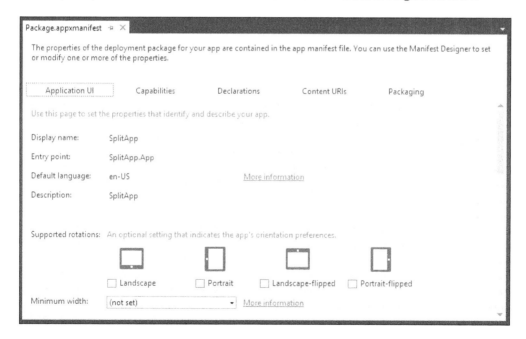

2. Select the **Capabilities** tab as shown in the following screenshot:

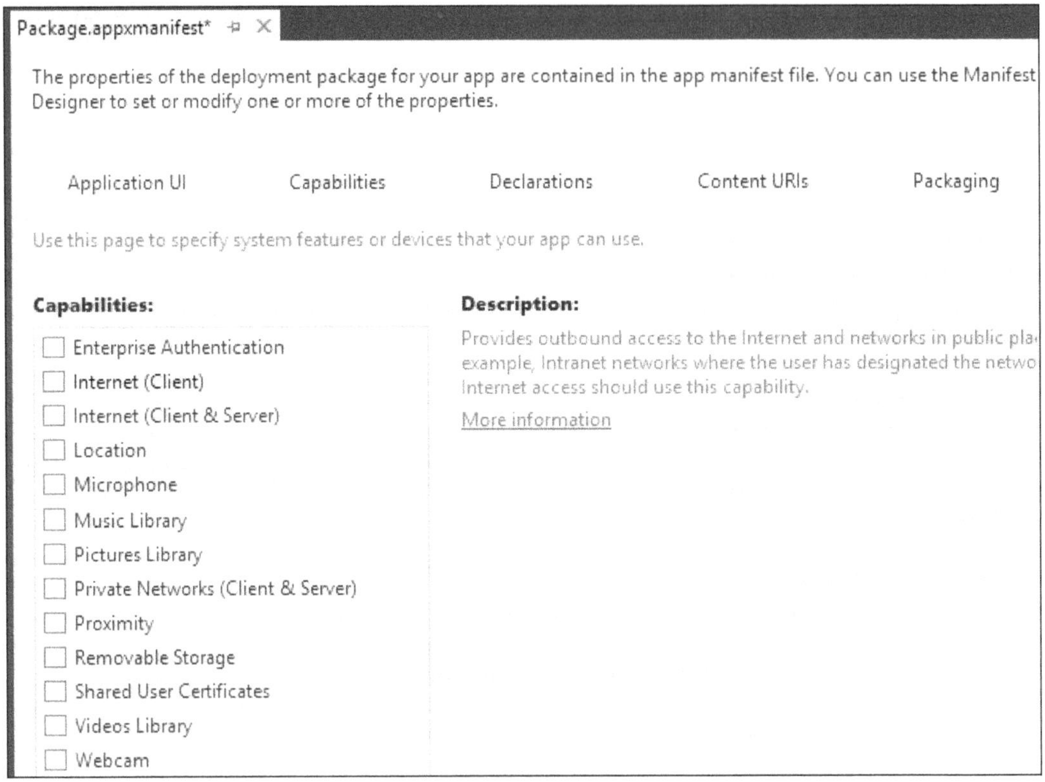

Package.appxmanifest* ⊣ ✕

The properties of the deployment package for your app are contained in the app manifest file. You can use the Manifest Designer to set or modify one or more of the properties.

| Application UI | Capabilities | Declarations | Content URIs | Packaging |

Use this page to specify system features or devices that your app can use.

Capabilities:

☐ Enterprise Authentication
☐ Internet (Client)
☐ Internet (Client & Server)
☐ Location
☐ Microphone
☐ Music Library
☐ Pictures Library
☐ Private Networks (Client & Server)
☐ Proximity
☐ Removable Storage
☐ Shared User Certificates
☐ Videos Library
☐ Webcam

Description:

Provides outbound access to the Internet and networks in public pla example, Intranet networks where the user has designated the netwo Internet access should use this capability.

More information

3. You should only declare the capabilities you actually need and as our app does not require any **Internet (Client)** access, deselect this capability.

4. Select the **Declarations** tab.

5. From the **Available Declarations** dropdown, select **File Type Associations** and then click on the **Add** button as shown in the following screenshot:

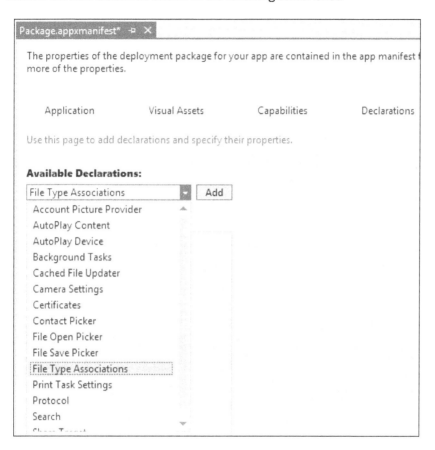

6. At this point, you are registering the `SplitApp` to handle and to be available for opening a specified file type. So if we wanted `SplitApp` to handle opening JPEG (JPG) files, we could use the settings shown in the following screenshot.

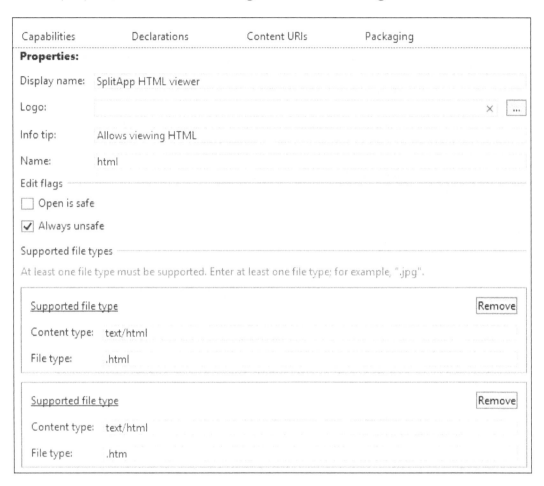

7. As shown in the previous screenshot, several fields are available to provide details. **Display name** is used to identify the app making the declaration. **Logo** can be used to specify a custom logo for this association to more easily identify your app—if left blank the app logo will be used. **Name** is a lower-case identifier for a group of files that share the same characteristics (logo, info, tip, edit flags, and so on). **Edit flags** are used to regulate how files opened from an untrusted source are handled. Since we are dealing with HTML, the previous example specifies that content should be treated as **Always unsafe**. Finally, we have setup this Declaration to address HTML files ending in `.html` and `.htm`.

8. You're not going to implement a full app as part of this recipe; so, for now just click on the **Remove** button next to **File Type Associations** in the Supported Declarations section.

How it works...

One of the design goals for Windows Store apps is that they should be portable, meaning that it should be easy to download them from the Windows Store and run them on any computer the user desires without needing any special permissions. By requiring an App Manifest to be bundled with every app, Windows itself can manage the app's installation without allowing the user to unknowingly compromise their system's security.

The App Manifest is a critical file for any Windows Store app and you need to pay attention to it. It contains all of the declarative information to inform Windows of the capabilities it needs as well as the contracts that it satisfies.

There's more...

There are numerous capabilities and contracts you can declare, but instead of describing all of the possible contracts that you can implement, let's have a look at the ones you are most likely to consider for your apps.

Contact Picker

Let's say, your app exposes information from your company address book. The Contact Picker contract will let other apps wanting to retrieve contact information use your app as a source of contact details.

File Open Picker

This provides the ability to serve files to other apps. The benefit here is that it makes your app's content available to other apps in a custom way. For example, rather than just present a list of 3D object files, an app with this contract could provide a 3D object browser that lets users see the actual model in action to help them pick the file they are looking for.

Search

The Search contract, as we saw in our recipe, allows the end user to search for information from within your program. Any program that implements the Search contract item template will be listed as a search source when the Search charm is used. Note that in Windows 8.1, an app using the Search contract will only show on the Search charm from within that app. For example, as shown in the following screenshot, the **Wikipedia** app implements the Search contract:

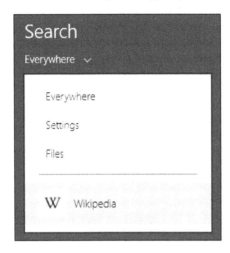

File Type Associations

This declaration allows you to specify one or more file types that your app will work with. For example, a photo app may specify types such as .jpg or .png while a music app may specify .mp3.

Certain file types are prohibited because they are reserved or for security reasons. For a list visit: http://msdn.microsoft.com/en-us/library/windows/apps/hh452684.aspx.

Share Target

The Share Target contract is used when you want to share something with someone else. For example, sharing web addresses on Twitter or Facebook, or sharing a picture with friends. The contract definition lets you determine what type of files or data can be shared (for example, image files, e-mail addresses, or URLs).

This contract is a little different to the previous ones you've seen. The contract is indicating that the app is a consumer of the shared information, not a source as with the other contracts.

Capabilities

As with the contracts, not all capabilities are going to be of interest for most developers. The following are some of the more important ones that you should be aware of.

Internet (Client)

The Internet (Client) capability lets Windows know that your app will be making requests to Internet-based resources but it will not be receiving any connections. It is for outbound connections on public networks only.

Given that most Windows Store apps are expected to have some level of Internet connectivity, this is enabled by default in the project templates.

Internet (Client & Server)

The Internet (Client & Server) capability informs Windows that your app will not only request data but will also be serving data and can accept inbound connections. Even if you specify this capability, you cannot accept inbound connections on critical ports. Specifying this capability means you do not need to specify the Internet (Client) capability, and if you do, it will have no effect.

Home or Work Networking

Windows 8 maintains the concept of network profiles for your machine and the Home and Work networks are considered to be private networks with separate security profiles from the public Internet. The Home or Work Networking capability allows you to make both inbound and outbound connections on these trusted networks.

As with the Internet (Client & Server) capability, you cannot accept connections on critical ports.

Library access

Windows Store apps have limited access to the underlying filesystem and must request access as part of their capabilities. The Music Library Access, Pictures Library Access, and Videos Library Access capabilities must be selected in order to access files in each of those locations.

When accessing a library, only files with extensions listed in the **File Type Association** contract will be available.

For a complete list of app contracts, refer to the following MSDN article, *App contracts and extensions (Windows Store apps)*: `http://msdn. microsoft.com/en-us/library/windows/apps/hh464906.aspx`.

See also

▶ This recipe provides an introduction to using Visual Studio's tools for editing a `.appxmanifest` file. You may also create and edit this manifest (which is an XML file) directly with an editor of your choice. For more information, visit: `http://msdn. microsoft.com/en-us/library/windows/apps/br211476.aspx`

Analyzing your App's performance

Visual Studio 2013 has added additional app performance and diagnostic tools over what was found in VS2012. The **Performance and Diagnostics** menu provides the following tools:

- ▶ **CPU Sampling**: This tests what parts of your app are CPU intensive.
- ▶ **Energy Consumption**: This runs your app to determine how much power it consumes. It is a useful guide to maximize battery life when your app is being run on a portable device.
- ▶ **XAML UI Responsiveness**: Ensuring your app feels fast to users is critical to its adoption. This tool helps you monitor where your app may need optimization.

Getting ready

For this example, we will continue to use the SplitApp project created in the *Using the Windows Store app simulator* recipe.

How to do it...

The following are steps to analyze your app's performance:

1. With SplitApp open, open the **Performance and Diagnostics** screen. For Visual Studio Express, this is found under the menu **Debug | Performance and Diagnostics**. For the paid editions (Professional and greater), this is located under the menu **Analyze | Performance and Diagnostics**. In either case, the hot key is *Ctrl + Alt + F9*.

2. On the screen that appears next, select the **Energy Consumption** test. Then click on **Start**.

3. After starting the test, your Visual Studio will start your app. Operate it as you expect a typical user would if you would like an overall report, or focus on a specific area if you feel something is especially draining. When you are done, close your app as usual (*Ctrl + Alt + F4*).

4. Visual Studio will prepare a report of your app's energy usage after closing your app as seen in the following screenshot:

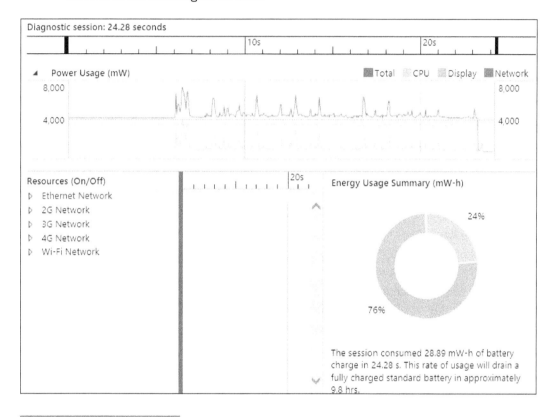

How it works...

Visual Studio monitors your apps' power usage via the emulator as you operate the app. It collects this information for your review at the conclusion of the simulator.

There's more...

Your app may use different hardware features of a device, and have different usage patterns. You can configure specific pieces of hardware via the emulator to be active or not based on those patterns, for example, comparing the differences in power usage between the wireless Ethernet versus a physical hardware connection.

Packaging your Windows Store app

For Windows 8 to correctly load and run a Windows Store app, it must be packaged in a particular format. The information contained in the package includes the capabilities and contracts that your app uses as well as information on the app user tile, the splash screen, and more.

This recipe will show you what you need to do to package your Windows Store app so that it is ready for the world to use.

Getting ready

Open the `SplitApp` project that you created in the *Using the Windows Store app simulator* recipe.

How to do it...

Perform the following steps for packaging your Windows Store app:

1. Open the `Package.appxmanifest` file from **Solution Explorer**.

2. Examine the fields in the **Application UI** tab. Add a space to the **Display Name** field so that it reads as **Split App** instead of `SplitApp`.

3. Add a useful description in the **Description** field. For example, `A sample app using the Split layout`.

4. Moving to the **Visual Assets** tab, under the **Tile** section, confirm the **Show name** field is set to **Square 150x150 Logo** as shown in the following screenshot. This setting will make the name of the app appear on the **Tile** on the Windows Start screen.

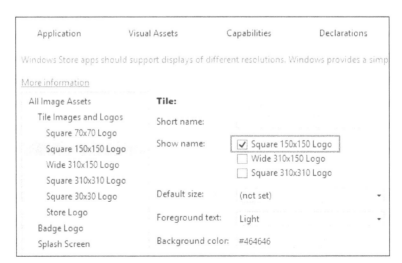

5. In the **Packaging** tab, adjust the **Package Display Name** to include a space so that the package name is **Split App**.

6. Save your changes to the manifest file.

7. Build the solution.

8. In Visual Studio, right-click on the solution in **Solution Explorer** and select **Deploy Solution**. This will deploy the Split App to your local machine ready for use.

9. In **Solution Explorer**, select the SplitApp project and then click on the **Show All Files** icon as shown in the following screenshot:

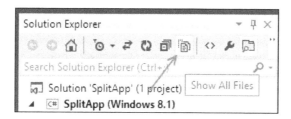

10. Navigate to the bin\Debug folder so that you can see the output from the build. This is the output that will be uploaded to the Windows store when you publish your app. It should look something like the following screenshot:

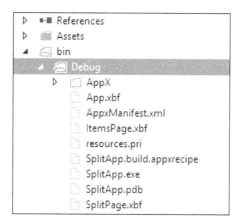

11. Press the Windows key to bring up the Start screen and scroll as needed to locate your new app. (Alternatively you can start typing the app's name at the Start screen to search for it.) You should see an icon for the **Split App** as shown in the following screenshot:

12. Deploying locally is great, but if you want to test your app on another machine, you will need to create a package. Right-click on the `SplitApp` project in **Solution Explorer** and navigate to the **Store | Create App Packages...** option from the context menu (Depending on your version of Visual Studio, you may have to be signed in for this option to be available, and you may also find it directly in the main menu **Store | Create App Package...**). If you choose the context menu route, it will look similar to the following screenshot:

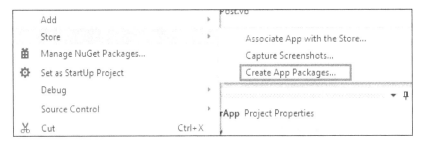

13. Select **No** when asked to build a package for the Windows Store and click on **Next**. (Packaging for the Windows Store is discussed in the *Appendix, Visual Studio Medley*.)

14. For the **Create App Packages** dialog box, leave all settings at the default. After you have reviewed the screen click on the **Create** button shown in the following screenshot:

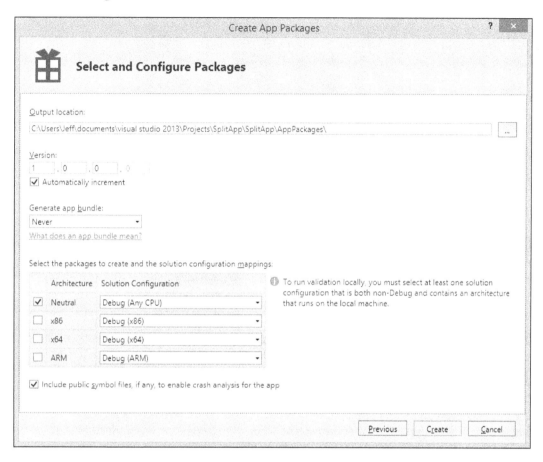

15. Wait until the package creation process completes and click on **OK** to dismiss the notification dialog.

16. Once the package finishes building, refresh **Solution Explorer** and you should now see an **AppPackages** folder appear that contains the package ready for local deployment as shown in the following screenshot:

```
Solution 'SplitApp' (1 project)
  ▲  C# SplitApp (Windows 8.1)
      ▷  🔧 Properties
      ▷  ■·■ References
      ▲  📁 AppPackages
          ▲  📁 SplitApp_1.0.0.0_AnyCPU_Debug_Test
              ▷  📁 Add-AppDevPackage.resources
                  📄 Add-AppDevPackage.ps1
                  📄 SplitApp_1.0.0.0_AnyCPU_Debug.appx
                  📄 SplitApp_1.0.0.0_AnyCPU_Debug.appxsym
                  📄 SplitApp_1.0.0.0_AnyCPU_Debug.cer
              📄 SplitApp_1.0.0.0_AnyCPU_Debug.appxupload
```

How it works...

You may notice in the `bin\Debug` folder that there are a few extra files generated, namely the `resources.pri`, `AppxManifest.xml` and `SplitApp.build.appxrecipe` files. The `AppxManifest.xml` file is simply a renamed copy of the `package.appxmanifest` file.

The `resources.pri` file contains the app resources in a binary format and the `SplitApp.build.appxrecipe` file is used for incremental builds of the package so that each time the package is rebuilt, the package version number is automatically incremented.

Moving to the **AppPackages** folder, there is a file with an `.appxupload` extension, which is a ZIP archive containing the app and any debug symbols, and there is a layout folder with a name based on the app, the CPU type, and so forth. In this case, the layout folder is called `SplitApp_1.0.0.0.AnyCPU_Debug_Test`.

Doing a deployment of the app to a test machine is simply a matter of copying this layout folder to the test machine and running the `Add-AppDevPackage.ps1` PowerShell script from that folder.

There's more...

Packages need to be signed in order to be uploaded to the Windows Store. When developing locally, Visual Studio uses a temporary certificate. However, deploying to the Windows Store will require a certificate issued by the store.

See also

▶ The *Submitting apps to the Windows Store* recipe in *Appendix, Visual Studio Medley*

Validating your Windows Store app

Every app submitted to the Windows Store will be validated by Microsoft before being listed. Part of that validation process involves running the app through an automatic certification tool that Microsoft has included with Visual Studio. You should check that your app passes the certification tool before beginning the Windows Store submission process.

Getting ready

Ensure the `SplitApp` project you were using in the *Packaging your Windows Store app* recipe is working correctly and has been deployed.

For the certification process to work, your deployed version must be in the **Release** mode.

How to do it...

The following steps need to be performed in order to validate your Windows Store app:

1. From the Windows Start screen, launch the **Windows App Cert Kit**. The app will prompt for elevation and then start a wizard as shown in the following screenshot:

2. Select the **Validate Windows Store App** option. The tool will search for Windows Store apps installed on your machine and list them.

3. Packages are listed by the `Display Name` listed in each app's manifest file (manifest files have the extension `.appxmanifest`). Locate your app and highlight it, and click on **Next**.

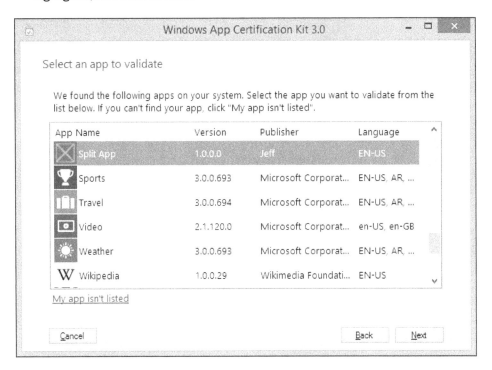

4. The Kit will then allow you to select the tests you would like to run. The default technique to test everything is what we will use here, so click on **Next**.

5. The certification process will then proceed by running your app multiple times to test its various characteristics.

6. When the certification process completes, you will be immediately prompted to save an XML file containing the report. Choose a location to save the file to and once the file is saved, you will see the completion dialog.

7. Click on the link in the dialog to view the report. Windows will prompt for a program with which to view the report, pick an editor of your choice, or use Internet Explorer. Scan the file for warnings and errors.

How it works...

The certification kit runs your app in order to verify each of the rules it has. It does not perform tests of your app's functionality, but rather validates how well the app behaves within the context of the Windows operating system and whether the rules for listing the app in the store are satisfied.

When your app passes the certification kit tests with no warnings or errors, it is ready for submission to the Windows Store where Microsoft will perform additional content and behavioral checks.

See also

- The *Submitting apps to the Windows Store* recipe, in *Appendix, Visual Studio Medley*
- Microsoft's official guide, *App certification requirements for the Windows Store*, is available online at `http://msdn.microsoft.com/library/windows/apps/hh694083.aspx`
- Further background on the app certification process and tips for a successful distribution are available at `http://msdn.microsoft.com/en-us/library/windows/apps/hh694079.aspx`

3
Web Development – ASP.NET, HTML5, CSS, and JavaScript

In this chapter, we will cover:

- ▸ Getting started with Bootstrap
- ▸ Previewing changes across multiple browsers
- ▸ Creating HTML5 web pages
- ▸ Taking advantage of CSS editor improvements
- ▸ Understanding the JavaScript editor improvements
- ▸ Adding bundling and minification to JavaScript and CSS files
- ▸ Verifying pages with the Page Inspector tool

Introduction

Application development based on web technologies continues at a breakneck pace with increasingly advanced functionality being enabled by ever-improving tools. With Windows 8, languages that originated for the Web (HTML5 and JavaScript) have found a place in the creation of Windows Store apps.

In addition to improving the JavaScript support that began with VS2012, VS2013 sees the arrival of **One ASP.NET**, which is designed to maximize the availability of all of Microsoft's current web technologies for use in any scenario. As a developer, you are no longer forced to choose at the start of a project which type of framework to use, instead you may start making your web application in the .NET language you prefer. Incorporate what you need, when you need it, whether that means web forms, MVC, Web API, or some combination of them all.

In this chapter, we will look at different areas where VS2013 can help make your web development tasks easier; from editor enhancements to specific tools such as Page Inspector.

Getting started with Bootstrap

Visual Studio 2013 changes the default template used for MVC-based projects to use the open source Bootstrap framework. Bootstrap provides a dynamic design that automatically reacts in a useful way to the resizing of browser windows, which also lends itself to easily accommodate the wide range of phones and tablets in use today.

You may recall the default MVC template from VS2012, which is shown as follows:

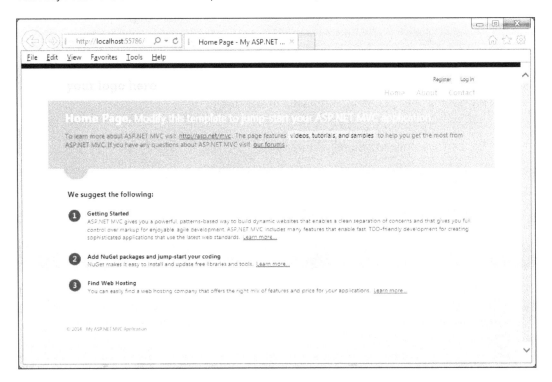

In VS2013, a One ASP.NET project using MVC with Bootstrap looks like the following screenshot:

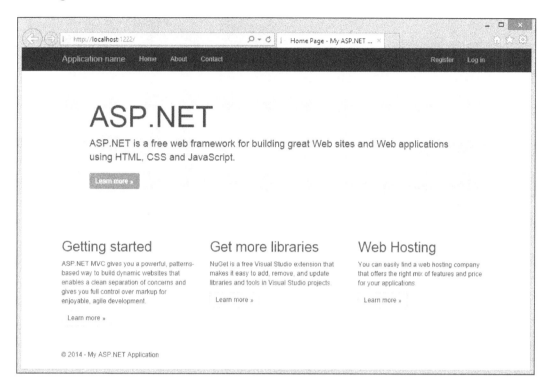

In this recipe, we will create a new MVC application to see Bootstrap in action.

Getting ready

You can use Visual Studio Express 2013 for Web or any of the premium versions for this recipe.

How to do it...

We'll start off creating a new project to see what is provided out of the box and then see what options exist for customization. This is performed with the following steps:

1. Start up your copy of VS2013.

2. Create a new project by navigating to **Visual C# | Web | ASP.NET Web Application**, accepting the default project name or one of your own choice.

3. On the next dialog box, choose **MVC** as shown in the following screenshot:

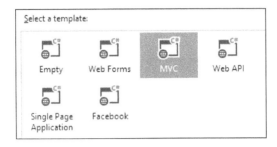

4. After Visual Studio finishes creating the project files, you may be prompted to select a source control system **Team Foundation Version Control** or **Git**. For the purposes of this recipe, we will just click on the **Cancel** button, but if you have a preference, feel free to make your choice.

5. At this point, you can preview your application if you want to see what you are starting with. Pressing *F5* or navigating to **Debug | Start Debugging** will bring up the default Bootstrap template as shown in the introduction to this recipe. If you decide to review/debug the app, please stop debugging before continuing.

6. The default MVC application that we've created uses the default Bootstrap theme. It's not a bad theme, but you will probably want to customize it a bit so that your site doesn't remain a clone. The CSS files that define your site's theme are located in the **Content** directory shown as follows:

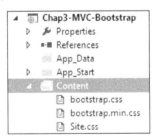

7. As you may surmise from the filenames, the `bootstrap.css` file contains a more human-friendly definition of the site while the `bootstrap.min.css` file is the minimized version intended to reduce loading time.

8. Before replacing the `bootstrap.css` file, rename it to avoid overwriting it by right-clicking on the file in the **Solution Explorer** window and clicking on the **Rename** option. Feel free to use a name of your choice.

9. Let's get a new theme from Bootswatch to personalize our site. Navigate to `http://bootswatch.com/`.

10. You can review the themes there and pick one that appeals to you. For this recipe, we'll choose `United`. The CSS file is found at `http://bootswatch.com/united/bootstrap.css`.

11. Download this new theme file to the **Content** directory of your Visual Studio project. (If you are using the defaults, your project will be in the `Documents\Visual Studio 2013\Projects\` directory, where `Documents` should be adjusted depending on your version of Windows.)

12. Once downloaded, it will have to be added to your project. Right-click on the **Content** directory in **Solution Explorer** and navigate to **Add | Existing Item...** as shown in the following screenshot:

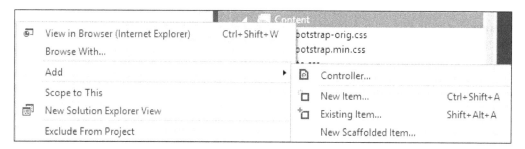

13. Choose your newly downloaded file, and add it to the project.

14. Preview the changes by pressing *F5* or navigating to **Debug | Start Debugging** as described in step 5:

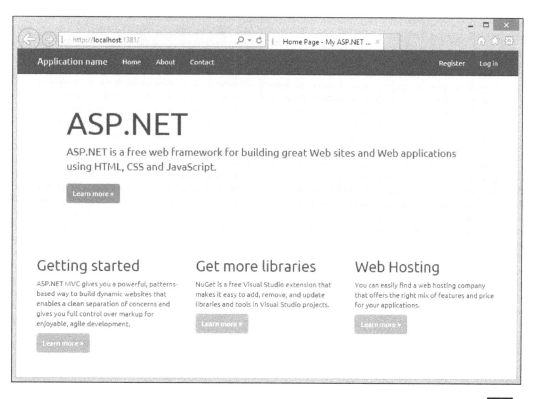

15. Note that you will want to download the minimized version of the theme when you are ready for a production release.

There's more...

The new templates based around MVC5 are not the only templates that ship with VS2013.

Visual Studio 2012 Templates

Depending on your particular development scenarios, you may need to create a new web application using the older MVC4. VS2013 supports this, letting you use the new editor features while maintaining compatibility with legacy environments. Instead of creating your web application with the One ASP.NET approach, use a template under **Web** | **Visual Studio 2012** as shown in the following screenshot:

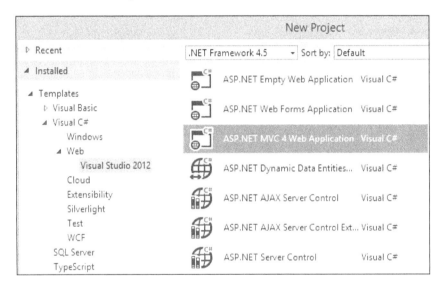

All of your familiar project types from VS2012 are available, with the sole exception of the ASP.NET MVC 3 Web Application template.

See also

▶ For more information on the Bootstrap framework, and to examine the source code, visit the project's home page at http://getbootstrap.com/. Specifically, your customization is described at http://getbootstrap.com/getting-started/#customizing.

▶ If you would like to know more about MVC5, check out Microsoft's official tutorial at http://www.asp.net/mvc/tutorials/mvc-5/introduction/getting-started.

▸ See the *Adding bundling and minification to JavaScript and CSS files* recipe later in this chapter.

Previewing changes across multiple browsers

A common task faced by HTML designers is the constant workflow of editing web pages and reviewing their changes. With the large number of web browsers in the market, it can be tedious to keep them all in sync as changes are made. VS2013 seeks to address this with the advent of the **Browser Link** feature. The Browser Link feature allows you to select any number of browsers available on your development machine and have them refreshed after making changes to your web pages. This feature makes it very easy to make changes to your website and preview them across your site's supported browsers in a streamlined way.

In this recipe, we will look at how to set up Browser Link and how it can help you with your projects.

Getting ready

You can use Visual Studio Express 2013 for the Web or any of the premium versions for this recipe. You should also install any web browser you plan to use (Google Chrome, Mozilla Firefox, and so on) before we start, but you can also just use Internet Explorer if you prefer.

How to do it...

We'll start this recipe by enabling support for Browser Link and then seeing it in action, by performing following steps:

1. Open up a web-based project in Visual Studio.

2. Ensure that your project's `Web.config` supports Browser Link by adding the following configuration option to `system.webServer` (note that it may be present so be sure to avoid any duplication):

```
<configuration>
  <system.webServer>
    <modules runAllManagedModulesForAllRequests="true" />
  </system.webServer>
  <system.web>...</system.web>

</configuration>
```

3. In the following snippet, you can see that the `<system.webServer>` element is added, and within that a setting for `modules`:

```
<system.webServer>
  <modules runAllManagedModulesForAllRequests="true" />
</system.webServer>
```

This enables Browser Link for all files in your project, including the HTML-based ones. If this is not set in your `Web.config` file, you will see the following error message on your **Browser Link Dashboard** window:

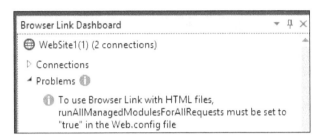

4. Once this change has been made, open an HTML page in your editor. To browse with Browser Link, you will have to open the web browsers as follows. For this example, we will be using **Firefox** and **Internet Explorer**:

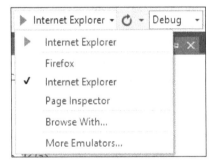

5. Click on **Browse With...**, which will open the following dialog box. While holding down *Ctrl*, click on **Firefox**. If **Internet Explorer** is not selected, *Ctrl* click on its title as well. The following screenshot shows the desired selections:

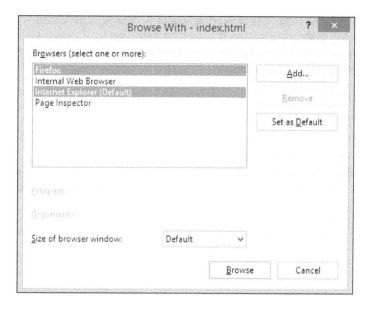

6. After making those selections, click on the **Browse** button. This will open up your web page in each browser selected.

7. You can verify this connection by leaving the browsers open and switching back to Visual Studio. Then open the **Browser Link Dashboard** window (if it is not already open) using the menu shown as follows:

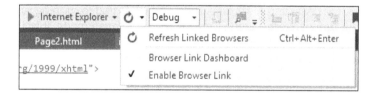

8. Opening the dashboard will show that the following connections are present:

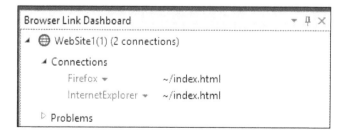

9. Returning to your main editor window, make a change, such as adding a few lines of text. You can instantly view the changes by reloading your website across all browsers with the hot key *Ctrl + Alt + Enter* or clicking on the **Browse** button under the **Browser Link** menu as shown in step 6.

How it works...

Visual Studio is able to make this feature work by injecting a snippet of JavaScript into the web pages served by Visual Studio's internal web server. This code is added transparently behind the scenes, and does not affect your source in any way (it is not saved to the disk or entered into your source control system). The following screenshot shows the code that is added:

```
83  <!-- Visual Studio Browser Link -->
84  <script type="application/json" id="__browserLink_initializationData">
85
    {"appName":"InternetExplorer","requestId":"4940829c4d194b9094a840a9585baa32"}
86  </script>
87  <script type="text/javascript"
    src="http://localhost:1242/ad1436d90c7c447bb804f72159c98525/browserLink"
    async="async"></script>
88  <!-- End Browser Link -->
```

There's more...

This doesn't apply to just HTML pages; other components of your project will work just as well including CSS, CSHTML, and ASPX files. Browser Link is tied to running your site through Visual Studio in the **Debug** mode; when switching to the **Release** mode, it will turn itself off. The following code added to your project's Web.Config file under the appSettings tag can force Browser Link to always be ON (true) or always OFF (false) depending on your needs:

```
<appSettings>
  <add key="vs:enableBrowserLink" value="true"/>
</appSettings>
```

Creating HTML5 web pages

VS2012 increased its support for the current web standards (including HTML5), and VS2013 continues this emphasis. The HTML editor used in VS2012 traced its roots to the code originally written in the 1990s (for developers with long memories that means it originated with Microsoft FrontPage). VS2013 is debuting a new editor for web applications built around managed code, which Microsoft promises will offer greater extensibility going forward as well as greater stability. Web forms-based applications (files ending with the .aspx or .ascx extensions) will still be using the older editor, but in any case, Visual Studio will automatically pick the correct editor transparently on your behalf.

Let's take a look at this new editor by creating some pages following the HTML5 standard.

Getting ready

Just start up VS2013 or Visual Studio Express 2013 for the Web. We will be creating a brand new project for this recipe.

How to do it...

This recipe will walk through editing files in the new editor. Let's get started!

1. Create a new **ASP.NET Web Application** project using C# and ensure that you are targeting .NET Framework 4.5+. When prompted to select the template, choose the **Web Forms** project template.

   The following screenshot indicates the type of project to create, along with the appropriate .NET Framework:

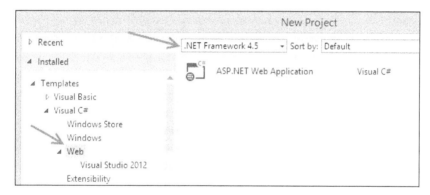

2. Open the project's `Site.Master` page (located at the top level of your project) and switch to the **Source** view in the editor.

3. In the toolbar, you can change the target schema that the IDE uses to validate the markup. By default, this will be based on the `DOCTYPE` tag in the page, though it can be changed manually. Verify that the schema is currently **DOCTYPE: HTML5** as shown in the following screenshot:

4. At present, the code in the editor is valid HTML5. Visual Studio is aware of the different standards and can assist you in writing compliant code. Edit the DOCTYPE tag from `<!DOCTYPE html>` to the following code snippet:

```
<!DOCTYPE HTML PUBLIC "-//W3C//DTD HTML 4.01//EN"
    "http://www.w3.org/TR/html4/strict.dtd">
```

The result should be like the following screenshot:

```
<!DOCTYPE HTML PUBLIC "-//W3C//DTD HTML 4.01//EN" "http://www.w3.org/TR/html4/strict.dtd">
<html lang="en">
<head runat="server">
    <meta charset="utf-8" />
    <meta name="viewport" content="width=device-width, initial-scale=1.0" />
    <title><%: Page.Title %> - My ASP.NET Application</title>
```

You will see that Visual Studio updates to report several errors as the `Site.Master` page is not compliant with this older standard. The first one is shown in the following screenshot, the `<meta/>` element in the document is now underlined in green, indicating a validation problem:

```
<head runat="server">
    <meta charset="utf-8" />
    <meta
    <title    Validation (HTML 4.01): Attribute 'charset' is not a valid attribute of element 'meta'.
```

```
100 %    ◄
⌞ Design    ▣ Split    ‹› Source
```

```
Error List
▼ ▾   ⊗ 0 Errors    ! 6 Warnings    ① 0 Messages
```

5. At the bottom of the screenshot, note that a total of 6 warnings were found. What you are seeing is how Visual Studio can help you develop your web pages according to the standards you wish to follow. Before continuing, undo the changes and switch the schema back to **DOCTYPE: HTML5** by editing the element back to the `<!DOCTYPE html>` tag. You can verify the switch was successful by noting that the errors disappear. Visual Studio uses the DOCTYPE tag to dynamically validate the HTML on your page.

6. Find the `asp:LoginView` tag in the source and click on it. You will see the standard **Smart Tasks** helper indicator appear as follows:

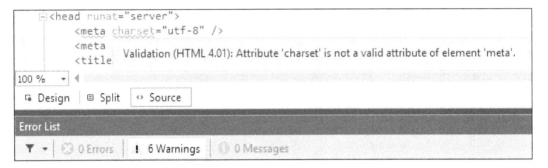

```
<asp:LoginView runat="server" ViewStateMode="Disabled">
    <AnonymousTemplate>
        <ul class="nav nav-pills nav-stacked pull-right"
            <li class="navbar-text"><a id="registerLink"
            <li class="navbar-text"><a id="loginLink" ru
        </ul>
```

7. Assume you need to set the users and permissions on the website. Hover over the Smart Tasks indicator until it expands to show an arrow. Click on the arrow to see the available tasks. Alternatively, you can press *Ctrl + .* (*Ctrl* + Period) to achieve the same result. From the pop-up task menu (shown in the following screenshot), select the **Administer Website** option to open the standard ASP.NET website administration page in a browser. Make any changes to the permissions you want and then close the browser:

 Feel free to explore the contents of the Smart Tasks helper and remember that it changes based on the context. For example, the tasks available for the `asp:LoginView` tag will differ from that of the `asp:ScriptManager` tag.

There's more...

IntelliSense in the HTML editor will filter what it displays based on the target schema used for validation. If you were to change the schema to HTML 4.01 as you did earlier in the recipe and then try a HTML5-based snippet, it would not be listed as it is not applicable to HTML 4.01. When you edit the tag name of an element that has an opening and closing tag, Visual Studio will automatically keep both tags synchronized to avoid common editing errors such as forgetting to change the matching tag or changing the wrong tag.

These improvements and in particular the inclusion of the Smart Tasks in the **Source** view, mean there are very few reasons for web developers to switch to the **Design** or **Split** views in the editor. For most developers, this will be a cause for minor celebrations.

Taking advantage of the CSS editor improvements

Just as in the HTML editor we looked at in the previous recipe, the CSS editor in Visual Studio has been improved. In this recipe, we'll take a look at these improvements by tweaking the default CSS of a web project.

Getting ready

Simply start Visual Studio Express 2013 for Web or any of the premium versions for this recipe. We will create a fresh project, but if you have an existing project in mind that has a relevant CSS file, that should work just as well.

How to do it...

There are several features that are helpful when editing CSS files, so let's take a look at what VS2013 offers by performing following steps:

1. Open the sample project `WebApp3`, or a project of your own choice that uses CSS files.

2. Open the `StyleSheet1.css` file.

3. Move your cursor to the hex color value in the `background-color` element of the `html` style and press *Ctrl* + Space bar to activate the CSS color picker as shown in the following screenshot:

```
html {
    background-color: #ffffff;
}
```

4. Click on the down chevrons (the icon with downward facing arrows) to expand the picker to show the full gamut of colors from which you can choose. Note that the picker also lets you change the opacity of the color selected:

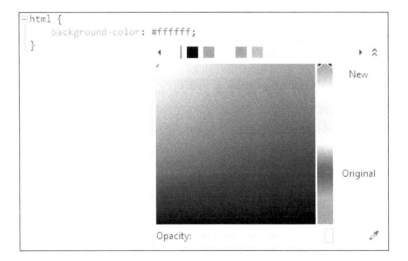

5. Also to note in the preceding screenshot is the color picker highlighted at the bottom-right corner. When building CSS for a site, sometimes you need to use a color from a picture supplied by a designer but don't have the hex value of that color. In these cases, you can use the color picker to select the color value. To test this out, click on the color picker button at the bottom-right corner of the Color Chooser window and then click anywhere on the screen where the color you need to use is currently showing. The color of the pixel where you click will be automatically selected for you.

6. The *Ctrl* + Space bar technique works on other fields too. Navigate to the `body` style and you will see that options are available for other items including `font-weight` or `text-decoration`.

7. To ensure your page is even more attention grabbing, you really should shout at your visitors. Go to the end of the `body` style and add a new blank line after the `font-weight` attribute. Type the text, then press *Ctrl* + Space bar, and Visual Studio will show you a list of style attributes that can be used. Select the `text-transform` attribute from the list and press *Tab*, as shown in the following screenshot:

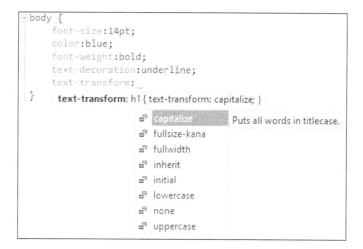

8. Visual Studio will now display a list of possible transforms that can be applied. Select the `uppercase` transform and press *Tab* to add it. Add a semicolon to complete the `style` attribute, and this will ensure that your web page really shouts at your visitors.

9. Locate the `ul` style. You should see a number of other styles indented beneath it as shown in the following screenshot. The CSS editor has a new hierarchical indentation feature that can be used to indicate specificity for your styles. For example, the `ul li a` style is indented because it has greater specificity than the `ul li` style, as shown in the following screenshot:

```
body {
    font-size: 14pt;
    color: blue;
    font-weight: bold;
    text-decoration: underline;
    text-transform: uppercase;
}

ul {
    color: orangered;
    font-weight: 200;
}

    ul li {
        color: green;
    }

        ul li a {
            color: yellowgreen;
        }
```

10. Let's add some finishing touches to the styles. Just below the `ul li a` style, add a new style with a selector of `ul li a:hover`.

11. Add a color property to the rule using any color you wish. Then press *Ctrl + K* and *Ctrl + D*. This will format the document and indent it according to specificity. Your stylesheet should now look similar to the following screenshot:

```
body {
    font-size: 14pt;
    color: blue;
    font-weight: bold;
    text-decoration: underline;
    text-transform: uppercase;
}

ul {
    color: orangered;
    font-weight: 200;
}

    ul li {
        color: green;
    }

        ul li a {
            color: black;
        }
        ul li a:hover {
            color: yellowgreen;
        }
```

12. CSS files often have a large number of rules in them, grouped into areas, the rules for the menu being a good example. You might not want to see them all the time. The CSS editor now supports regions so you can logically group your style rules and hide them when you don't need to see them. Head up to the comment `/* List comment */`. Add a new line, `/* #region List */`, below it. Then move to the end of the list-related styles and add a new line, `/* #endregion */`. As soon as you close the comment, Visual Studio will show a document outlining indicator:

```
/* #region List */
ul {
    color: orangered;
    font-weight: 200;
}

ul li {
    color: green;
}

ul li a {
    color: black;
}
ul li a:hover {
    color: yellowgreen;
}
/* #endregion */
```

13. Collapse the region by clicking the minus icon next to the opening of the `#region` comment, which will look like the following screenshot:

How it works...

IntelliSense in Visual Studio not only understands CSS 3.0 but also understands common browser hacks such as the star (*) and underscore (_) hacks used to target various IE specific styles. IntelliSense for style properties will still work if you start typing with a star or underscore.

When using CSS 3.0, the editor supports vendor-specific extension attributes such as the `moz` and `webkit` attributes for targeting specific browsers. You can see examples of this in the `bootstrap.css` file that is now a part of the default template.

If you don't like the **Hierarchical Indentation** setting, you can turn it off in the Visual Studio options. Go to **Tools | Options | Text Editor | CSS | Advanced | Formatting** and deselect the **Hierarchical Indentation** checkbox. (Or use **Quick Launch** by pressing *Ctrl + Q*, entering CSS, and pressing the down arrow key to select **Text Editor | CSS | Advanced**.)

Understanding the JavaScript editor improvements

As you have seen in the previous two recipes, the HTML and CSS editors have been greatly improved in Visual Studio and you'll be pleased to know that the JavaScript editor has also received a significant overhaul. With HTML and JavaScript being first-class choices for developing Windows Store apps, it's not really a surprise that this happened.

Within the HTML5 specification, the marquee tag is of course not valid, but thanks to Aaron Powell (http://www.aaron-powell.com/doing-it-wrong/marquee), we have a way to implement a marquee tag using JavaScript and jQuery. In this recipe, we will write a JavaScript script to emulate a marquee tag so that we can learn how the editor works.

Getting ready

Simply start Visual Studio Express 2013 for Web or any of the premium versions and you are good to go.

How to do it...

As previously noted, JavaScript's popularity makes having a powerful editor very useful. Let's see what VS2013 provides, with the help of following steps:

1. For this example, we will create a C#-based application using the One ASP.NET application. When prompted, select the **Web Forms** template.

2. Add a new JavaScript file named marquee.js to the Scripts folder in your solution.

3. The original marquee tag scrolled a block element horizontally across the page. For this to work in JavaScript, you first need to know the width of the element you will be animating. In your empty marquee.js file, start by typing the jQuery shortcut $ character followed by a period (.) to bring up the IntelliSense options. IntelliSense should now be showing you all the valid jQuery functions you can use along with their method signatures as in the following screenshot:

This is page 103, Chapter 3.

4. Enter the following JavaScript script in the `marquee.js` file:

```
$.fn.textwidth = function () {
  var calc = '<span style="display:none">' + $(this).text()
    + '</span>';
  $('body').append(calc);
  var width = $('body').find('span:last').width();
  $('body').find('span:last').remove();
  return width;
};
```

5. At this point, you have a simple method for returning the width of the text. You can now start writing the `marquee` function by adding the following JavaScript script at the bottom of the `marquee.js` file:

```
$.fn.marquee = function () {
  var that =$(this),
  calculatedWidth = that.textwidth(),
  offset = calculatedWidth,
  width = offset;
};
```

6. Before you go any further, put your cursor on the `textwidth()` method call in the line you just added and either press *F12* or right-click on it and select the **Go To Definition** option.

7. Visual Studio will navigate to where the `textwidth()` method definition is declared (in this case, the preceding function). In the `textwidth()` method, move the cursor onto the call to the jQuery `append()` method and press *F12* to go to its definition. You will be taken to the method in the `jquery-1.8.2-intellisense.js` file.

If you update your jQuery version, either manually or via NuGet, then you will be taken to a different version of the `intellisense.js` file than the one shown in the recipe.

8. It's time to finish off the JavaScript you were working on before. Navigate back to the `marquee.js` file by pressing *Ctrl + -* (*Ctrl* and the minus key) to navigate backwards. Complete the first part of the `marquee` function by ensuring the CSS used in the animation is defined. Start by replacing the existing `width = offset;` statement in the following code (note the change of the semicolon to a comma on the first line):

```
$.fn.marquee = function () {
  var that = $(this),
  calculatedWidth = that.textwidth(),
  offset = calculatedWidth,
  width = offset;
  css = {
    'text-indent': that.css('text-indent'),
    'overflow': that.css('overflow'),
    'white-space': that.css('white-space')
  };
  marqueeCss = {
    'text-ident': width,
    'overflow': 'hidden',
    'white-space': 'nowrap'
  };

  function go() {
    if (width == (calculatedWidth * -1)) {
      width = offset;
    }
    that.css('text-indent', width + 'px');
    width--;
    setTimeout(go, 1e1);
  };
  that.css(marqueeCss);
  width--;
  go();
};
```

9. The method ends with the addition of the `go()` function. The `go()` function is used as the main loop of the `marquee` effect and adjusts the CSS of the element each time through the loop, before using the `setTimeout` method to pause execution before looping again.

10. You may have noticed that, as you typed the inner `go()` function in the editor, the outlining tips appeared. This feature helps with document outlining. The collapsed `go()` method is shown in the following screenshot:

```
    };
+   function go() ...;
    that.css(marqueeCss);
    width--;
    go();
```

11. Now all that's left is to apply the `marquee` function to a web page. In the **Solution Explorer** window, navigate to the `About.aspx` page and view the HTML source. Move to the bottom of the HTML file and just before the closing `</asp:Content>` tag, add a reference to the `marquee` script:

```
<script src="/Scripts/marquee.js"></script>
```

12. The `<p>` element would make a good target for your `marquee` script. Add another script block directly below the reference that was added in the previous step and enter `$('p').marquee();` surrounded by the script element pair. As you type, IntelliSense will provide information on the available methods, including your newly-created `marquee` method, as shown in the following screenshot:

13. After making the edits to the `About.aspx` file, the resulting section of code should look like the following screenshot:

```
    </div>
    <script src="/Scripts/marquee.js"></script>
    <script>
        $('p').marquee();
    </script>
</asp:Content>
```

14. Run the application and navigate to the `About.aspx` page to see the `marquee` tag in action.

How it works...

When you first started typing the `marquee` script and IntelliSense displayed the jQuery information, you may have been wondering where that information came from. IntelliSense uses the contents of the `_references.js` file to discover information about the JavaScript libraries for your project.

If you don't like this file or have another convention you wish to use, then you can customize this behavior through the Visual Studio menu options under **Text Editor | JavaScript | IntelliSense | References**, selecting the **Implicit (Web)** reference group.

There's more...

Visual Studio supports ECMAScript 5, and IntelliSense will show ECMAScript methods whenever appropriate. For example, the `trim()` method will be displayed for string variables but not for numeric variables.

If you want good page load times with JavaScript, you should be placing your scripts at the bottom of your page, with the exception of the `Modernizr` library. In the `About.aspx` page, you placed the scripts at the bottom of the page, but since that page is actually loaded into an ASP.NET content control on a master page, the scripts would be rendered mid page. Not quite what you want.

For more information on the impact of JavaScript positioning and the impact on page load times, see the *Yahoo! Best Practices for Speeding up Your Web Site* list at `http://developer.yahoo.com/performance/rules.html`.

A better approach might be to add a new content placeholder to the master page called, for example, `EndOfPageScripts`, and place it below the `<footer/>` element. In the `About.aspx` file, you can then add a second ASP.NET content control for the `EndOfPageScripts` placeholder and place the scripts there.

The JavaScript editor does not support regions out of the box. If you would like to use them with your JavaScript editing, there are solutions available. In particular *Mads Kristensen* maintains the Web Essentials Visual Studio extension that provides this functionality (and much more). Visual Studio 2012 users should try `http://visualstudiogallery.msdn.microsoft.com/07d54d12-7133-4e15-becb-6f451ea3bea6`, while Visual Studio 2013 users should use `http://visualstudiogallery.msdn.microsoft.com/56633663-6799-41d7-9df7-0f2a504ca361` or visit `http://vswebessentials.com/`.

See also

▸ The *Fortifying JavaScript applications with TypeScript* recipe in *Chapter 9, Languages*

Adding bundling and minification to JavaScript and CSS files

One of the common techniques for improving website performance is to reduce the number of requests a browser needs to make in order to get the resources required for the page, and to compress any resources that are requested to reduce bandwidth.

When it comes to both JavaScript and CSS, this generally means combining all of the files of the same type into a single large file (**bundling**) and then removing unnecessary whitespace from them and renaming variables to use the minimum amount of space possible, while still leaving the functionality unchanged (**minification**).

Since version 4.5, ASP.NET supports automatic bundling and minification; in this recipe, you'll add bundling and minification to a site and see how it impacts your development activities.

Getting ready

We're going to use the project from the previous recipe, *Understanding the JavaScript editor improvements*. If you haven't already done so, complete that recipe first.

If you don't have time, the completed code from the previous recipe is located in the `Chapter 3\Marquee.zip` archive for you to use as your starting point.

This recipe assumes that your browser of choice has developer tools that are able to capture network traffic. If you use Internet Explorer, you will need Internet Explorer 11 or higher, which is what this recipe assumes you are using.

How to do it...

Bundling and minification are important steps to remember when moving your code into production (even if just testing for production-like environments). Let's see how to do it:

1. Build the application and run it without the debugger by pressing *Ctrl + F5* or navigating to **Debug | Start Without Debugging** from the menu.
2. Navigate to the `http://<yoursite>/About.aspx` page in your browser and open the browser's developer tools. If you are using Internet Explorer 11, you can press *F12* to open them.

3. Go to the **Network** tab (*Ctrl + 4*) and click on the **Start Capturing** (*F5*) button. In the browser window, press *Ctrl + F5* to force a complete refresh of the page. The network trace should show that a lot of files are required to load the page as shown in the following screenshot:

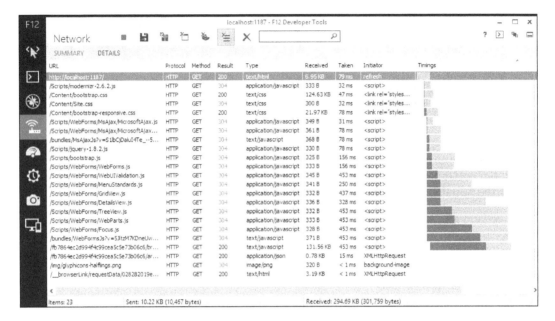

4. Look at all those requests! If you want a faster loading page, you need to reduce this. Leaving the browser open, switch back to Visual Studio and in the **Solution Explorer** window, find and open the `Site.Master` file.

5. In that file, at line 12, you will find the code shown in the following screenshot:

```
<asp:PlaceHolder runat="server">
    <%: Scripts.Render("~/bundles/modernizr") %>
</asp:PlaceHolder>
```

6. The `Scripts.Render()` statement is outputting a `~/bundles/modernizr` file. Look at the **Solution Explorer** window again. There is no `bundles` folder. What's going on here? This is shown in the following screenshot:

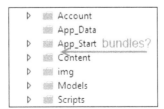

7. In **Solution Explorer**, expand the `App_Start` folder and then open the `BundleConfig` file within that. The third statement of the `RegisterBundles()` method defines the missing file, whose code is as follows:

```
bundles.Add(new ScriptBundle("~/bundles/modernizr").
  Include("~/Scripts/modernizr-*"));
```

8. In your project, you will no doubt want the `bundles` file for your own custom JavaScript; so, we are going to follow the preceding example and create one now by adding a new statement to the `RegisterBundles()` method as follows:

```
bundles.Add(new ScriptBundle("~/bundles/customjs").
  Include("~/Scripts/marquee.js"));
```

9. Go back to the `Site.Master` file and at the bottom of the page include a reference to your `customjs` bundle, as shown in the following screenshot:

```
    </form>
    <%: Scripts.Render("~/bundles/customjs") %>
</body>
```

10. Next, go to the `About.aspx` page and remove the script reference for the `marquee.js` file. Since the marquee function won't be present when it's called in the `About.aspx` page, change the call to only happen when the page is ready, as follows:

```
<script>
  $(function () { $('p').marquee(); });
</script>
```

11. Now is a good time for a checkpoint. Rebuild the solution, switch over to your browser and perform a full page refresh (that is, press *Ctrl* + *F5* in Internet Explorer). Assuming the network tab is still open in the developer tools, you should see the `marquee.js` file being loaded and the marquee effect still working.

12. While you have defined the bundles, they still aren't actually being bundled or minified. Switch back to Visual Studio, and in **Solution Explorer**, find and open the `Global.asax.cs` file. In the `Application_Start()` method, add the following highlighted line of code to enable optimizations:

```
void Application_Start(object sender, EventArgs e)
{
    // Code that runs on application startup
    BundleConfig.RegisterBundles(BundleTable.Bundles);
    RouteConfig.RegisterRoutes(RouteTable.Routes);
    BundleTable.EnableOptimizations = true;
}
```

> The `EnableOptimizations` property forces bundling to occur. Without this call, bundling only occurs when running the site in **Release** mode. In other words, when the `debug="true"` attribute of the `system.web.compilation` tag of the `web.config` file is specified, bundling optimizations are disabled.

13. Rebuild the application, switch over to the browser and perform a full page refresh again. The network trace will now show that JavaScript bundles are being downloaded instead of individual script files and that the download size of the bundle files is less than the download size of the original JavaScript files, as shown in the following screenshot:

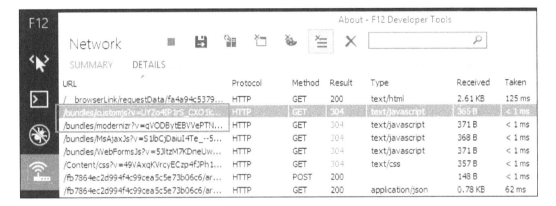

14. It's worth confirming that the scripts are not only bundled but also minified. Navigate to the **Debugger** tab (*Ctrl + 3*) in the browser developer tools and select the `customjs` file from the scripts' drop-down list, as shown in the following screenshot:

15. Use the search box on the right-hand side to locate the `marquee` function as shown in the following screenshot. In the following script you can see that, not only has the whitespace been removed, but the variable names have also been shortened and the code slightly optimized. Exactly what you should expect minification to do:

How it works...

Inside the ASP.NET runtime, when a browser requests a page with a bundle in it, ASP.NET will either render the names of the individual files in the bundle or the bundle name itself, depending on whether optimizations are turned on or not. When optimizations are on, browsers will request bundles by their name and ASP.NET will group the individual bundled files into a single larger file before minifying them and sending the result back to the browser. The resulting minified file is cached by ASP.NET so that future requests do not impact site performance.

You can create your own custom bundle types by subclassing the `Bundle` class. This allows you to provide your own minification rules and bundling mechanisms, which is useful if you want to support web technologies such as LESS, Sass, or CoffeeScript.

See also

▶ The *Understanding the JavaScript editor improvements* recipe.

Verifying pages with the Page Inspector tool

Page Inspector is a tool included with Visual Studio built around a web browser that runs inside Visual Studio. It provides a range of features for page inspection similar to what is provided with the Internet Explorer developer tools, but with the ability to map elements back to the line of code that generated them.

Let's have a look at what Page Inspector can really do for your debugging experience by following this recipe.

Getting ready

Page Inspector requires Internet Explorer 9 (or higher). If you are developing on a Windows Server operating system, you must have **Internet Explorer Enhanced Security Configuration** disabled.

How to do it...

This recipe will show how mapping a web page's code to what is displayed can make development easier as follows:

1. For this example, we will create a C#-based application using the One ASP.NET application. When prompted, select the **Web Forms** template.

2. You can launch the Page Inspector tool by navigating to **View | Other Windows | Page Inspector**, the **Quick Launch** tool by right-clicking a page and selecting the **View In Page Inspector** option; by clicking the Page Inspector icon in the toolbar; or by pressing *Ctrl + K* and *Ctrl + G*.

   For this recipe, right-click on the `Views\Home\Index.cshtml` page and select **View in Page Inspector**.

3. The **Page Inspector** window will open next to the main document area and display the site's home page.

4. In the bottom half of the **Page Inspector** window, is a toolbar with a number of inspection tabs and also an **Inspect** button. Click on that and then hover over various elements of the web page in the top section of the inspector. As you do, you will notice that the HTML tab adjusts to show the relevant part of the DOM, and that the code where the text came from is shown in the document pane. In our following example, `"We suggest the following"` is highlighted by both the **Page Inspector** window and in the HTML code:

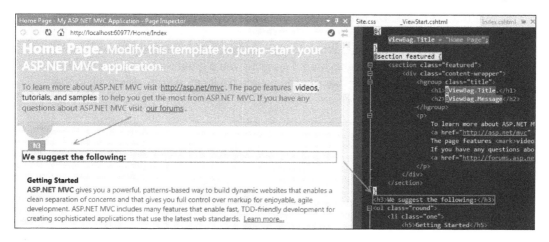

5. Inside the `Views\Shared\_Layout.cshtml` file, which should currently be open in the document area, move to the bottom of the file and locate the footer element. Highlight a section of the copyright notice, as shown, and note how the matching text in **Page Inspector** is highlighted. You will also see that the HTML tab of the **Page Inspector** updates to show the page's DOM and that the other **Page Inspector** tabs update to reflect the details of the selected item. This bidirectional selection is very useful, which is shown in the following screenshot:

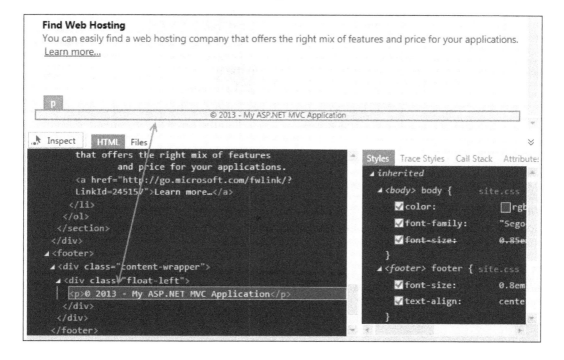

6. With the text still highlighted, select the **Trace Styles** tab in the **Page Inspector** screen and scroll down to the `margin-top` attribute. Expand the item and click on the `footer p` selector. When you do so, the `site.css` file will be shown and the `footer p` style is highlighted. This gives you a great way to trace a style you see on a page directly back to the source file it came from, as shown in the following screenshot:

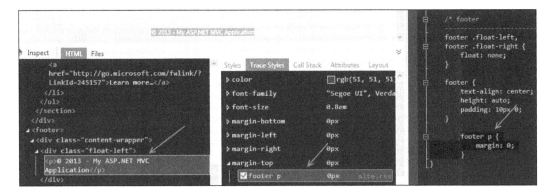

 If you can't find the style, you may have accidentally changed the selected content on the **Page Inspector** screen. Try reselecting the copyright notice and then looking at the **Trace Styles** tab again.

7. Change the `margin` properties of the style in the `site.css` file to `margin: 10px 0 0 0;` as this will make a noticeable change to review.

8. Page Inspector detects that a change has occurred and the page is updated to reflect the change dynamically. This makes it easy to find the exact settings needed for the layout you desire.

How it works...

When you first launched the Page Inspector tool, you didn't need to compile the web application or launch IIS Express. Page Inspector did that for you automatically, making the process of getting started very simple.

The mapping of the page elements and styles back to the source only works if those elements are statically generated. In other words, they have to map back to the actual source and can't be the result of any dynamic DOM manipulation performed via JavaScript. The mapping of page elements to the JavaScript that created them is not supported by Page Inspector.

There's more...

One thing you didn't look at in the recipe was the **Files** tab, located next to the **HTML** tab in the **Page Inspector** window. The **Files** tab shows all the source files that were used in the construction of the layout for the page, excluding CSS and JavaScript files, as shown in the following screenshot:

Partial pages and user controls

If you right-click on a partial view or a user control in the **Solution Explorer** window and select **View in Page Inspector**, the **Page Inspector** screen may not be able to determine how to launch those pages because the routing rules aren't specific enough. When this happens, the **Page Inspector** screen will prompt you for a URL to navigate to that includes the view or control you are interested in, as shown in the following screenshot:

Enter an absolute or relative URL and then click on the **Set** button to define the mapping. The next time you inspect the user control or partial page, the Page Inspector tool will remember your mapping and launch the appropriate page for you, allowing you to inspect your element in the context of the containing page.

If Page Inspector is too narrow

By default, Page Inspector is loaded in a tool window on the left of the IDE and renders the page in a very narrow window.

You don't have to live with it this way. If you have multiple monitors, then you can undock the Page Inspector tool and drag it over to your second monitor. You will then be able to see the full page in Page Inspector as well as your code, and the two-way synchronization of code and HTML will be easy to track.

Alternatively, you can move Page Inspector to the main document area, though doing so will mean that you have to use *Ctrl + Tab* to switch between Page Inspector and the source files. Of course, the final option is to simply widen the Page Inspector tool window, though doing so reduces the size of the main document area. Regardless, if the window is too narrow for your liking, change it. It's your Visual Studio; make it work the way you want it to.

4

.NET Framework 4.5.1 Development

In this chapter, we will cover:

- ▶ Adding the Ribbon to a WPF application
- ▶ Creating a state machine in Visual Studio
- ▶ Creating a task-based WCF service
- ▶ Managing packages with NuGet
- ▶ Unit testing .NET applications
- ▶ Sharing class libraries across runtimes
- ▶ Detecting duplicate code

Introduction

In *Chapter 3, Web Development – ASP.NET, HTML5, CSS, and JavaScript*, we looked at web development and how Visual Studio supports web developers. Whether it is used for traditional desktop applications or designing apps for Windows 8.1, the .NET Framework remains both popular and powerful.

In this chapter, we turn the spotlight on Visual Studio 2013's support for the .NET platform for non-web applications. We will look specifically at functionality that has been added or enhanced. This chapter will start by discussing what was included with the .NET Framework 4.5 and then move on to discuss the new features found in 4.5.1.

You should be aware that like its previous version, the .NET Framework 4.5, Framework 4.5.1 is an in-place upgrade of its 4.X predecessors. While 4.5 and 4.5.1 are mutually exclusive (you can only have one of them installed), they will run side by side with earlier versions of the framework (version 3.5 SP1 and its predecessors).

 Be aware that the .NET Framework 4.5 is not supported on Windows XP, Windows Vista, or Windows Server 2003. Extended support for Windows XP SP3 ends in 2014. Extended support for Windows Server 2003 ends in 2015. The .NET Framework 4.5.1 ships with VS2013 and is a part of Windows 8.1 and Windows Server 2012R2. It is also available for use on Windows Vista, Windows 7, and Windows Server 2008R2. Your application's targeted audience should be a consideration when choosing which framework to use, but most new applications should use the latest version of the framework available.

Adding the Ribbon to a WPF application

Windows Presentation Foundation (**WPF**) remains the recommended choice for developing desktop applications on the Windows platform. Visual Studio 2013 itself is a WPF application and, even with Windows 8, there are still many applications that target the Windows Desktop. This recipe will show how Microsoft's Ribbon control can be used in your applications.

Getting ready

You'll need some icons for this recipe. If you have your own set available, feel free to use them. Otherwise, for this recipe we used an icon set available at PC Unleashed, via `http://pcunleashed.com/download/icon-sets/`, specifically the **Icons Unleashed Vol. 1 - Computer Hardware** set. Regardless of the icons that you use, make sure you have downloaded these icons before starting this recipe; alternatively have a set of your own you can use instead.

How to do it...

Here, we will see how to add the Ribbon control and how quickly it can be customized. Let's get started!

1. Start Visual Studio and create a new **WPF Application** under **Visual C#** using the default name.

2. You need to add a reference to the Ribbon control in order to use it. Right-click on the project in the **Solution Explorer** window and add a reference to the `System.Windows.Controls.Ribbon` assembly. (Note that you can use the search box for a faster search.)

3. The easiest way to work with the Ribbon control is to edit the XAML file directly as there are a number of child controls that need to be added. Open the `MainWindow.xaml` file and change the markup so that the base class is no longer a `<Window>` control but a `<RibbonWindow>` control, as shown in the following screenshot:

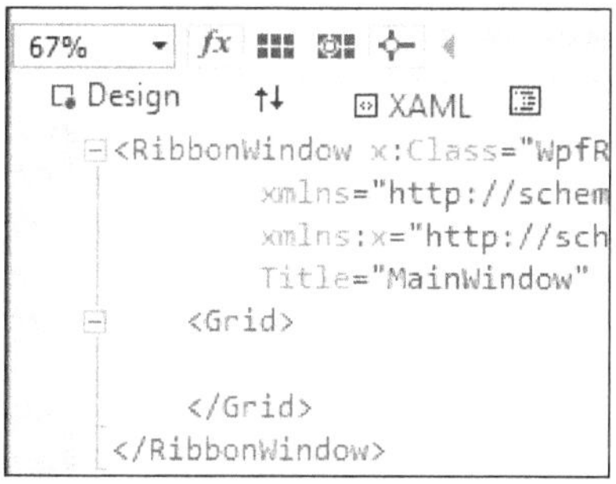

4. You need to make a similar change in the code-behind file. Navigate to the `MainWindows.xaml.cs` file and change the base class from `Window` to `RibbonWindow` and add a using statement for the `System.Windows.Controls.Ribbon` assembly to the file as well, as shown in the following screenshot:

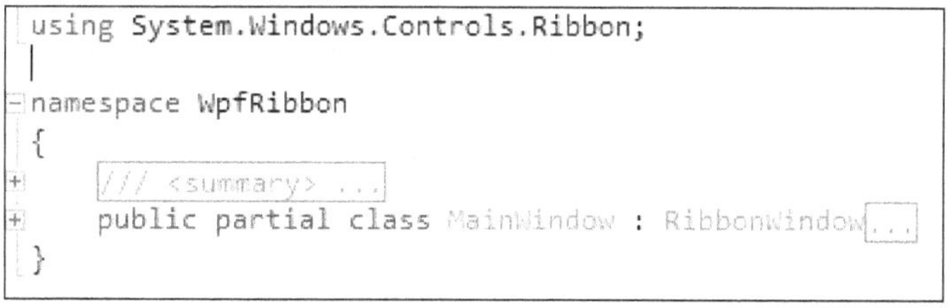

5. Switch back to the designer. Add a Ribbon control to the form by adding a `<Ribbon>` element inside the `<Grid>` element as shown. As you do so, the Ribbon will appear in the designer window as shown in the following screenshot:

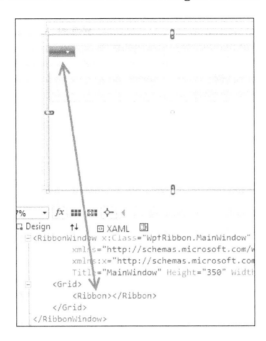

6. The Ribbon hosts tabs, groups, and buttons (amongst other things); so, populate the Ribbon element by adding the following XAML code:

```xml
<RibbonTab x:Name="FirstTab" Header="Tab1">
  <RibbonGroup Header="Group 1">
    <RibbonButton Background="Azure" Label="Button 1" />
    <RibbonButton Background="AliceBlue" Label="Button 2"
      />
  </RibbonGroup>
  <RibbonGroup Header ="Group 2">
    <RibbonButton Background="Bisque" Label="Button 3" />
    <RibbonButton Background="MintCream" Label="Button 4"
      />
  </RibbonGroup>
</RibbonTab>
<RibbonTab Header="Tab2">
  <RibbonGroup Header="Group 3">
    <RibbonButton Background="Purple" Label="Button 5" />
    <RibbonButton Background="Pink" Label="Button 6" />
  </RibbonGroup>
</RibbonTab>
```

7. Now would be a good time to run the application to verify that the Ribbon control appears correctly and that you can switch between tab groups. The application should look like the following screenshot. Close the running application when you have confirmed things are working:

8. The Ribbon control also features a Quick Access Toolbar and an Application Menu. Add a Quick Access Toolbar by adding the following code between the `<Ribbon>` and `<RibbonTab>` elements:

```
<Grid>
<Ribbon>
  <Ribbon.QuickAccessToolBar>
    <RibbonQuickAccessToolBar>
      <RibbonQuickAccessToolBar.Items>
        <RibbonButton Background="Red" />
        <RibbonButton Background="Orange" />
      </RibbonQuickAccessToolBar.Items>
    </RibbonQuickAccessToolBar>
  </Ribbon.QuickAccessToolBar>
<RibbonTab x:Name="FirstTab" Header="Tab1">
```

9. Run the application again to confirm that the Quick Access Toolbar is appearing correctly, as shown in the following screenshot;

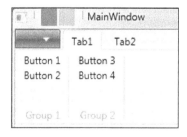

10. At this point, it's time to add some images to those buttons. Start by adding an `Images` folder to your project. (Right-click on your project, navigate to **Add**, and select **New Folder**.)

11. From Windows Explorer, copy your icons (you should have downloaded this before starting the recipe) into the `Images` folder.

12. In Visual Studio, click on the **Show All Files** icon in **Solution Explorer**. Select all the files in the `Images` folder, right-click on them, and select **Include in Project**.

13. Hover the mouse over one of the image files in the `Images` folder. You will see a preview of what each image looks like as you hover over each filename, making it easier to identify the files you are working with. The following screenshot demonstrates this behavior:

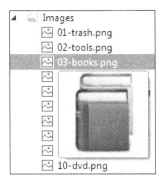

14. Edit the `MainWindow.xaml` file to replace each button background color with an image. The `QuickAccessToolbar` element uses the `SmallImageSource` attribute for images and the main `RibbonTab` buttons use the `LargeImageSource` attribute. Make the changes for as many buttons as you like using the images you prefer. You can avoid typing full path names by entering just the attribute name and then dragging the image to use onto the XAML editor from **Solution Explorer** as shown in the following screenshot. Just remember to change the image path so that it is a relative path, not an absolute one:

```
1    <RibbonQuickAccessToolBar.Items>
        <RibbonButton SmallImageSource="" />
        <RibbonButton Background="Orange" />

2    <RibbonQuickAccessToolBar.Items>                      08-desktop.png
        <RibbonButton SmallImageSource=""                  09-usb.png
        <RibbonButton Background="Orange" />               10-dvd.png

3    <RibbonQuickAccessToolBar.Items>
        <RibbonButton SmallImageSource="c:\users\jeff\documents\visual studio 2013
        <RibbonButton Background="Orange" />

4    <RibbonQuickAccessToolBar.Items>
        <RibbonButton SmallImageSource="Images\08-desktop.png" />
        <RibbonButton Background="Orange" />
```

15. Now, let's run the program to see what it looks like with all of the icons added:

How it works...

While this recipe shows you how to lay out the new WPF Ribbon, it is hardly an exhaustive run through the Ribbon control and nor is it meant to be. The recipe is to show you how Visual Studio assists you when developing WPF applications. You should have also noticed that the WPF designer feels better to use and is more responsive than previous versions of Visual Studio designer (especially the 2010 edition) and that it keeps up with your XAML changes better than before. This will make developing WPF and XAML applications in general a lot smoother than before and it should remove some of the angst people have had with Visual Studio's XAML designer.

Beyond the Ribbon, WPF also includes features such as asynchronous validation and the ability to access collections on non-UI threads without needing to marshal calls. These extra features, along with the improved binding, async language features, and general .NET 4.5 runtime enhancements should help you to deliver Windows Desktop applications that feel more responsive for your users and don't suffer from the white screen of death anywhere near as often.

See also

▸   The *Making your code asynchronous* recipe in *Chapter 6, Asynchrony in .NET*

Creating a state machine in Visual Studio

Windows Workflow underwent a major overhaul for .NET 4.0 and was largely a ground-up rewrite. As part of that rewrite, the workflow designer was also rebuilt; however, it was still fairly slow, and with medium to large workflows, it was more than capable of crashing Visual Studio, taking all your unsaved changes with it and generally annoying anyone who had to use it for long periods of time.

What is a workflow? Developer Dino Esposito has said, "... a workflow-based solution consists of making complex processes simpler to model and implement..." Microsoft's MSDN provides in-depth information on creating workflows, starting with a conceptual overview available at `http://msdn.microsoft.com/en-us/library/dd489465(v=vs.110).aspx`.

In Visual Studio 2012 and higher, the workflow designer has been given some additional attention to improve its stability and performance. For the workflow engine itself, Microsoft has added much needed support for state machines. Let's have a look at how to put a state machine together.

Getting ready

Start a premium version of Visual Studio and create a new project by navigating to **Visual Basic | Workflow | Activity Library**.

How to do it...

Workflows are used to model a structured activity (typically, but not always, a business process). We will create a simple workflow here to show what is available by performing the following steps:

1. The `Activity1.xaml` file should be open in the designer when the project is created, but if it isn't, open it now.

2. In the **Toolbox**, you will see the workflow activities as well as a new group called **State Machine**. (If you don't see the **Toolbox**, you can get it by navigating to **View | Toolbox** or *Ctrl +Alt + X*.) From within that group, drag a **StateMachine** activity onto the `Activity1.xaml` designer, as shown in the following screenshot:

You must drag it onto the **Drop activity here** text; the cursor will change when you are on the target.

3. Add a second state by dragging a **State** activity onto the state machine you just added in the designer. You should now have two states as shown in the following screenshot:

4. Next, position your mouse near the edge of **State1** as shown in the following screenshot. A connector drag handle will appear (**1**). Click-and-drag it to join **State1** to **State2** (**2**). When you let go of the mouse, the transition will be given a default name of **T1** (**3**).

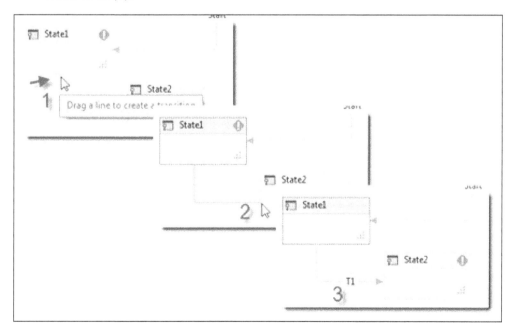

5. All state machine workflows need a final state, so drag a **FinalState** activity onto the state machine and add transitions from the existing states to the final state as shown in the following screenshot:

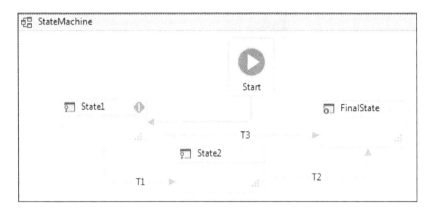

6. The default naming of states doesn't make much sense from a usability perspective, especially if more states are added in the future. Before we rename them, notice that the use of "breadcrumbs" can make navigating back to the **StateMachine** activity easier. The following screenshot illustrates this:

7. Click on the headers of each state to edit their names and name them **New Task**, **In Progress**, and **Closed** as shown in the following screenshot:

8. To rename the state transitions, you will need to double-click on each one and then click on the header to edit the description. Change the transition names to **Commenced**, **Cancelled**, and **Completed** as shown in the following screenshot:

9. At the top-right corner of the **New Task** state is a blue warning symbol. This exists because there are two possible transitions from **New Task** to other states. The workflow engine needs a way to choose between the two transitions. Add an argument to your workflow by clicking on the **Arguments** tab at the bottom of the designer as shown in the following screenshot:

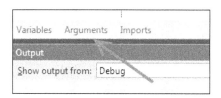

10. Click on the **Create Argument** line to create a new entry. Leave the argument name as the default one but change the **Argument type** field to **Boolean** as shown in the following screenshot:

Name	Direction	Argument type	Default value
argument1	In	Boolean	Enter a VB expression
Create Argument			

11. Double-click on the **Commenced** transition in the designer, and in the **Condition** field, enter `argument1 = True` as shown in the following screenshot:

 Because `argument1` is a Boolean, the `= True` comparison is redundant. It is used here to aid readability and maintainability.

12. Return to the state machine view in the designer by clicking on the **StateMachine** activity in the breadcrumbs, located at the top of the designer (as shown in step 6).

13. Set the **Condition** on the **Cancelled** transition to `Not argument1`, using the same method you used in step 10.

14. Return again to the state machine view and note how the **New Tasks** state no longer shows you the warning icon because there is now a way to choose between the transitions. Build the application to ensure the workflow is defined correctly. (You won't be able to run this directly without adding an executable project, but building is sufficient to check for errors.)

How it works...

State machines are a very welcome addition to the Windows Workflow functionality and are useful in many situations. In addition, each state has entry and exit actions that are activated as the state machine transitions between states and can be used to customize how the workflow behaves.

Upon entering a state, the entry action is processed and when the action is complete the trigger for each possible state transition is prepared. Triggers are effective event listeners and state transitions only occur when a trigger event has been received and the condition evaluates to true. The Workflow runtime provides a number of trigger activities, though in many cases, you will need to create your own trigger activities specifically for your purposes.

There's more...

You can now search within workflows! If you've ever dealt with large workflows, then you'll be well aware of the pain of not having a search feature.

Quick Find (Visual Studio's normal find function) will match on object properties, variables, arguments, and expressions.

Find in Files will search the XAML representation of the workflow and match on anything it finds in there. When double-clicking a search result, the designer will navigate to the activity that matches the search result location.

Panning

Pan the designer either by dragging with the middle mouse button, or by holding down space and dragging with the left mouse button.

Alternately, click on the panning icon at the bottom-right of the designer:

C# Workflows

In previous versions of Visual Studio, all workflow projects required expressions to be entered using the Visual Basic syntax. With Visual Studio 2012/2013 C# workflow, projects will now use C# expressions.

If you upgrade an existing workflow from .NET 4.0 to .NET 4.5, a compatibility flag is set on the workflow so that any existing Visual Basic expressions will still work.

Versioning your workflows

Versioning problems have long hindered the adoption of Windows Workflow. Changing a workflow definition could easily break long running, persisted workflows, and cause applications to crash or data to be lost.

With Visual Studio 2012/2013, a new `WorkflowIdentity` class has been added for dealing with persisted workflows. This class allows you to host multiple versions of a workflow side by side so that your old persisted workflows can still run through to completion, while new workflows will use the new definitions you provide.

In addition, Dynamic Update can be used to amend the definition of older, persisted workflows if you want to bring them in line with your newer workflow definitions. For more information refer to: `http://msdn.microsoft.com/en-us/library/hh314052(v=vs.110).aspx`

Creating a task-based WCF service

There's not a great deal of change in Visual Studio 2013 for **Windows Communication Foundation** (**WCF**) development. However, don't misread that as there's not a lot of improvement for WCF developers in the .NET Framework 4.5.X. It's simply that since WCF is a technology focused on network communications, the visible changes in Visual Studio are quite small.

> WCF is Microsoft's framework designed for use in creating applications based on service-oriented architecture. Some of the features provided by WCF include interoperability, service metadata, data contracts, and security. For in-depth information on using WCF, refer to `http://msdn.microsoft.com/en-us/library/dd456779(v=vs.110).aspx`.

The only visible changes are in the **Add Service Reference** dialog box and the IntelliSense support for WCF configurations.

In this recipe, you'll create a task-based WCF service so that you can see what has changed. A sample WPF application will call this sample WCF service.

Getting ready

Simply start a premium version of Visual Studio and you're ready to go.

How to do it...

As you create these WCF applications, you will see how Visual Studio simplifies the process. Let's get started:

1. Create a new project by navigating to **Visual C# | WCF | WCF Service Application** and give it the default name.

2. Add to the solution another project by navigating to **Visual C# | Windows | WPF Application**, also giving it the default name.

3. Compile the solution and start the WCF service to make sure it starts correctly and so that you have a working service for the next few steps. Stop the application once you are satisfied that it's working.

4. Back in Visual Studio, right-click on the WPF application and select **Add | Service Reference**.

5. Click on the **Discover** button. The **Service1** web service should be discovered, as shown in the following screenshot:

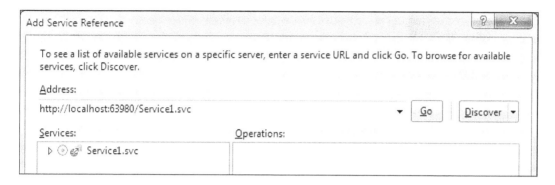

6. Click on the **Advanced** button in the bottom-left corner of the **Add Service Reference** dialog box. Ensure that, in the options for service generation, **Generate task-based operations** is selected and **Allow generation of asynchronous operations** is turned ON as shown in the following screenshot:

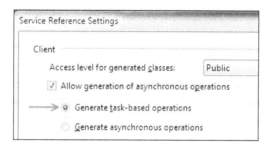

7. Click on **OK** in this options' dialog box (**Service Reference Settings**) and then again in the **Add Service Reference** dialog box to generate the service proxy. (In some cases, Visual Studio may erroneously throw an error here, such as **Unable to check out the current file**. If you get bit by this bug, simply restart Visual Studio and try again.)

8. Go to the `app.config` file for the WPF application, locate the `<endpoint>` configuration section, and hover the mouse over the `name` attribute. A tooltip will appear to explain what this attribute is for as shown in the following screenshot. Given the issues people historically have had with understanding the details in WCF configuration, this IntelliSense information is very welcome:

```
<endpoint address="http://localhost:63980/Service1.svc" binding="basicHttpB
    bindingConfiguration="BasicHttpBinding_IService1" contract="ServiceRefe
    name="BasicHttpBinding_IService1" />
lient   Optional string attribute. This attribute uniquely identifies an endpoint for a given contract.
n.ser
```

9. Start adding a new endpoint configuration to the `<client />` section by typing `<endpoint binding=`. IntelliSense will kick in to show you the values that can be placed inside the quotes. That makes editing WCF configurations much simpler than trying to remember what all the valid values are. Select the `basicHttpBinding` value as shown in the following screenshot:

10. Continue building the `endpoint` configuration by adding a `bindingConfiguration` attribute. When you type the `=` (equals), IntelliSense will pop up again and show you the binding configurations available as well as a tooltip about the binding. Select the `BasicHttpBinding_IService1` option and then close the `endpoint` configuration element with `/>`, as shown in the following screenshot:

```
<client>
  <endpoint address="http://localhost:63980/Service1.svc" bindin
      bindingConfiguration="BasicHttpBinding_IService1" contract
      name="BasicHttpBinding_IService1" />
  <endpoint binding="basicHttpBinding"
          bindingConfiguration="BasicHttpBinding_IService1"/>
</client>
```

The recipe asks you to add it here so you can see the new IntelliSense support for WCF configurations. A complete WCF tutorial is outside the scope of this book, but once you finish the recipe, try manually adding support for https using the `basicHttpsBinding` class. For now, we will comment out the second endpoint that we just added.

11. Returning to the WPF project, open the `MainWindow.xaml` file and change the `<Grid>` element to a `<StackPanel>` element. Add a button and a textbox to the `<StackPanel>` element as listed in the following code:

```
<StackPanel>
  <Button x:Name="btnAsync" Click="btnAsync_Click_1">click!
    </Button>
  <TextBlock x:Name="txtText">Not yet populated</TextBlock>
</StackPanel>
```

12. Navigate to the code-behind file, `MainWindow.xaml.cs`, and add code for the button click event handler so that it calls out to the WCF service, as follows:

```
async private void btnAsync_Click_1(object sender,
  RoutedEventArgs e){
    using (var client = new
      ServiceReference1.Service1Client())
    {
      var result = await client.GetDataAsync(3);
      txtText.Text = result;
    }
}
```

13. In **Solution Explorer**, right-click on the solution and select the **Set StartUp Projects** option.

14. Choose **Multiple startup projects** and set **Action** to **Start** for both projects. Click on **OK** to save the changes:

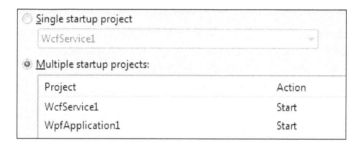

15. Press *F5* to start debugging and when the WPF application appears, click on the **click!** button to make the async call to the WCF service.

    The text below the button should update to say **You entered: 3**, proving the call to the service worked.

How it works...

As mentioned, the **Add Service Reference** dialog box can generate task-based proxy classes that you can call from your code with an await keyword. This makes asynchronous calls to services much easier to write, though you can still call the blocking, synchronous methods if you need to. The generated code contains both the synchronous method call as well as the task-based call.

WCF's **ServiceModel Metadata Utility Tool** (`svcutil.exe`) can also be used to generate task-based proxies if you prefer to use the command-line tool instead of Visual Studio.

See also

▶ The *Making your code asynchronous* recipe *Chapter 6, Asynchrony in .NET*

Managing packages with NuGet

Microsoft's approach to open source software and open source projects, in general, has softened over the years from the "open source is evil" stance it took at the turn of the century to the one where open source is now valued, embraced, and recognized as an integral part of the development ecosystem. Microsoft is now so committed to open source that they are developing a number of frameworks in an open manner including the ASP.NET Web Stack (`http://aspnetwebstack.codeplex.com`) and providing contributions for a number of third-party open source projects such as jQuery, Node.js, and Git.

With the amount of open source now available and the acceptance of open source as a normal part of development, developers needed an easy way to locate and find open source packages that could be used in their own projects; much like the package managers of other languages such as Ruby and Python. As a result, Microsoft supported an open source project to create a package manager for Visual Studio called the NuGet package manager. NuGet (`https://www.nuget.org/`) allows developers to download packages of libraries that will install themselves into a project, configure themselves, and then be ready for use by the developer. The package manager also does the work of looking for new updates and applying those updates when they are available.

In this recipe, you'll see the ways to use the NuGet package manager in Visual Studio.

Getting ready

Create a new **ASP.NET Web Application** under **Visual C#**, select the **MVC 5** project template, and give it a name of your choosing.

How to do it...

1. In **Solution Explorer**, right-click on the references node for the project and select **Manage NuGet Packages**.

2. The **Manage NuGet Packages** dialog box will appear. Under the **Online** grouping, make sure **nuget.org** is selected on the left-hand side column and then in the search box at the top-right corner, enter `EntityFramework` and wait a moment for the results, as shown in the following screenshot:

3. As you can see, **EntityFramework** appears as the first result. Note the check mark indicating that the package is already installed.

4. Now, let's add a new package. Replace the `EntityFramework` search text with `json.net`.

5. The first result should be the **Json.NET** JSON framework. Click on the **Install** button. Once the package has been installed, close the **Manage NuGet Packages** dialog box using the **Close** button.

6. Close the NuGet window and then expand the **References** node for the project in **Solution Explorer**. You should see not only the **EntityFramework** and Json.NET assemblies but also assemblies for other packages that the bundler relies on. A partial listing of the references is shown in the following screenshot:

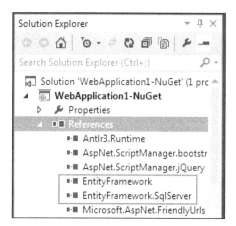

7. Open the NuGet window again by right-clicking on the **References** node and selecting **Manage NuGet Packages**.

8. Over time, the packages you have installed will become stale as the package owner releases new and updated versions. In the NuGet package manager, select the **Updates** node on the left-hand side column of the dialog box. Wait for a moment to see if there are any available updates, as shown in the following screenshot:

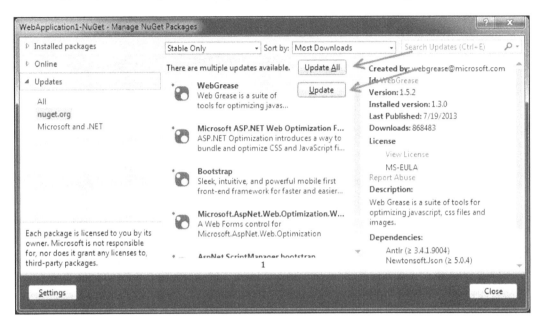

9. In the preceding screenshot, you can see buttons labeled **Update All** and **Update**. These give you the option of quickly updating all of the installed packages from `nuget.org` or individually choosing which packages you would like to update. We will continue and show how to do a bulk update from the **Package Manager Console**.

10. From Visual Studio's main menu, navigate to **View | Other Windows** and select **Package Manager Console**.

11. The console will appear at the bottom of the screen. So, click inside it and enter the command `Update-Package` and press *Enter*, as shown in the following screenshot:

12. Since a particular package is not specified, NuGet will iterate over all installed packages to see if any updates exist. Alternatively, you may enter a specific package to check for updates on that single package (for example, `Update-Package jquery`).

13. NuGet will then locate and install updates for all packages automatically. Because package installation in web projects often affects the `Web.config` file, you may get prompted to reload it a number of times. Each time you do, just click on **Yes**.

    The results of the update will be shown in the **Package Manager Console**, as shown in the following screenshot (note you may receive a notice to restart Visual Studio depending on the scope of the update):

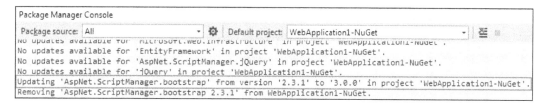

14. Compile and run the application to check that everything still works as expected.

How it works...

NuGet uses a central, well-known location for storing packages located at `http://www.nuget.org`. Anyone can create and upload packages to this site and the site features a gallery allowing you to search and browse all available packages. For many people, the NuGet site is the first port of call when looking for a package to help them in their development efforts.

With Visual Studio 2012 Update 4 and Visual Studio 2013, Microsoft is using NuGet to deliver their own packages via NuGet. As you may have noticed in earlier screenshots, this feed is labeled Microsoft and .NET. This provides Microsoft with an easier way to deliver updates and provides you with an easier way to install them on your system.

There's more...

We just scratched the surface of what NuGet can do, but it offers a couple of more useful abilities. Let's take a look.

Automatically loading packages

If you are sharing solutions with different developers—perhaps you would like to try an open source project or have recently changed your programming environments for example—you will inevitably run into a situation where packages needed by your project are missing.

Visual Studio provides an option to automatically retrieve these packages for you, which can be especially helpful in these situations when you want to focus on learning the code and not be mired in troubleshooting build settings. To turn this feature ON or verify your current settings, navigate to **Tools** | **Library Package Manager** | **Package Manager Settings** as shown in the following screenshot:

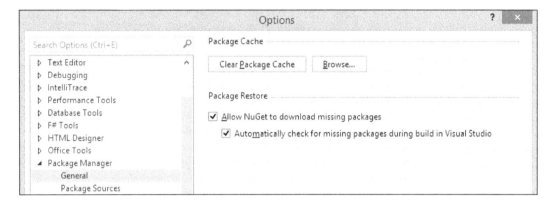

Selecting both options (as shown in the preceding screenshot) will allow NuGet to download missing packages automatically.

Using custom package locations

A lot of organizations build their own utilities, frameworks, and helpers for use in development and share them across various projects. Managing these dependencies can become difficult over time. Fortunately, NuGet can be configured to use local locations for packages, either using a filesystem location or your own internal NuGet server.

> If you wish to host your own NuGet server, instructions can be found at `http://github.com/NuGet/NuGetGallery/wiki/Hosting-the-NuGet-Gallery-Locally-in-IIS`. If you wish to host just your own project-specific server via a custom feed, check out `http://docs.nuget.org/docs/creating-packages/hosting-your-own-nuget-feeds`.

To configure Visual Studio to use a local location for NuGet packages, go to **Tools** | **Options** | **Package Manager** | **Package Sources** and add entries by filling in the **Name** and **Source** fields and then clicking on the add button. The following screenshot shows two extra entries: one configured to point to a local NuGet server and the other pointing to a network share:

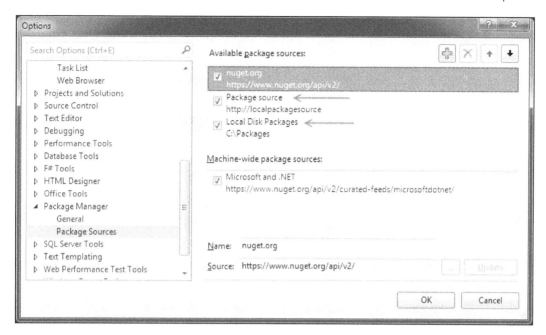

Unit testing .NET applications

When it comes to unit testing, Visual Studio has always been tightly tied to the MSTest framework. The inclusion of a unit test framework inside Visual Studio has been excellent. It has encouraged developers to improve their quality by writing tests to prove code functions as expected. On the flip side, many developers regard MSTest as an inferior unit test framework when compared to NUnit, XUnit, MbUnit, and other frameworks. The problem stems from the fact that MSTest does so much more than unit testing and as a result suffers from poor speed and bloat. Additionally, its assertion methods are fragmented across multiple classes and it has a cumbersome approach to data-driven tests and expected exceptions. MSTest has also been tied to the release cycle of Visual Studio, so updates have been very slow and it lags behind when compared to the other test frameworks.

Microsoft is ending the tight coupling between Visual Studio and MSTest by making the unit test framework pluggable. MSTest is still provided out of the box but now developers can choose the framework that they like the most, as long as their choice of framework implements a Visual Studio adapter.

Microsoft is also removing Test Impact Analysis from Visual Studio (it's still there in Microsoft Test Manager) and replacing it with a Continuous Testing style feature instead. Continuous Testing is an approach that has been gaining popularity because of the incredibly rapid feedback cycle it gives developers. The idea is that each time a change is saved in the source files, the unit tests are run to see if anything has broken. This works well with dynamic languages such as Ruby; however, as .NET is a static language, this approach is not so simple. In Visual Studio 2012 and 2013, instead of having all tests run whenever the source is saved, you can have them run automatically each time the code is compiled.

This overall testing functionality is viewed and controlled by Test Explorer. In this recipe, you will use the XUnit testing framework in a test first manner to implement a very simple calculator and you'll see how the Continuous Testing feature works. The important part of this recipe isn't so much the code you will write, but in seeing how Visual Studio can change your development practices when it comes to unit testing. Let's get to it!

Getting ready

You are going to need a premium version of Visual Studio (Professional or higher) for this recipe. Install the xUnit.net runner for Visual Studio 2012 and 2013. You can do so by navigating to **Tools | Extensions and Updates** (search for xUnit) or download the `.vsix` file from the Visual Studio gallery and install it manually (`http://visualstudiogallery.msdn.microsoft.com/463c5987-f82b-46c8-a97e-b1cde42b9099`). In either case, you will have to restart Visual Studio after installing it.

How to do it...

1. Open Visual Studio and create a new **Class Library** under **Visual C#** and name it `UnitTests`.

2. Use NuGet to add the package xUnit.net to your project. See the *Managing packages with NuGet* recipe in this chapter for a refresher on NuGet if needed.

3. Rename `Class1.cs` to `CalculatorOperations.cs`. You will be prompted to rename all references to `Class1`. Click on **Yes** so that Visual Studio will rename `Class1` to `CalculatorOperations` in the code itself.

4. In the `CalculatorOperations` class file, add the following test method. Don't worry if the code doesn't compile yet. In a test-driven approach, you write the tests first to work out how your code should behave before you implement anything. Then, you write the following implementation code to make the test(s) succeed:

```
using Xunit;

namespace UnitTests
{
  public class CalculatorOperations
  {
```

```
[Fact]
public void Adding_1_and_2_should_give_3()
{
  var calculator = new Calculator();
  var result = calculator.Add(1, 2);
  Assert.Equal(3, result);
}
  }
}
```

5. You now need to add a `Calculator` class, but good practice dictates that we shouldn't place it in your test assembly. Add a new C# class library to the unit test solution and call it `CalculationEngine`.

6. Rename the `Class1.cs` file to the `Calculator.cs` file and when prompted, allow Visual Studio to rename `Class1` to `Calculator`.

7. Switch back to the `UnitTests` project and add a project reference to the `Calculator` project. To do this, right-click on the **References** node for `UnitTests` and select **Add Reference....** Make sure **Projects** is selected on the right-hand side column and then click on the checkbox for **CalculationEngine**, as shown in the following screenshot:

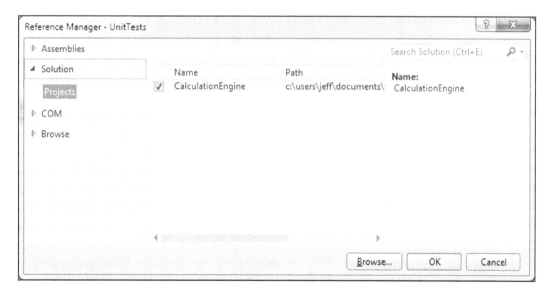

8. Place the cursor on the `Calculator()` constructor call in the unit test and either mouse over and click on the actions drop down or press *Ctrl + .* (*Ctrl* + Period) to show the available actions. Select the **using CalculationEngine;** option to add the required using statement to your test code.

9. Now place the cursor on the `Add()` method on the next line and bring up the available tasks. Again, do this either by hovering over the code with the mouse and then clicking on the options drop down when it appears or by pressing *Ctrl + .* and selecting the only available option to generate the method stub.

10. Open **Test Explorer** by navigating to **Test** | **Windows** | **Test Explorer**.

11. Select the **Run All** option in the **Test Explorer** window to compile the code and run the tests in the project for the first time.

12. The unit test should fail at this point because the method stub you generated for the `Add()` method simply throws a `NotImplementedException` as shown in the following screenshot:

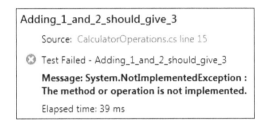

13. Switch to the `Calculator` class file and implement the `Add()` method by using the following code:

```
public class Calculator
{
    public object Add(int p1, int p2)
    {
        return p1+ p2;
    }
}
```

14. Press *Ctrl + Shift + B* to rebuild the solution. Right-clicking on the solution and selecting **Build All** will have the same result.

15. The **Test Explorer** screen will now reflect a passing test as you have implemented the method correctly.

How it works...

When using projects and unit testing frameworks supported by the test adapters, they will take care of the discoverability aspects for you. The adapter driven approach has also allowed Microsoft to create a unit test optimized version of MSTest that is fast and light and can be used in standard class libraries without a problem.

You can also mix and match your unit test frameworks. It is entirely valid to have MSTest, xUnit, and NUnit tests in one assembly. For example, you may have a suite of older tests in one framework and may want to transit to a new framework without reworking all those old tests. Now you can, without any problem at all.

Out of the box, Visual Studio only supports the MSTest framework; however, adapters are available in the Visual Studio Gallery for the major test frameworks, and the **Chutzpah** test adapter adds support for both the QUnit and Jasmine JavaScript unit test frameworks. (Chutzpah is available at `http://chutzpah.codeplex.com/`.)

 As mentioned, MSTest no longer requires a TestSettings file for unit test projects. TestSettings files can still be used with MSTest unit test projects; however, if they are included, MSTest reverts to Visual Studio 2010 compatibility mode and you will have much slower execution of unit tests.

There's more...

The changes in the test runner are fairly dramatic and with it come a number of other changes you should be aware of.

Can I restrict the unit tests that automatically execute?

In many projects, it is common to have unit tests in one test project and integration tests in a second project. Unit tests are considered to be those tests that execute entirely in memory and have no interactions with external systems such as the network, filesystem, screen, or database. Integration tests are those tests that interact with external systems.

If you want to restrict the tests that run so that only unit tests run, and slower integration tests are excluded, you will need to use the Test Explorer filter to limit the tests to run. If you have your unit and integration tests in separate assemblies, then the `FullName` filter is likely to be the filter that will help you the most.

Asynchronous tests

In .NET 4.5, MSTest now supports asynchronous tests that make use of the await keyword. You can see this in the following code where the method signature is no longer a `public void` method, but rather an `async` task:

```
[TestMethod]
async public Task Can_load_Bing_home_page()
{
    var client = new System.Net.WebClient();
    var page= await client.DownloadStringTaskAsync("http://www.bing.
com");
    StringAssert.Contains(page, "bing");
}
```

The asynchronous test ensures that the test runner will wait for the test to end before starting the next test. It does not mean that multiple tests will be run in parallel; it is just that you can test methods that use the `async` and `await` keywords.

Automatically trigger test execution

With Visual Studio Premium and Ultimate, the Test Explorer presents an additional feature: automatically executing tests every time a build is made. To select this, use the icon located on the **Test Explorer** as shown in the following screen:

See also

▸ The *Managing packages with NuGet* recipe

▸ The *Touring the VS2013 IDE* recipe of *Chapter 1, Discovering Visual Studio 2013*

Sharing class libraries across runtimes

There are a number of managed runtimes and profiles for .NET development, including the .NET Framework, Silverlight, Windows Phone, and now the WinRT profile for Windows 8 (also known as Windows Store). If you have to write code that can be shared across more than one of these runtimes, it usually involves either the use of copy-and-paste development (never a good idea!) or multiple versions of the same project and the use of linked files. The linked files approach is cumbersome and error prone and often a pain to work with when Visual Studio is telling you it can't open a file as it is already open in another project.

The solution to this is to use Portable Class Libraries. The idea here is that you can build a class library that works across all desired runtimes by ensuring that only code that works on all runtimes is used. Further, the compiler only builds the project once, regardless of the number of runtimes supported, making the overall solution faster to build.

Let's look at a quick example of how a Silverlight application might talk to a .NET application using this approach. To keep the recipe focused, we're only going to look at the connection between the two runtimes, not building a full application.

Getting ready

This requires a premium version of Visual Studio. Start the one that you have available and you're ready to go.

How to do it...

1. Create a **Silverlight Class Library** project by navigating to **Visual Basic | Silverlight** and giving it the default name. When you are prompted for the Silverlight version to use, choose **Silverlight 5**. (Depending on your system, you may be prompted to install the Silverlight runtime and SDK, install it if prompted.)

2. Right-click on the solution and add a **Class Library** project under **Visual Basic**, again giving it the default name.

3. Right-click on the solution one more time and add a Portable Class Library project under **Visual Basic**, once again giving it the default name.

4. When you are prompted to choose **Target frameworks**, change the selections so that only **.NET Framework 4.5 and higher** and **Silverlight 5** and higher are selected and then click on the **OK** button as shown:

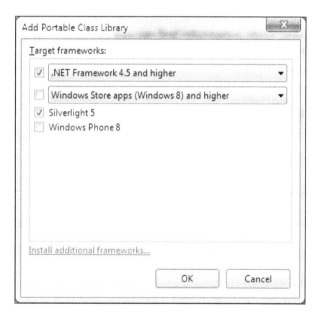

5. Right-click on the Silverlight project in **Solution Explorer** and select **Add Reference**. In the **Reference Manager** dialog box, navigate to **Solution | Projects** and select the checkbox next to `PortableClassLibrary1`. Click on **OK** to add the reference to the project as shown in the following screenshot:

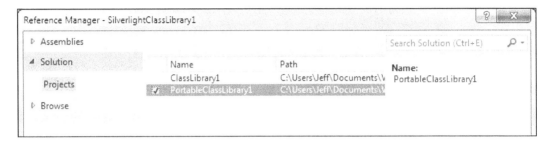

6. Likewise, right-click on the .NET class library project and add a reference to the `PortableClassLibrary1` project. You will get a warning about referencing a project using a different .NET runtime and that you will need to compile the project for IntelliSense to work correctly. Click on **OK** to dismiss the warning.

7. Navigate to the `Class1.vb` file in the `PortableClassLibrary1` project and add a method to the `Class1` class as shown:

```
Public Class Class1
  Public Function SharedMethod() As Integer
    Return 42
  End Function
End Class
```

8. Compile the solution.

9. In the `Class1.vb` file of the `ClassLibrary1` project, check that you can make a call to the portable library using the following code:

```
Public Class Class1
  Public Sub CallPortableCode()
    Dim portable As New PortableClassLibrary1.Class1()
    Dim result = portable.SharedMethod()
  End Sub
End Class
```

10. Navigate to the `Class1.vb` file in the Silverlight project and add the same code that you used in step 9 to check that a call to the portable library can be made from Silverlight as well.

11. Compile the solution to confirm that there are no compiler errors and prove that you can make calls from both the .NET Framework 4.5 code and Silverlight code to a single shared, portable library.

How it works...

The portable libraries themselves are just standard .NET class libraries with restrictions on the framework calls that can be made from within them. The set of calls that can be made is determined by the methods that are supported across all target runtimes selected in the project's properties.

A good practice to follow when writing your portable libraries is to avoid adding references to other libraries. Instead, try and design your PCLs as standalone libraries. Since most people tend to use portable library classes for WCF contracts, data transfer objects, or calculation libraries, this is unlikely to be too limiting.

One example of a PCL that demonstrates the advantages of PCLs is the `HttpClient` library (`https://www.nuget.org/packages/Microsoft.Net.Http`) published by Microsoft. This library allows an application to have a uniform way of making web calls without having to write specific code for each platform.

There's more...

Coinciding with the release of Visual Studio 2013, Microsoft has loosened the license restrictions on the portable class library reference assemblies. From a licensing standpoint, this increases the utility of using PCLs across all of your target platforms for your client software. Take advantage of PCLs to make your development process more efficient.

Xamarin offers products to add support to VS2013 for the iOS and Android platforms. This includes support for writing PCLs. For more information on the integration, see `http://blog.xamarin.com/pcl-projects-and-vs2013/` and for information on PCLs, check `http://docs.xamarin.com/guides/cross-platform/application_fundamentals/pcl/`.

Detecting duplicate code

Copy and paste development is generally regarded as a bad practice because bug fixes or enhancements in one area of code have to be repeated in all the other copies of the same code. Not only is this time consuming and tedious, but in large code bases, it's very easy to miss a change, leading to bugs and lower overall quality.

With Visual Studio, Microsoft has provided a way to detect duplicate code so that you can take remedial action to clean it up. Let's see how this is done.

Getting ready

You will need Visual Studio Premium or Ultimate for this recipe. Start it up and you're ready to go.

How to do it...

1. Create a new **Class Library** project under **Visual C#** and name it `OriginalLibrary`.

2. Rename the `Class1.cs` file to the `OriginalClass.cs` file and allow Visual Studio to rename the class itself when prompted.

3. Add a second C#-based **Class Library** project to the solution giving it the name `DuplicateLibrary`.

4. Rename the `Class1.cs` file to the `DuplicateClass.cs` file, and as in step 2, allow Visual Studio to rename the class itself when prompted.

5. In `OriginalClass`, add the following method:

```
public string StringWithSillyCheckDigit(int x, int y)
{
  if (x <= 0)
  throw new ArgumentOutOfRangeException("x", "must be
    positive");
  if (y <= 0)
  throw new ArgumentException("I don't like negatives",
    "y");
  var counter = "";
  for (int i = 0; i < x; i++)
  {
    counter += y;
  }
  var checkDigits = new List<char>() { 'a', 'b', 'c', 'd',
    'e' };
  var checkDigit = checkDigits[y % 5];
  counter += checkDigit;
  return counter;
}
```

6. Copy and paste the code you just added into `DuplicateClass`, renaming the method to `DuplicatedCheckDigit`.

7. Rename the parameters in the `DuplicatedCheckDigit` method to `p1` and `p2`.

8. Rename i to loop and counter to outString. Your duplicated method should now look like the following code:

```
public string DuplicatedCheckDigit(int p1, int p2)
{
  if (p1 <= 0)
  throw new ArgumentOutOfRangeException("p1", "must be
    positive");
  if (p2 <= 0)
  throw new ArgumentException("I don't like negatives",
    "p2");
  var outString = "";
  for (int loop = 0; loop < p1; loop++)
  {
    outString += p2;
  }
  var checkDigits = new List<char>() { 'a', 'b', 'c', 'd',
    'e' };
  var checkDigit = checkDigits[p2 % 5];
  outString += checkDigit;
  return outString;
}
```

9. From the Visual Studio menu, navigate to **Analyze | Analyze Solution for Code Clones**. The **Code Clone Analysis Results** window will be displayed and will show you where the duplication exists, as shown in the following screenshot:

10. Right-click on the **Weak Match 1(2 Files)** result and select **Compare**, as shown in the following screenshot:

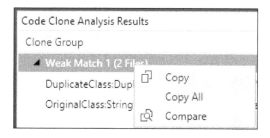

11. The two sections of duplicated code are shown in Visual Studio's new diff viewer and you can decide what remedial action to take from there:

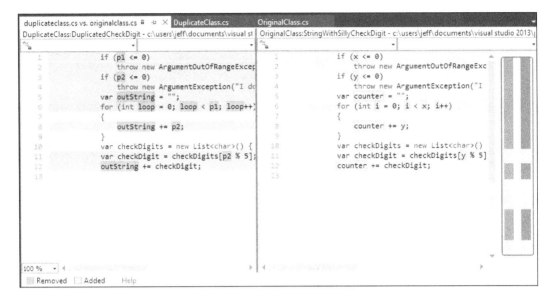

This code would have been hard to find using just **Find in Files** and looking for variable names or a single line of code. The clone detection algorithm in Visual Studio ignores differences in variable names and instead looks at the structure of the code itself. It also limits searches to duplicates that are a minimum of 10 statements long to prevent detection from taking a very long time.

If you do want to search for smaller or specific sections of code, you can highlight code in the editor, right-click on it, and select **Find Matching Clones in Solution** as shown in the following screenshot:

```
    throw new ArgumentExcep
var counter = "";
for (int i = 0; i < x; i++)
{
    counter += y;
}
var checkDigits = new List<char>() { 'a', 'b', 'c', 'd', 'e' };
var checkDigit = checkDigits[y % 5];
counter += checkDigit;
return counter;
```

Copy		Ctrl+C
Paste		Ctrl+V
Outlining		▶
Find Matching Clones in Solution		

There's more...

There are a number of items that get ignored by the detection algorithm to help improve the speed of detection and to exclude files that you are unlikely to be interested in. The following files can be ignored or excluded:

▸ Type declarations are ignored. Two classes with the same properties are not considered to be clones, nor are classes with the same method signatures. Only the code within the methods and properties is examined.

▸ The `*.designer.cs` and `*.designer.vb` files are automatically excluded, as is code within any `InitializeComponent` methods.

You can add a `.codeclonesettings` file to your project to exclude certain paths or file types from the comparison. For example, if you are using T4 code generation, you may want to place all the generated code in a subfolder and then exclude that folder from the clone detection engine by adding an entry for it in the settings file.

A sample exclusion could be like the following code snippet. This file was named `sample.codeclonesettings` and placed in the top level of the project `DuplicateLibrary` used in the previous recipe. In this case, it blocks our `DuplicateClass` file from being examined.

```
<CodeCloneSettings>
  <Exclusions>
    <File>DuplicateClass.cs</File>
  </Exclusions>
</CodeCloneSettings>
```

It can be modified to use wildcards, and also ignore a whole directory as shown in the following code snippet:

```
<CodeCloneSettings>
  <Exclusions>
    <File>ExcludeTheseFiles\*.cs</File>
  </Exclusions>
</CodeCloneSettings>
```

5
Debugging Your .NET Application

In this chapter, we will cover:

- ▶ Maximizing everyday debugging
- ▶ Debugging on remote machines and tablets
- ▶ Debugging code in production with IntelliTrace
- ▶ Debugging parallel code
- ▶ Visualizing concurrency

Introduction

It's an unfortunate reality, but modern software development still requires developers to identify and correct bugs in their code. The familiar edit-compile-test cycle is as familiar as a text editor, and now, the rise of portable devices has added the need to measure for battery consumption and optimization for multiple architectures. Fortunately, our development tools continue to evolve to combat this rise in complexity, and Visual Studio continues to improve the arsenal.

Multi-threaded code and asynchronous code are probably the two most difficult areas for most developers to work with and also the hardest to debug when you have a problem like a race condition. A race condition occurs when multiple threads perform an operation at the same time and the order in which they execute makes a difference to how the software runs or how the output is generated. Race conditions often result in deadlocks, incorrect data being used in other calculations, and random, unrepeatable crashes.

The other painful area to debug is the code running on other machines, including code in production. Hooking up a remote debugger in previous versions of Visual Studio has been less than simple, and as for debugging code in production, the experience was frustrating. In this chapter, we're going to see how the improvements to the debugging experience that began with Visual Studio 2012 has been expanded in Visual Studio 2013, and how it can help you diagnose the root cause of a problem faster so you can fix it properly and not just patch over the symptoms.

Maximizing everyday debugging

Given the frequency of debugging, any refinement to the tools used can pay immediate dividends. Visual Studio 2013 brings the popular Edit and Continue feature into the 21st century by supporting 64-bit code. Added to that is the new ability to see the return value of functions in your debugger. The addition of these features combines to make debugging code easier, allowing you to solve problems faster.

Getting ready

For this recipe, you will just need a premium version of VS2013 or you may use VS Express for Windows Desktop. Be sure to run your choice on a machine using a 64-bit edition of Windows. Note that Edit and Continue previously existed for 32-bit code.

How to do it...

Both features are now supported by C#/VB, but we will be using C# for our examples. The features being demonstrated are compiler features, so feel free to use code from one of your projects if you prefer. To see how Edit and Continue can benefit 64-bit development, perform the following steps:

1. Create a new **C# Console Application** using the default name.

2. To ensure the demonstration is running with 64-bit code, we need to change the default solution platform.

3. Click on the drop-down arrow next to **Any CPU** and select **Configuration Manager...**:

4. When the **Configuration Manager** dialog opens, we can create a new Project Platform targeting 64-bit code. To do this, click on the drop-down menu for **Platform** and select **<New...>**:

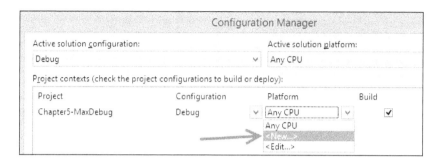

5. When **<New...>** is selected, it will present the **New Project Platform** dialog box. Select **x64** as the new platform type:

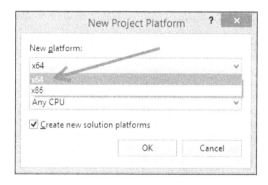

6. Once **x64** has been selected, you will return to the **Configuration Manager**. Verify that **x64** remains active under **Platform** and then click on **Close** to close this dialog. The main IDE window will now indicate that x64 is active:

7. Now, let's add some code to demonstrate the new behavior. Replace the existing code in your blank class file so that it looks like the following listing:

```
class Program
{
    static void Main(string[] args)
    {
        int w = 16;
        int h = 8;
```

```
                    int area = calcArea(w, h);
                    Console.WriteLine("Area: " + area);
            }

            private static int calcArea(int width, int height) {
                    return width / height;
            }
    }
```

8. Let's set some breakpoints so that we are able to inspect during execution. First, add a breakpoint to the `Main` method's `Console` line. Add a second breakpoint to the `calcArea` method's `return` line. You can do this by either clicking on the left side of the editor window's border or by right-clicking on the line, and selecting **Breakpoint | Insert Breakpoint**:

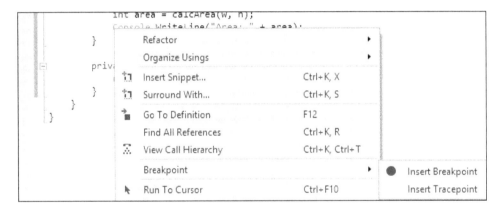

9. If you are not sure where to click, use the right-click method and then practice toggling the breakpoint by left-clicking on the breakpoint marker. Feel free to use any method that you find most convenient.

   Once the two breakpoints are added, Visual Studio will mark their location as shown in the following screenshot (the arrow indicates where you may click to toggle the breakpoint):

```
namespace Chapter5_MaxDebug
{
    class Program
    {
        static void Main(string[] args)
        {
            int w = 16;
            int h = 8;
            int area = calcArea(w, h);
            Console.WriteLine("Area: " + area);
        }

        private static int calcArea(int width, int height) {
            return width / height;
        }
    }
}
```

10. With the breakpoint marker now set, let's debug the program. Begin debugging by either pressing *F5* or clicking on the **Start** button on the toolbar:

11. Once debugging starts, the program will quickly execute until stopped by the first breakpoint. Let's first take a look at **Edit and Continue**. Visual Studio will stop at the `calcArea` method's `return` line. Astute readers will notice an error (marked by **1** in the following screenshot) present in the calculation as the area value returned should be `width * height`. Make the correction.

12. Before continuing, note the variables listed in the **Autos** window (marked by **2** in the following screenshot). If you don't see **Autos**, it can be made visible by pressing *Ctrl + D, A* or through **Debug | Windows | Autos** while debugging.

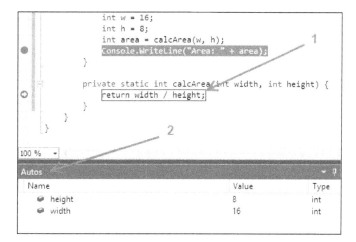

13. After correcting the area calculation, advance the debugging step by pressing *F10* twice. (Alternatively make the advancement by selecting the menu item **Debug | Step Over** twice). Visual Studio will advance to the declaration for `area`. Note that you were able to edit your code and continue debugging without restarting.

14. The **Autos** window will update to display the function's return value, which is **128** (the value for `area` has not been assigned yet):

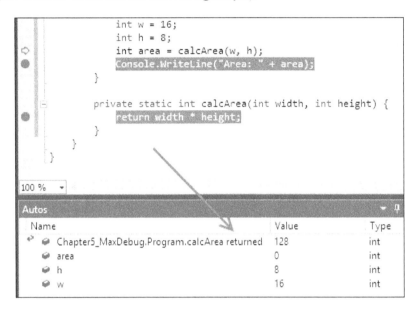

Programmers who write C++ already have the ability to see the return values of functions; this just brings .NET developers into the fold. Your development experience won't have to suffer based on the languages chosen for your projects.

The **Edit and Continue** functionality is also available for ASP.NET projects. New projects created in VS2013 will have Edit and Continue enabled by default. Existing projects imported to VS2013 will usually need this to be enabled if it hasn't been already. To do so, right-click on your ASP.NET project in **Solution Explorer** and select **Properties** (alternatively, it is also available via **Project** | <Project Name> **Properties...**). Navigate to the **Web** option and scroll to the bottom to check the **Enable Edit and Continue** checkbox. The following screenshot shows where this option is located on the properties page:

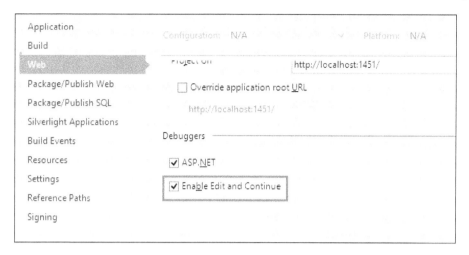

Debugging on remote machines and tablets

For most developers, debugging an application means setting a breakpoint with *F9* on a line of code, and then pressing *F5* (or **Debug | Start Debugging**) and stepping into and over statements with *F10* and *F11*.

The experience is great when you're debugging code on your local machine, but what if you need to debug code running on a different machine and Visual Studio isn't installed on that machine? This is where remote debugging tools come into play.

Even though many developers aren't aware of this functionality, debugging code on remote machines with Visual Studio isn't anything new. It's just that until now, the debugging experience has been limited and unrefined. With Visual Studio 2013, the experience is much improved, and combined with speed improvements and an increasing range of devices that applications need to run on, remote debugging is something every developer should know.

This recipe shows how to configure a machine for remote debugging and then debug an application that you have deployed to that machine.

Getting ready

For this recipe, you will need a second machine to act as your remote machine. It doesn't matter if it's a virtual or physical machine as long as your development machine and the remote machine can communicate over a network connection.

The remote machine will need **Remote Tools for Visual Studio 2013** installed before starting. If you don't have the Remote Tools already installed, download them from the Microsoft website at `http://www.microsoft.com/en-us/download/details.aspx?id=40781` and then install them. Versions exist for each CPU architecture that Windows 8.1 supports: x86, x64, and ARM. This recipe assumes that your local machine has a premium edition of VS2013, but note Remote Tools does support Express for Windows Desktop and Express for Windows.

Using the Remote Tools enables you to debug on a remote machine that does not have Visual Studio installed, especially important for ARM-based devices such as the Surface RT where there is no native version of Visual Studio available. It also saves time and the hassle of maintaining a working development environment on each end-device you are targeting.

How to do it...

Remote debugging makes it easier to see how your application performs for end users by minimizing the influence of your development environment. Let's see how to do it:

1. Create a new **C# Console Application** using the default name.

2. Open the `Program.cs` file and fill in the body of the `Main()` method as shown in the following code snippet (there is an intentional bug in the code):

```
static void Main(string[] args)
{
    Console.Out.WriteLine("Press any key to begin");
    Console.ReadKey();  // Wait for keypress to start
    var charCode = 97;
    var outputBuilder = new StringBuilder();

    for (int i = 1; i < 26; i++)
    {
      outputBuilder.Append((char)(charCode + i));
    }

    var output = outputBuilder.ToString();
    Console.WriteLine(output); // should write "abcd...z"
    Console.ReadKey();
}
```

3. Run the program locally by pressing *F5*. When the console window appears, press any key and you should see a string of characters appear. Press any key again to close the program.

4. You should now check if it works on the remote machine. On your remote machine, start the **Remote Debugger Configuration Wizard** and ensure that the **Run the "Visual Studio Remote Debugger"** service checkbox is deselected. Also ensure that the firewall configuration is set appropriately for your network and then complete the remaining steps of the wizard by taking the default values.

5. Now that you have configured it, start the **Remote Debugger** on your remote machine.

6. When the application appears, you should see a message showing the machine name and port number that the debugger is listening on. Take a note of the machine name as you'll be using it later on. In the following screenshot, the machine is named **WIN81VM** and it is running on port **4018**:

7. For the smoothest development and debugging experience, the remote machine will need to run the code from your development machine via a network share. Either add a specific share to the `debug` folder under the `bin\debug` path of your development machine or access it via the inbuilt `C$` share, for example, `\\dev-machine\C$\Users\Richard\Documents\Visual Studio 2013\Projects\ConsoleApplication1\bin\debug` (your location will vary).

>
> Ensure that you can connect to your network share from the remote machine. Code Access Security is not applied to .NET 4.0 applications by default, but it is for .NET 2.0 applications. To debug a .NET 2.0 application on a remote machine via a file share, you need to make sure that the share is a trusted location. Use the `caspol.exe` utility in both the x86 and x64 versions of the framework to modify the security settings of your machine. `CasPol.exe -m -pp off -ag 1.2 -url "file://\\server\share\*" FullTrust` will set full trust permissions on a file share.

8. In Visual Studio, on your development machine, open the project's properties by right-clicking on the project in **Solution Explorer** and choosing **Properties**. Select the **Debug** tab.

9. Change the **Start Action** to **Start external program** and enter the path to the compiled application using the path that will be used by the remote machine to start the application, for example, `\\dev-machine\sharename\ConsoleApplication1.exe`.

10. In the **Start Options**, check the **Use remote machine** checkbox and enter the name of the remote machine. This is the machine name you noted in step 6. Your **Debug** tab should now look similar to the following screenshot:

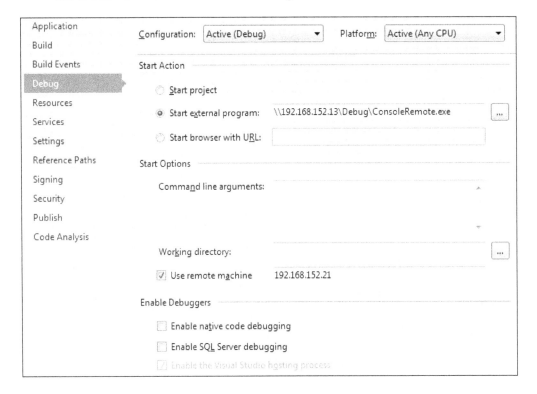

11. On your development machine, press *F5* to start debugging. Assuming there are no firewall issues and your permissions are ok, Visual Studio will communicate with the remote machine and launch the application for you automatically. Note that, depending on the accounts used on each machine, you may be prompted for login credentials. If that happens, enter the details of the user running the debugging monitor on the remote machine.

12. If you have a problem communicating with the remote machine, check that the firewall on the remote machine is allowing incoming connections. If it isn't, you can either rerun the **Remote Debugger Configuration Wizard** to confirm the firewall settings or manually add a rule to allow a connection on the port number that the **Remote Debugger** is using (the port number is shown in step 6).

13. The application is now waiting for you to press a key. Go back to your development machine and set a breakpoint in the `Main()` method of `Program.cs`, somewhere after the `ReadKey()` method. A good place would be where the `outputBuilder` variable is initialized.

14. Switch back to the remote machine and press a key to continue program execution.

15. Switch back to the development machine. You should find that your breakpoint has been hit and that the application is ready for you to continue debugging.

16. Step through the code in Visual Studio to get a feel of how quick the remote debugging experience is and then continue executing down to the second `Console.ReadKey()` statement. The easiest way to do this rather than looping through the `for` loop 26 times is to right-click on the `Console.ReadKey()` statement and select **Run to Cursor**.

17. You may notice that the output has dropped the `'a'` at the start of the output string. Is that a display problem or a bug in the code? You can check the string length to be sure. Navigate to the **Immediate Window** and type `?output.Length` to see how long the output string is.

18. If the **Immediate Window** isn't visible, you can display it by pressing *Ctrl + Alt + I* or choosing **Debug | Windows | Immediate** from the menu.

19. You should see the value **25** displayed. Note that this value is not from a process on the local machine; it is from the process running on your remote machine. To verify this, navigate to **Debug | Attach to Process** from the menu bar. In the **Qualifier** drop-down, select the remote machine. If it does not appear, use the neighboring **Find...** button. It will be suffixed by the port number that the remote debugger is listening on. When the **Available Processes** list is populated, you should see that your application is the only process on the remote machine that the debugger is attached to (titled **ConsoleRemote.exe** in the following screenshot).

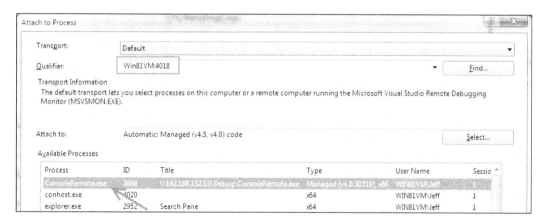

20. Stop debugging by either pressing *Shift + F5* and clicking on the Stop button in the debugging toolbar, or choosing **Debug** | **Stop Debugging** from the menu. This will also terminate the process on the remote machine.

21. Fix the bug in the `for` loop by altering the loop variable to start from `0` instead of `1`. Your `for` loop should now look like the following code:

```
for (int i = 0; i < 26; i++)
{
    outputBuilder.Append((char)(charCode + i));
}
```

22. Without changing any other setting, press *F5* to start debugging again. Visual Studio will compile the application and launch it on your remote machine for you.

23. Run through the application again to verify that the output is now correct.

How it works...

The main thing to keep in mind when using the remote debugger is that you are looking at data from the remote machine. The debug experience can feel so smooth and so normal that it's easy at times to forget that a path name for a file, for example, is a path relative to the remote machine and not your local machine.

Normally, the debugger runs using Windows authentication; however, it can be switched over to the **No Authentication** mode. The No Authentication mode enables debugging scenarios for managed and native debugging across versions of Windows that were previously not possible. The danger of this approach is that it opens up a security hole, including allowing attackers to launch any application they choose. Do not run the remote debugger on production machines in this way. The remote debugger is a developer tool and should only be run when developers require it.

There's more...

If you don't want to install the remote debugger on the remote machine, you can run it directly from a file share; however, you won't be able to debug Windows Store apps in Windows 8 or debug JavaScript.

Another thing to note is that when you are debugging a Windows Store app on Windows 8, you will not need to change the **Start Action** of the project to start an external program. Leaving it set to **Start project** and then ticking the checkbox and setting the value of the **Use remote machine** field will tell Visual Studio that the project should be packaged and deployed to the remote machine before debugging commences.

Debugging an ASP.NET process

To debug ASP.NET websites running under IIS, you do not need to make any changes to the project properties to configure the remote debugger. In fact, you can't. The options aren't available.

For remote debugging, you will either need to run the remote debugger as a service or run the application as an administrator. On your development machine, you then use the **Attach to Process** dialog to connect to the ASP.NET worker process and begin the debugging session.

To configure the remote debugger as a service, rerun the **Remote Debugger Configuration Wizard** and check the option to run it as a service.

Much like you did in this recipe, for the best debugging experience, you should configure the IIS application on the remote machine to run from a network share, pointing to the web application's source folder on your development machine.

Once the web application is running in Visual Studio, navigate to the **Debug | Attach to Process** menu option. The **Qualifier** drop-down is the name of the debugger instance you are connected to, and this should be the remote machine. If your target machine is not already listed, you can use the **Find** button to locate available debuggers.

Once you are connected to the correct machine, locate the ASP.NET worker process (w3wp) from the list, select **Attach**, and then close the window. You are now connected to the remote debugger for the web application and can set breakpoints in your pages and step through code just as you would expect.

Deploying directly to a remote machine

The suggestion to run the programs on the remote machine via a file share is just a tip to make the development process simpler and to eliminate the time it takes to redeploy the application you are trying to debug each time you make a change.

If you don't want to run the application from a file share, then you will need to deploy the application to the remote machine and use the **Attach to Process** dialog to connect the debugging session each time.

Missing symbols

While debugging remote processes, you may find that after you attach to a process and set a breakpoint, it will look similar to the following screenshot:

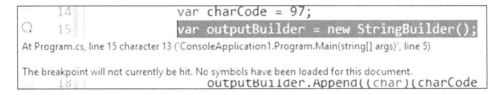

This message appears because Visual Studio either can't load the symbol information (the PDB file) of the executable file or the version that is running on the remote machine is not the same as the one on your development machine. For example, you may have recompiled the code on your development machine since you last deployed to the remote machine, causing the two environments to no longer match.

There's a way to fix this. Follow the given steps:

1. Navigate to the **Debug | Windows | Modules** menu entry to display the **Modules** window. You have to be actively running the debugger for this option to be available.

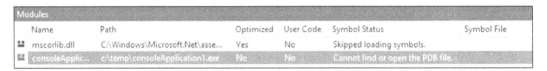

2. Right-click on the entry with the missing symbols, and from the options, choose **Load Symbols From | Symbol Path**.

3. From the file selection dialog box, locate the correct symbol file (PDB file) to load. Once you do this, the debug breakpoints will change to show filled-in red dots, as expected, and the **Modules** window will indicate that symbols are loaded.

Debugging code in production with IntelliTrace

Applications frequently seem to have the frustrating characteristic of performing very well during the development and test cycle, only to be followed up by randomly misbehaving in production environments for no apparent reason. This results in a frantic effort to try and figure out what's going wrong from bug reports such as "it just stopped working" and "nothing updated but I don't know why". Diagnosing these problems in a production environment can be rather tricky, especially if you are in an environment where you have no production access. This is where **IntelliTrace** can help.

A traditional dump file only provides a capture of the runtime environment as a moment in time; with IntelliTrace, a more lengthy and detailed record is made. IntelliTrace was introduced in Visual Studio 2010 as a way for developers and testers to record what they'd just done, leading up to a bug, and then step back through those actions to make a diagnosis of the bug simpler. In Visual Studio 2012, this feature was extended so that system administrators can capture IntelliTrace information from live, running production systems and send the logs to developers for diagnosis.

With Visual Studio 2013, IntelliTrace has been expanded further. It can be used directly to debug apps within VS2013, monitor a session in Test Manager, or it can also be used in conjunction with Microsoft Monitoring Agent on production systems.

This recipe will show you how to gather information from a live application running in a production environment and then diagnose and debug problems.

Getting ready

You will need a machine to use as your "production" machine. Of course, it doesn't have to be a genuine production machine, just a second machine without Visual Studio Ultimate installed. A virtual machine is perfectly acceptable. For this recipe, a Windows Server 2012 R2 environment was used. The recipe does require Visual Studio 2013 Ultimate on your development machine.

Your nominated production machine will need to have .NET Framework 4.5, PowerShell, and as you will be diagnosing a web application, Internet Information Server, installed on it.

 If you are really tight for machines and can't even run a virtual machine, then you can use your development machine as your "production" server for the purposes of this recipe.

How to do it...

1. On your development machine, create a new application with the default name by selecting **Visual Basic | ASP.NET Web Application**, and on the ensuing dialog, select **Web Forms** as the type of project.

 If you receive any errors regarding the PowerShell scripts not being able to execute, you will need to change your `Set-ExecutionPolicy` via PowerShell and restart Visual Studio. For a development environment, this would typically mean changing the policy to `RemoteSigned`. For more information, visit `http://technet.microsoft.com/en-us/library/ee176961.aspx`.

2. Open the `Default.aspx` page and add a button to the bottom of the page (just before closing the `asp` tag). Give it an ID of `ClickMe`, set the text attribute to `Click Me`, and ensure that a button click event is created as shown in the following code snippet:

```
<p>
<asp:Button ID="ClickMe" runat="server" OnClick="ClickMe_Click"
Text="Click Me" />
</p>
</asp:Content>
```

3. In the code behind file, add code for the button's click event handler as shown in the following code snippet:

```
Protected Sub ClickMe_Click(sender As Object, e As EventArgs)
    Dim second As Integer = DateTime.Now.Second
    If (second Mod 2 = 0) Then
        Throw New ApplicationException("No clicky for you!")
    Else
        ClickMe.Text = "current second: " & second.ToString()
    End If
End Sub
```

4. Now, when you run the application and click on the button, an exception will be thrown whenever the current time has an even numbered second.

5. Deploy your web application to your production server. Confirm that it runs and throws exceptions randomly when the button is clicked. You will want to note the **Site Name** and the **Application Name** that you use here. In the following screenshot, the **Default Web Site** name was used and the application was installed as `VS2013`:

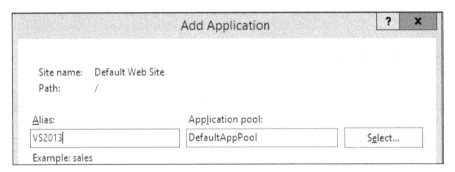

6. Create a location on the production server to store the logfiles that we will be generating. For this example, we will use `C:\IntelliTraceLogs`. In an actual production environment, it is important to choose a location that is secure as information in the IntelliTrace files can reveal potentially sensitive data from your application. A performance consideration should also be made to use a separate physical disk from the one hosting your application where possible.

7. Download the latest version of **Microsoft Monitoring Agent 2013** available at `http://www.microsoft.com/en-us/download/details.aspx?id=40316` and install it on your production environment.

8. Open a PowerShell prompt as an Administrator and enter the following command: `Start-WebApplication-Monitoring`.

9. You will be prompted for the name of the application to monitor, but you must also include the site it is located on. In our example, it is `Default Web Site\VS2013`. Next, you will be prompted for the mode of monitoring; enter `Trace`. Finally, you will be prompted for the location where the output should be logged. Enter `C:\IntelliTraceLogs`.

```
PS C:\IntelliTraceLogs> Start-WebApplicationMonitoring

cmdlet Start-WebApplicationMonitoring at command pipeline position 1
Supply values for the following parameters:
Name: Default Web Site\VS2013
Mode: Trace
OutputPath: C:\IntelliTraceLogs
Starting monitoring for 'Default Web Site/VS2013' ...
Monitoring started for 'Default Web Site/VS2013'

PS C:\IntelliTraceLogs>
```

10. If you want to now verify the status of your monitor, enter `Get-WebApplicationMonitoringStatus`, which will display the information we just entered for what is being monitored. Verify that your monitor is operational and then load your website and generate both some successful and unsuccessful clicks.

11. In true production environments, logging should have minimal interference with an application's performance. To obtain a trace file while the monitor continues to run, you can enter `CheckPoint-WebApplicationMonitoring`. This will prompt for the name of the site you want to generate a log for, and then, one will be saved to the previously stated output directory. In this case, we can stop the monitor and review our logs. Enter `Stop-WebApplicationMonitoring -all`, which will stop the monitoring service and a final log. The file will end in `.itrace` and be found in `C:\IntelliTraceLogs`.

12. Copy the logfile back to your development machine. Double-click on the `.iTrace` file to open it in Visual Studio. Alternately, if Visual Studio is already open, you can either press *Ctrl + O* or use the **File | Open | File** menu option to load it. Once the file loads, you should be able to see a **Web Requests** section that looks a little like the following screenshot:

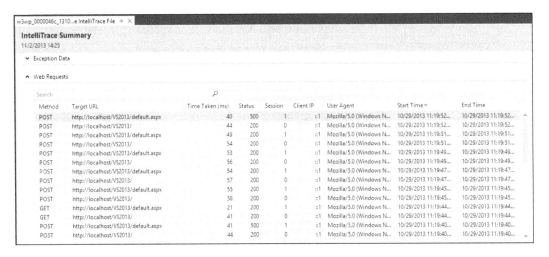

13. In the request list, find a request with a return code of **500**, select it, and then click on the **Request Details** button below the list, as shown in the following screenshot:

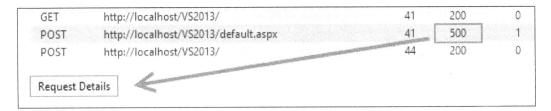

14. The details of the individual request are shown along with the actions that occurred and any exceptions that were thrown:

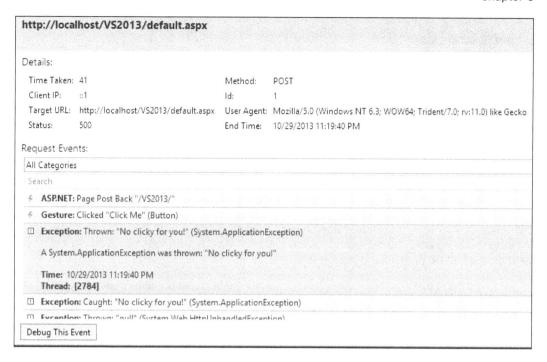

15. Select the entry in the list where the exception is first thrown, as shown in the previous screenshot in step 14, and click on the **Debug This Event** button.

16. The code will be displayed and the execution point will be positioned where the exception was thrown:

```
Protected Sub ClickMe_Click(sender As Object, e As EventArgs)
    Dim second As Integer = DateTime.Now.Second
    If (second Mod 2 = 0) Then
        Throw New ApplicationException("No clicky for you!")
    Else
        ClickMe.Text = "current second: " & second.ToString()
    End If
End Sub
End Class
```

17. You can then use the IntelliTrace debugging controls to move around the code and diagnose what occurred by following the execution path and inspecting parameters.

How it works...

No recompilation of code was required for this to work. The application is untouched and the website didn't need to be restarted. Collecting IntelliTrace data is something that your system administrators can do on your behalf, safe in the knowledge that the application will be unchanged, and that existing web requests will complete normally. This makes debugging and diagnosing those tricky production problems a much more viable prospect since checkpoints can be made periodically at intervals that minimize server disruption.

There's more...

The IntelliTrace settings used in the recipe are the detailed `Trace` settings. They will record execution flow as well as events and will have some impact on production performance. The alternative option is to use the `Monitor` setting, which has a minimal impact on performance as it focuses on exceptions and performance.

Don't forget that IntelliTrace files can get very big, very quickly. Make sure that the location you place them in has plenty of space if you want to capture data over a reasonable time period, and more so, if you have a busy production server. Logging directly to the system drive, like we did in the recipe, is generally not recommended since filling your system drive will bring your server to a grinding halt.

Finding the variable values

If you haven't used it before, you might expect IntelliTrace to be equivalent to the normal debugging experience. Unfortunately, the performance impact of recording all the data needed to simulate the full debugging experience makes this prohibitive.

By default, variable values are not recorded by IntelliTrace unless a breakpoint has been set or an event occurs. In the recipe, if you hovered your mouse over the second variable in the code window during the debugging session, you would see an indication that the data was not collected.

If you wanted to capture that information, you could configure IntelliTrace to record tracing information and add trace statements for your code, or you could write custom IntelliTrace events (outside the scope of this book) and add them to the IntelliTrace configuration. In either case, it would require recompiling and redeploying code to production, so there is an assumption that you know the level of trace information you will need ahead of time.

Debugging parallel code

With the prevalence of multi-core CPUs, we are seeing more and more applications taking advantage of parallel processing to improve performance. .NET Framework 4.0 added a number of features such as **Task Parallel Library** (**TPL**) and **Parallel LINQ** (**PLINQ**) to make the development of applications that take advantage of multi-core CPUs much simpler.

The debugging experience for threaded applications in Visual Studio has got better with each release, and VS2013 is no exception. Let's take a look at what is available.

Getting ready

Start a premium edition Visual Studio 2013 and create a new C# console application. For this recipe, call the application `ParallelDebugging`.

How to do it...

In order to debug the parallel code, perform the following steps:

1. Use the following code to populate the body of `Program.cs`. It's a pretty simple program that starts a parallel `for` loop, which in turn calls a method that performs meaningless calculations intended to keep the CPU busy.

```csharp
class Program
{
    static void Main(string[] args)
    {
        Parallel.For(0, 100000, i => SlowMethod(i + 1));
    }

    private static void SlowMethod(int i)
    {
        var total = 0;
        for (int loop = 0; loop < 1000000; loop++)
        {
            total += loop;
            total /= i;
        }
    }
}
```

2. Press *F5* to run the program, and after a second or two, break into the debugger either by pressing the pause button in Visual Studio or by pressing *Ctrl + Alt + Break*.

3. You will most likely break inside `SlowMethod()`. When you do, you should be able to see the current value of the variable `i` by hovering over the variable name as shown in the following screenshot:

```csharp
var total = 0;
for (int loop = 0; loop < 1000000; loop++)
{
    total += loop;
    total /= i;|
}                    ● i  411  ⇨
```

4. So far, this is standard behavior while debugging; however, you are only seeing the value of `i` for a single thread. What about the value of `i` on all the other threads? From the menu, navigate to **Debug | Windows | Threads**, and you will see all the threads in the application, including the threads that the parallel `for` loop has created.

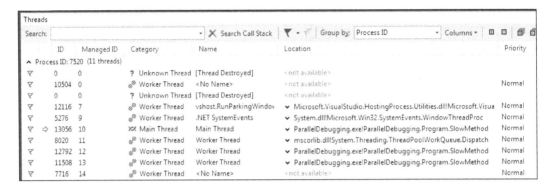

5. Right-click on a different thread from the one you are currently on and select **Switch To Thread** from the context menu. Now look at the values of `i`, `loop`, and `total`, and you will see that they are different.

6. This is useful but still fairly cumbersome if you want to see the value of `i` across all threads. For a more holistic view, from the menu, navigate to **Debug | Windows | Parallel Watch | Parallel Watch 1**. You will see all the current threads listed and an area in the header of the last column for adding watch expressions. Any expression entered will be automatically evaluated across all threads for you.

7. Add watch expressions for **i** and **1000000-loop** as shown in the following screenshot, so you can see how this works (click on the **<Add Watch>** column header to enter a watch):

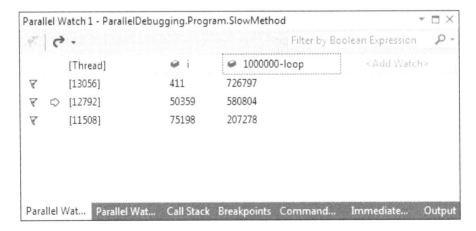

8. Stop debugging. In Visual Studio, add a second console application named **Parallel2** to the current solution. In `Program.cs`, use the following code for the body of the file:

```
class Program
{
    static void Main(string[] args)
    {
        Parallel.For(0, 100000, i => AnotherSlowMethod(i + 1));
    }


    private static void AnotherSlowMethod(int i)
    {
        var total = 0;
        var sb = new StringBuilder(1000 * i);
        for (int loop = 0; loop < 1000 * i; loop++)
        {
            sb.Append(loop);
        }
        total = sb.ToString().Length;
    }
}
```

9. Right-click on the solution in **Solution Explorer**, and in the context menu, select **Set Startup Projects**. Select **Multiple startup projects** and ensure that the **Action** value for both console applications is **Start**.

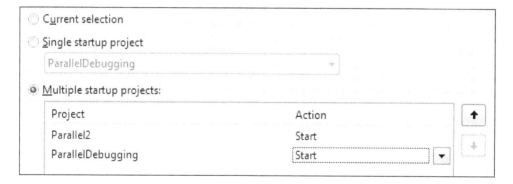

10. Click on **OK** to save the changes and then press *F5* to start debugging.

11. Wait for a short period of time and then break into the debugger using the same process as explained in step 2.

12. From the menu, navigate to **Debug | Windows | Tasks**. You will now see that you have multiple processes, each with multiple tasks. You can also see what thread each task is running on, as shown in the following screenshot:

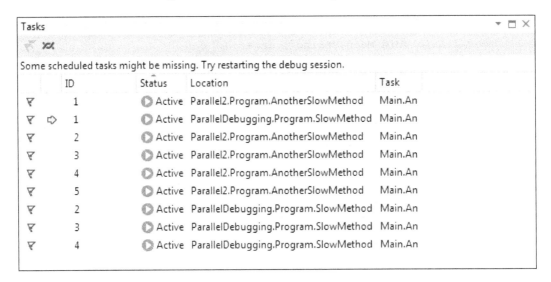

13. From the menu, navigate to **Debug | Windows | Parallel Stacks**. This view was added in Visual Studio 2010, and in Visual Studio 2012, it was extended to show stacks for multiple processes. As shown in the following screenshot, you now have two processes being displayed, each with a main thread and the spawned threads created by the parallel for loops of each process:

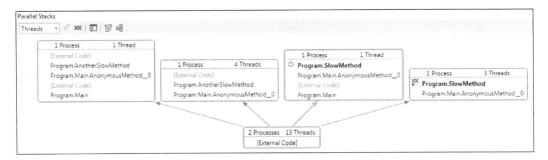

How it works...

Apart from the debugging improvements themselves, Microsoft has worked hard on the Task Parallel Library, PLINQ, and other multithreading-related framework features and gained some serious performance improvements in .NET 4.5. Since .NET 4.5 is an in-place replacement of the .NET 4.0 runtime, it means that any of your .NET 4.0 code that uses these libraries will automatically benefit from the performance improvements, without you making any recompilation or code changes.

See also

▸ The *Visualizing concurrency* recipe

▸ For more information on the *Task Parallel Library*, refer to the MSDN documentation at `http://msdn.microsoft.com/en-us/library/dd460717(v=vs.110).aspx`

▸ Information on *PLINQ* is available at `http://msdn.microsoft.com/en-us/library/dd460688(v=vs.110).aspx`

Visualizing concurrency

The **Concurrency Visualizer** is another tool that was added in Visual Studio 2010 to assist with multithreaded code, and just like the other features of Visual Studio related to threading in Visual Studio 2012, it too has been the subject of a number of improvements. With Visual Studio 2013, it has been pulled out of the default installation but is available on the Visual Studio Gallery.

In this recipe, we'll take a look at these improvements and see how you can understand better what is happening inside your application when it runs.

Getting ready

You will need to use a premium version of VS2013 for this recipe. Download and install the Concurrency Visualizer from the Visual Studio Gallery available at `http://visualstudiogallery.msdn.microsoft.com/24b56e51-fcc2-423f-b811-f16f3fa3af7a`. Once installed, reopen Visual Studio and create a new C# console application named `Concurrency`.

How to do it...

1. Open the `Program.cs` file and add the following statements to the `using` statements at the top of the file:

```
using System.Threading;
using System.Diagnostics.Tracing;
```

2. In the body of `Program.cs`, add the following code. It's fairly straightforward. You simply build up a list of tasks you want to run and then execute them. Each task then calls `SpinWait` on the thread for a period of time. It's similar to the `Thread.Sleep` method, but instead of the thread yielding back to the operating system's task scheduler, it keeps the CPU busy.

```
static void Main(string[] args)
{
    var taskList = new List<Task>();
    for (int i = 0; i < 10; i++)
    {
        taskList.Add(Task.Run(() =>
        {
            MyEventSource.Log.RecordAnEvent(DateTime.Now.Second);
            Thread.SpinWait(10000000);
        }));
    }
    Task.WaitAll(taskList.ToArray());
}
```

3. Next, add a custom event source as shown in the following code snippet. It will be called whenever a new task is created in the main program's loop.

```
[EventSource(Guid = "EE8B671C-90FA-4D6F-A238-F779DBCA6128")]
class MyEventSource : EventSource
{
    internal static MyEventSource Log = new MyEventSource();

    [Event(1)]
    public void RecordAnEvent(int data)
    {
        WriteEvent(1, data);
    }
}
```

4. Launch the **Concurrency Visualizer**, either by pressing the keyboard shortcut of *Alt + Shift + F5*, or from the menu by navigating to **Analyze | Concurrency Visualizer | Start with Current Project**.

> For the purpose of the recipe, if you are prompted to configure a symbol cache, or you see a warning about running without executive paging on an x64 machine, you can select **No** in each case.
>
> If you are prompted for elevation, then select **Yes** since the collection analyzer requires administrative privileges.

5. When the process completes and the data collection ends, you will see a window as shown in the following screenshot:

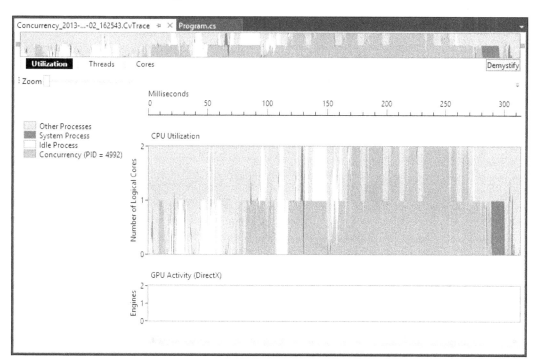

6. At the very top of the window is an overview area with drag handles that you can use to limit the amount of data displayed. Move the red drag handles toward each other so that the selected area contains the high activity area of the trace file as shown in the following screenshot:

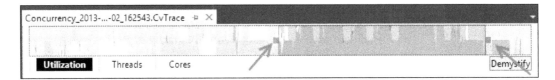

7. Navigate to the **Threads** view by clicking on the button just under the overview area. You will be shown what has been happening in each thread as seen in the following screenshot, but you can also see that your custom event isn't displaying yet. Let's figure out the reason behind this.

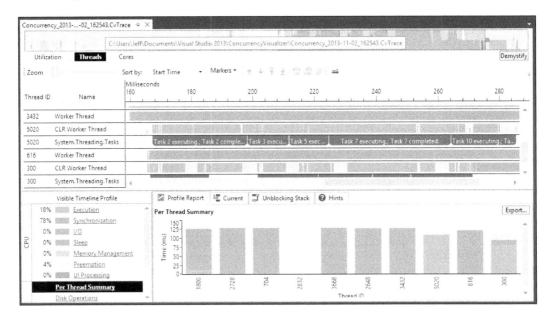

8. Navigate to **Analyze | Concurrency Visualizer | Advanced Settings** and select the **Markers** tab.

9. Click on the green plus icon to add a new marker. Enter `RecordAnEvent` as the name of the marker, and in the **Provider GUID** field, enter the GUID you used in the `MyEventSource Event` attribute. The following screenshot shows how this should look. Click on **OK** to close the dialog box:

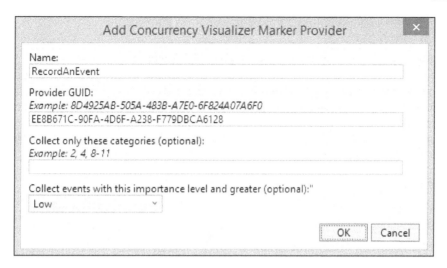

10. To make this step a little easier, copy the GUID from the code and paste it into the dialog. It'll help prevent errors while entering the GUID.

11. Repeat step 4 to reanalyze the application and collect updated results, including your newly-added event marker.

12. When the **Concurrency Visualizer** opens, switch to the **Threads** view as before. You should be able to find the custom event information as shown in the following screenshot:

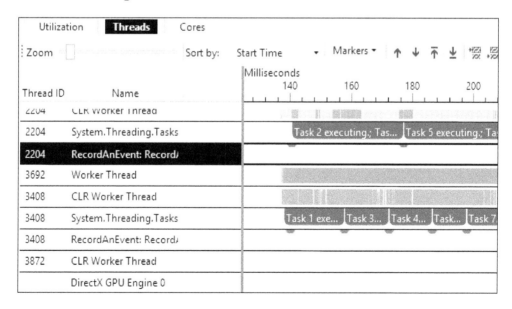

How it works...

The Concurrency Visualizer exists to help you understand what the CPU is doing when your application runs and where performance issues may originate from. The ability to add your own custom markers is very useful when you want to tie events that are specific to your application to the visualizer. Apart from custom event data, the visualizer also understands the events from the Task Parallel Library, PLINQ, synchronized data structures, and more. This information gives you a great insight into your code and will hopefully help you isolate performance bottlenecks and bugs.

See also

 ▸ The *Debugging parallel code* recipe
 ▸ Information on *PLINQ* is available at `http://msdn.microsoft.com/en-us/library/dd460688(v=vs.110).aspx`

6

Asynchrony in .NET

In this chapter, we will cover:

- ► Making your code asynchronous
- ► Understanding asynchrony and the Windows Runtime
- ► Using asynchrony with web applications
- ► Working with actors and the TPL Dataflow Library

Introduction

The use of asynchronous code has become more popular as a way for programmers to deal with latency and blocking operations. For example, an application running with the benefit of significant local resources is still at the mercy of the response time of other systems that it has to communicate with. Frequently, applications are waiting for the user to respond, but they shouldn't consume all available system resources while they wait.

To deal with these and similar challenges, a multithreaded code has been used. With this approach, the work that needs to be done is handled by multiple threads; so while one thread is handling network communication, another may update the display. Sometimes, this approach has its own limitations as additional threads increase complexity for the programmer and there are practical limitations on how many threads can be effectively created and utilized.

Whether your code is currently multithreaded or not, the use of asynchronous techniques can be beneficial as they eliminate blocking on an executing thread. This applies whether it is the sole main execution thread or a particular thread devoted to the task at hand.

Microsoft realized that while most developers understand the benefits of asynchronous code and the improvements it can bring about in their applications, the programming models involved in asynchrony were fairly cumbersome, verbose, and in some cases quite difficult to get right. As a result, most developers ignored asynchrony unless circumstances forced it upon them. The extra complexity, effort, time, chance for bugs, and difficulty in debugging meant that it simply wasn't worth it for most developers.

To ensure reading and writing asynchronous code is no longer restricted to the domain experts among us, Visual Studio 2012 and .NET 4.5 introduced the `async` and `await` keywords for both the C# and Visual Basic languages. These keywords make the asynchronous code as easy to read, write, and debug as a normal synchronous code.

As you saw in *Chapter 5, Debugging Your .NET Application*, the debugging experience for .NET code has been greatly improved. When this is combined with the improved language features, the implementation cost of asynchronous code has been made much easier and so should be considered for use to see if it is appropriate for your projects.

In this chapter, you'll be looking specifically at the `async` and `await` keywords and seeing how Visual Studio 2013 supports them.

Making your code asynchronous

So, you've got yourself an application that might be lacking in the performance department. If you're honest, it's probably horribly slow, and yet when you look at the performance counters on the host machine, it doesn't seem to be doing all that much. The odds are high that your existing code is operating slowly and blocking the execution thread, which prevents other code from executing.

It gets even worse in web applications that come under heavy load. Every request thread that gets blocked is a point where other requests can get queued, and before too long you've got yourself a server that is throwing `503 Service Unavailable` errors.

Time to take that synchronous code, stick an "a" on the front of it, and more efficiently take advantage of your production system's hardware. Keep in mind that before you make all of your code asynchronous, you should understand where it blocks and where it doesn't (refer to *Chapter 5, Debugging Your .NET Application*, for some tips on getting started with this).

 The overhead of using asynchronous code everywhere can actually make your application run slower if you aren't careful (this is similar to the fact that you cannot improve application performance solely by adding dozens of execution threads). While techniques such as multithreading and asynchronous programming can help in many situations, they do not represent a magical cure-all that is appropriate in every situation.

Getting ready

You will need an Internet connection for this recipe to work since you will be loading data from various RSS feeds and displaying it.

So, ensure you have a working connection, then simply start one of the premium editions of VS2013 or VS Express for Windows Desktop and you're ready to go.

How to do it...

Perform the following steps:

1. Create a C# **Console Application** named `FeedReader`. This application will read the feeds from a number of sites and display them on the console. At the end of the display, the total time required for the feeds to be fetched and displayed will be shown.

2. In the program, classes from a number of different namespaces will be used. To save some time, add the following code to the `using` statements at the top of `Program.cs`:

```
using System.Diagnostics;
using System.Net;
using System.Net.Cache;
using System.Xml.Linq;
```

3. Before you implement the main method, you need to create some supporting methods. Add a `ReadFeed()` private method, as shown after the `Main()` method. It creates a web client to read an RSS feed with the cache setting turned off. This will ensure that we always pull data from the Internet and not a local cached copy. The following is the code for `ReadFeed()`:

```
private static string ReadFeed(string url)
{
    var client = new WebClient()
    {
        CachePolicy = new RequestCachePolicy(RequestCacheLevel.
NoCacheNoStore)
    };
    var contents = client.DownloadString(url);
    return contents;
}
```

4. Add a `PublishedDate()` method below the `ReadFeed()` method. It will convert the dates in the feed, that `System.DateTime` doesn't handle, into dates that can be parsed. The following is the code for `PublishedDate()`:

```
public static DateTime PublishedDate(XElement item)
{
    var s = (string)item.Element("pubDate");
    s = s.Replace("EST", "-0500");
    s = s.Replace("EDT", "-0400");
    s = s.Replace("CST", "-0600");
    s = s.Replace("CDT", "-0500");
    s = s.Replace("MST", "-0700");
    s = s.Replace("MDT", "-0600");
    s = s.Replace("PST", "-0800");
    s = s.Replace("PDT", "-0700");
    DateTime d;
    if (DateTime.TryParse(s, out d)) return d;
    return DateTime.MinValue;
}
```

5. Now move back into the `Main()` method and create a variable for the list of feeds to read from as follows (feel free to customize to suit your personal tastes):

```
static void Main(string[] args)
{
    var feedUrls = new List<string>() {
    "http://massively.joystiq.com/rss.xml",
    "http://feeds2.feedburner.com/alvinashcraft",
    "http://blogs.msdn.com/b/pfxteam/rss.aspx",
    "http://feeds.feedburner.com/ScottHanselman",
    };
}
```

6. To continue in `Main()`, create a `Stopwatch` instance so that you can start timing how long the execution takes, and then add the code to load the data from the feeds as follows:

```
var stopwatch = Stopwatch.StartNew();
var feeds = (from url in feedUrls select ReadFeed(url)).ToArray();
```

7. You need to parse the feed so that you can extract something to show on screen. Add the following code in the `Main()` method:

```
var items = from feed in feeds
            from channel in XElement.Parse(feed).
Elements("channel")
            from item in channel.Elements("item").Take(1)
            let date = PublishedDate(item)
            orderby date descending
            select new
```

```
{
    Title = (string)channel.Element("title"),
    Link = (string)channel.Element("link"),
    PostTitle = (string)item.Element("title"),
    PostLink = (string)item.Element("link"),
    Date = date
};
```

8. Complete the `Main()` method by adding the following code to display an item from each feed on the console and show the total time it took to process all feeds:

```
foreach (var item in items)
{
    Console.WriteLine("Title: {0} [{1}]", item.Title, item.Link);
    Console.WriteLine("  Post: {0}[{1}]", item.PostTitle, item.
PostLink);
    Console.WriteLine("  Date: " + item.Date);
    Console.WriteLine("---------");
}

Console.WriteLine("Total Time: " + stopwatch.Elapsed);
Console.ReadKey(); // this line will be removed in Step 16
```

9. Compile the program and check if it runs. Don't panic if the console takes a little while to show some text, you've got some slow code running here. When it does eventually complete, you should see output similar to the following screenshot:

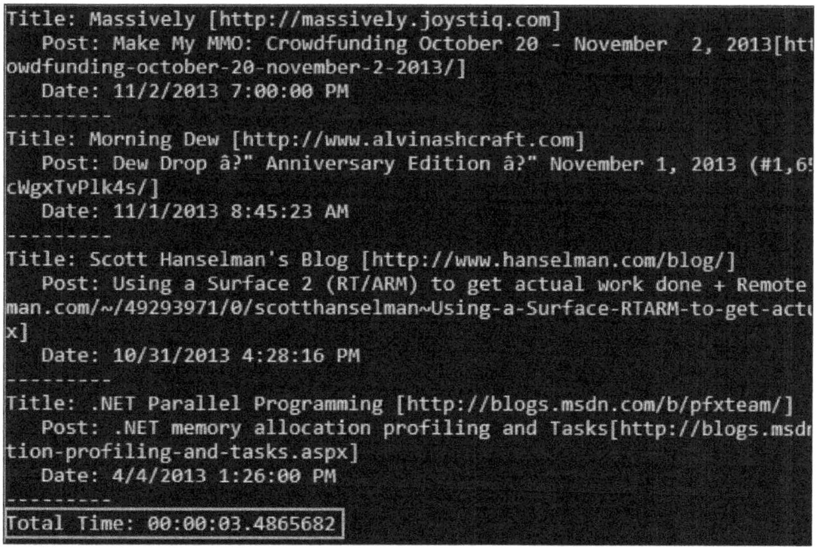

10. As you can see, since each request is being made in a synchronous manner, this does not execute very fast. This program contacts each site sequentially, waits for a response, and then contacts the next site in the list. Even though they are independent servers, each delayed response increases overall execution time. This isn't very efficient, so let's introduce the `await` and `async` keywords in an effort to improve our program's performance. First, locate the `ReadFeed()` method and change the return type from `string` to `Task<string>`.

11. You will then need to return a `Task<string>` object from the method, but you can't just cast the contents variable to that type. Fortunately, the `WebClient` class includes a task-based version of `DownloadString` called `DownloadStringTaskAsync` that returns a `Task<string>` object, which is perfect for our needs. Change the code to use `client.DownloadStringTaskAsync(url)` as follows:

```
private static Task<string> ReadFeed(string url)
{
    var client = new WebClient()
    {
        CachePolicy = new RequestCachePolicy(RequestCacheLevel.
NoCacheNoStore)
    };
    var contents = client.DownloadStringTaskAsync(url);
    return contents;
}
```

12. Navigate back up to the `Main()` method and you will see a problem with the `Parse()` method in the LINQ statement. The root cause is that the `feeds` variable is now an array of the `Task<string>` objects, and not `string` objects.

13. Change the code where `feeds` is assigned to wrap the LINQ statement in a `Task.WhenAll()` call instead of using `.ToArray()`. The `Task.WhenAll` method creates a task that waits until all of the inner tasks returned by the enclosed LINQ statement are complete. The `await` keyword tells the compiler that the task should be executed asynchronously and the result assigned to the `feeds` variable. The variable `feeds` is defined as follows:

```
var feeds = await Task.WhenAll(from url in feedUrls select
ReadFeed(url));
```

14. There is still a problem. The compiler is now complaining about the `await` keyword not being valid. Any method where the `await` keyword is used must have the `async` keyword in its declaration. Go to the declaration of the `Main()` method and add the `async` keyword as shown in the following code:

```
static async void Main(string[] args)
```

15. Compile the application. You will get an error indicating that the `Main` method can't be made asynchronous as it is the program entry point.

16. This is easy enough to work around. Retitle the `Main()` method to `static async Task ProcessFeedsAsync()` and insert a new `Main()` method above it, using the following code. Also, remove the `ReadKey()` method from the end of the `ProcessFeedsAsync()` method so that the user is not prompted for an input twice. The result should be like the following code:

```
static void Main(string[] args)
{
    Console.WriteLine("starting...");
    ProcessFeedsAsync().Wait();
    Console.WriteLine("finished...");
    Console.ReadKey();
}
static async Task ProcessFeedsAsync()
```

17. Compile and run the program. You should see an output somewhat similar to the following screenshot and the elapsed time should be shorter than before:

```
starting...
finished...
Title: Massively [http://massively.joystiq.com]
    Post: Warhammer Online goes free for final weeks[http://massively
or-final-weeks/]
    Date: 11/2/2013 9:00:00 PM
---------
Title: Morning Dew [http://www.alvinashcraft.com]
    Post: Dew Drop â?" Anniversary Edition â?" November 1, 2013 (#1,
cWgxTvPlk4s/]
    Date: 11/1/2013 8:45:23 AM
---------
Title: Scott Hanselman's Blog [http://www.hanselman.com/blog/]
    Post: Using a Surface 2 (RT/ARM) to get actual work done + Remot
man.com/~/49293971/0/scotthanselman~Using-a-Surface-RTARM-to-get-act
x]
    Date: 10/31/2013 4:28:16 PM
---------
Title: .NET Parallel Programming [http://blogs.msdn.com/b/pfxteam/]
    Post: .NET memory allocation profiling and Tasks[http://blogs.ms
tion-profiling-and-tasks.aspx]
    Date: 4/4/2013 1:26:00 PM
---------
Total Time: 00:00:01.6033822
```

How it works...

The final version of the program written using asynchronous techniques provides better results based on the nature of the work we are trying to accomplish (I/O dependent processing). The primary impediment to timely execution is the wait imposed by each server's response time. In the original program, even one slow server can impede the results as the delay cascades through each request. The asynchronous version avoids this by making each request in a non-blocking manner, so each request can be started without waiting for the preceding request to complete.

The `DownloadStringTaskAsync()` method shows off an important convention to be aware of in the .NET 4.5 Framework design. There is a naming convention to help you to locate the asynchronous versions of methods, where all the methods that are asynchronous have an "async" suffix on their names. In situations where an asynchronous method exists from previous framework versions, the newer, task-based, asynchronous methods are named with the "TaskAsync" suffix instead.

In step 16, the `ReadKey()` method was added to stop the `Main()` method just so that we can see the output of the program before the window closes. The line `ProcessFeedsAsync().Wait();` calls the `Wait()` method so that the program will not terminate before receiving a response from of all the asynchronous tasks that were started. This use of `Wait()` is what allows an overall program flow to run as we would expect it to: **starting** is printed, the feeds retrieved and displayed, and then **finishing** is printed when the program has completed its work.

As you've seen, Visual Studio offers enough warnings and errors through IntelliSense to make the conversion of synchronous code to asynchronous, reasonably straightforward, as long as you make changes in small, incremental steps. Large scale changes of code, regardless of what those changes may be, are always difficult and error prone, especially if you lack unit tests or other mechanisms to verify that your changes haven't broken any functionality.

There's more...

It's possible to overdo it. Every piece of asynchronous code comes with a certain amount of overhead. There is a CPU cost to context switching and a higher memory footprint used for maintaining the memory state of each asynchronous task/method, and it is possible to reduce the performance of your application when they are used inappropriately.

The design guideline for the Windows Runtime libraries in Windows 8 was that any method that was likely to take more than 50 ms to complete was changed to be asynchronous. Before you go and improve all the methods in your application, start by determining which of your current methods are the slowest. Also, take into consideration what a function is trying to do.

An initial step would be to start by improving only methods that take more than 500 ms to complete and resolve those first, before targeting the faster methods. Using asynchronous code for this example was ideal, since each feed is located on a separate server and obtaining results from one server isn't dependent on another.

When determining an appropriate balance between synchronous and asynchronous code, you should first define what your application's current performance profile is so that you can accurately measure what effect your changes have had. Because each and every application is different, finding the right mix can be an art. As a tip, identify the slowest areas of your application and target them first. I/O-based methods are good candidates for consideration. As you improve performance, keep an eye on how much time it costs you to make your code asynchronous versus the improvement you are seeing in the overall application performance.

See also

▸ Stephen Cleary has written an informative article for the MSDN magazine, *Best Practices in Asynchronous Programming*, available at `http://msdn.microsoft.com/en-us/magazine/jj991977.aspx`

Understanding asynchrony and the Windows Runtime

When developing the Windows Runtime for Windows 8/8.1, Microsoft followed a design guideline where any synchronous method that might take longer than 50 ms to complete was to be removed and replaced with an asynchronous version. The goal behind this design decision is to dramatically improve the chances of developers building applications that work smoothly without blocking threads on framework calls.

In this recipe, you're going to revisit the RSS feed reader concept, just as you did in the *Making your code asynchronous* recipe, though this time you're going to be creating a Windows Store application.

There are a few differences between a Windows Store application and a console application, which include differences in the classes available. For example, the WebClient class doesn't exist in WinRT, so you'll be using the HttpClient class instead.

For variety, you will be writing this code using Visual Basic.

Getting ready

Ensure you are running Windows 8.1 and then launch Visual Studio 2013. You will need either one of the premium editions or Visual Studio Express 2013 for Windows. You will also need an unexpired developer license, which Visual Studio will prompt for if you don't have it already. Simply log in with your Microsoft ID and obtain a current license.

How to do it...

Perform the following steps:

1. Create a new project by navigating to **Visual Basic | Windows Store | Blank App (XAML)** and name it `FeedReaderApp`.

2. Add a class named `Post` to the application using the following code. This class will hold the details of each post from the RSS feed that we will show on screen.

```
Public Class Post
    Public Property Title As String
    Public Property Link As String
    Public Property PostTitle As String
    Public Property PostLink As String
    Public Property PostDate As DateTime
End Class
```

3. Open `MainPage.xaml` and add the following XAML to the `<Grid />` element to define the markup of how the results should appear. The layout consists of a button to start the feed loading and a `ListBox` element in which the results are displayed. You also have a `TextBlock` element in which you'll post the time it takes to read the feeds.

```
<Grid Background="{ThemeResource
ApplicationPageBackgroundThemeBrush}">
    <Button Name="LoadFeeds" Margin="116,60,0,0"
VerticalAlignment="Top">
        Load Feeds
    </Button>
    <TextBlock Name="TimeTaken" HorizontalAlignment="Left"
Height="36" Margin="257,60,0,0" TextWrapping="Wrap"
                    VerticalAlignment="Top" Width="360"
FontSize="32">
                Waiting for click...
    </TextBlock>
    <ListBox Height="450" HorizontalAlignment="Left"
Margin="116,140,0,0" Name="PostsListBox" VerticalAlignment="Top"
Width="500" >
        <ListBox.ItemTemplate>
```

```
            <DataTemplate>
                <StackPanel Orientation="Vertical" Height="110">
                    <TextBlock Text="{Binding Title}" />
                    <TextBlock Text="{Binding Link}" />
                    <TextBlock Text="{Binding PostTitle}" />
                    <TextBlock Text="{Binding PostLink}" />
                    <TextBlock Text="{Binding PostDate}" />
                </StackPanel>
            </DataTemplate>
        </ListBox.ItemTemplate>
    </ListBox>
</Grid>
```

4. Next, navigate to the code behind the file `MainPage.xaml.vb`, and add a couple of `Imports` statements that you will need later as follows:

```
Imports System.Net.Http
Imports System.Net.Http.Headers
```

5. Now, add some initial code to define the RSS feeds our program will use and a collection to hold the `Post` objects as follows:

```
Public NotInheritable Class MainPage
    Inherits Page

    Public Property Posts As List(Of Post)
    Dim feedUrls As New List(Of String)

    Public Sub New()
        InitializeComponent()
        feedUrls = New List(Of String) From {
        "http://massively.joystiq.com/rss.xml",
        "http://feeds.feedburner.com/ScottHanselman",
        "http://www.nasa.gov/rss/dyn/breaking_news.rss"
        }
        Posts = New List(Of Post)
    End Sub
End Class
```

6. Add the `PublishedDate()` helper method to the class after the `New()` method as follows:

```
Public Function PublishedDate(item As XElement) As DateTime
    Dim s As String = CType(item.Element("pubDate"), String)
    s = s.Replace("EST", "-0500")
    s = s.Replace("EDT", "-0400")
    s = s.Replace("CST", "-0600")
```

```
        s = s.Replace("CDT", "-0500")
        s = s.Replace("MST", "-0700")
        s = s.Replace("MDT", "-0600")
        s = s.Replace("PST", "-0800")
        s = s.Replace("PDT", "-0700")

    Dim d As DateTime
    If DateTime.TryParse(s, d) Then
        Return d
    End If
    Return DateTime.MinValue
End Function
```

7. Add the `ReadFeed()` helper method below the `PublishedDate()` method using the following code:

```
Private Async Function ReadFeed(url As String) As Task(Of String)
    Dim client As New HttpClient
    Dim cacheControl As New CacheControlHeaderValue With {
        .NoCache = True,
        .NoStore = True
    }
    client.DefaultRequestHeaders.CacheControl = cacheControl
    client.MaxResponseContentBufferSize = Integer.MaxValue
    Dim response As HttpResponseMessage = Await client.
GetAsync(url)
    Dim content As String = Await response.Content.
ReadAsStringAsync()

    Dim _posts = From channel In XElement.Parse(content).
Elements("channel")
    From item In channel.Elements("item").Take(1)
    Let _date = PublishedDate(item)
    Order By _date Descending
    Select New Post With {
        .Title = CType(channel.Element("title"), String),
        .Link = CType(channel.Element("link"), String),
        .PostTitle = CType(item.Element("title"), String),
        .PostLink = CType(item.Element("link"), String),
        .PostDate = _date
    }
    Dim post = _posts.First
    Posts.Add(post)
    Return content
End Function
```

8. It's now time to add some functionalities to the button that loads the feeds. Write a handler for the `LoadFeeds` button's click event using the following code:

```
Private Async Sub LoadFeeds_Click(sender As Object, e As
RoutedEventArgs) Handles LoadFeeds.Click
    Dim _stopwatch = Stopwatch.StartNew
    Await Task.WhenAll(From url In feedUrls Select ReadFeed(url))
    Dim _timespan As TimeSpan = _stopwatch.Elapsed
    TimeTaken.Text = _timespan.ToString
    PostsListBox.ItemsSource = Posts
End Sub 'End of method
```

9. Compile and run the program. When the UI appears, click on (or press if your machine is touch-enabled) the **Load Feeds** button, wait a few seconds, and you should see the results of your work appear as in the following screenshot:

How it works...

In step 8, you added a `LoadFeeds.Click` event handler. The important thing to note about this method is that it is a `async` method and that `await` is used with the `Task.WhenAll` method. When the application runs and you click on the button, the click event fires the event handler, which in turn starts the background processing that reads the feeds. While the application is waiting for that background process to complete, control is returned to the main application for any other work that needs to be done, ensuring that you do not block the application while waiting for the feeds to be retrieved. When the feed retrieval completes, execution returns to the click event handler, which then updates the UI with the results.

In step 7, the `ReadFeed()` method looks similar to what you used in the console application in the *Making your code asynchronous* recipe; however, you will now see that you are using the `HttpClient` class instead of the `WebClient` class as it isn't available in the Windows Runtime. The `HttpClient` class also requires different code to set up the cache control values and you have to specify the response buffer size; otherwise, you can get runtime exceptions on long feeds.

Since this is a Windows Store app and you are coding against WinRT and the .NET Framework 4.5 Windows Store app profile, you cannot produce a synchronous version of the application. The synchronous API calls that you might have used with a console or WPF application simply aren't available. This makes the `await` and `async` keywords critical for Windows Store apps. Get familiar with them, know them, and use them. Without these keywords, developing asynchronous applications that meet modern design guidelines would be so much harder to do and so much more fragile and difficult to debug. These two little keywords make asynchronous programming much easier.

Using asynchrony with web applications

Internet Information Server (**IIS**) has limits on the number of requests and I/O threads it can use. Blocking any of these threads means IIS is forced to wait until the thread is released before another request can be processed. When there are no threads available to process requests (because of blocking or a high-server load), requests start to queue up, and over time, that queue can grow until it reaches its maximum size, at which point the dreaded `503 Service Unavailable` message will be displayed to the visitors on your site. This is not really what you want.

Historically, developers may have overlooked the benefits of using an asynchronous design when it came to web application design. This oversight may have been due to a mindset or limitations of the available technology. The rise of `Node.js` and similar asynchronous-based technologies demonstrates that this mentality is quickly changing. Most developers want a responsive, scalable web application that can support hundreds, if not thousands, of users and are willing to consider new approaches if that would mean better results.

High-server load due to a large volume of visitors is not something you can control. What is in your control, however, is your ability to write code that doesn't block threads and allows IIS to scale and process more requests than would have been possible otherwise. If you want a responsive, scalable web application that supports hundreds or thousands of users per server, you need to make the best use of the hardware you are on and you must consider the problems that are caused by blocking threads.

Once again, you'll use the feed reader scenario, but for simplicity, you'll just make the network calls to retrieve the RSS feeds and then display the time it took to do so.

Getting ready

Simply start a premium edition of Visual Studio or VS2013 for Web and you're ready to go.

How to do it...

Create an asynchronous web application by the following steps:

1. Start a new C# **ASP.NET Web Application** and then choose the **Web Forms** project type. Keep the default project name or pick one of your own.

2. Add a new **Web Form** item to the project using the default name of `WebForm1`.

3. In `WebForm1.aspx`, add `Async="true"` to the end of the page directive. This tells ASP.NET to allow the page life cycle events prior to the `PreRender` event to execute asynchronous tasks. This insertion is shown in the following screenshot:

4. Further down in the page body, add an `id` attribute to the `<div>` element and a `runat="server"` attribute as shown in the following code so that you can place the timing results in it when the page executes:

```
<body>
    <form id="form1" runat="server">
        <div id="timeTaken" runat="server" />
        <div>
        </div>
    </form>
</body>
```

5. Now, navigate to the `WebForm1.aspx.cs` code behind the file and add the following `using` statements to what is already listed:

```
using System.Diagnostics;
using System.Threading.Tasks;
using System.Net;
using System.Net.Cache;
```

6. Next, add the supporting `ReadFeed()` method to read a single RSS feed:

```
private async static Task<string> ReadFeed(string url)
{
    var client = new WebClient()
    {
        CachePolicy = new RequestCachePolicy(RequestCacheLevel.
NoCacheNoStore)
    };
    return await client.DownloadStringTaskAsync(url);
}
```

7. Now that you have the `ReadFeed()` method implemented, you should implement the `Page_Init()` method to read all the feed information during page startup. Because you want the page to load asynchronously, you will need to register a `PageAsyncTask` object. This lets ASP.NET know that you are performing an asynchronous operation, which is important since page life cycle events themselves are not asynchronous and without them the page would render before your tasks were complete. The following code is the implementation for `Page_Init()`:

```
private TimeSpan duration;

protected void Page_Init(object sender, EventArgs e)
{
    var feedUrls = new List<string>() {
            "http://massively.joystiq.com/rss.xml",
         "http://feeds.feedburner.com/ScottHanselman",
         "http://www.nasa.gov/rss/dyn/breaking_news.rss"
    };

    RegisterAsyncTask(new PageAsyncTask(async (ct) =>
    {
        var stopwatch = Stopwatch.StartNew();
        var feeds = await Task.WhenAll(
            from url in feedUrls select ReadFeed(url));
        foreach (var feed in feeds)
        {
            Debug.WriteLine(feed.Length);
        }
```

```
        duration = stopwatch.Elapsed;
        timeTaken.InnerText = duration.ToString();
    }));
}
```

8. Finally, add code to the `Page_PreRender()` method so that the duration of the entire page lifecycle, inclusive of the RSS reading, can be seen in the debug console in Visual Studio.

```
protected void Page_PreRender(object sender, EventArgs e)
{
    Debug.WriteLine("Duration: {0}", duration);
}
```

9. Press *F5* to start debugging the application. After a few seconds, the page load should complete and render a screen similar to the following screenshot:

10. Leaving the page open, switch back to Visual Studio, which should still be in debug mode. Look at the contents of the **Output** window and the **Debug** messages in particular. As shown in the following screenshot, you should see that the debug message from the `PreRender` event is displayed before the four numbers, showing the size of data pulled from the RSS feeds.

The duration shows as zero because the `Page_Init` method has been completed, but `PageAsyncTask` you registered has not yet been executed by the time the `PreRender` method is called.

How it works...

It's important to keep in mind that with ASP.NET Web Forms, the page methods are executed synchronously, even if you put the `async` keyword on the method declarations. You must use `RegisterAsyncTask`, just as you needed to in the previous .NET versions.

Because of the `async` keyword, the registering of tasks is now simply a matter of including a lambda in the code. You don't need to follow the old style of asynchronous programming anymore and you don't have to write any `begin` and `end` methods for the framework to call.

You will also notice that the page itself still took a while to load. The asynchronous approach you used allows the web server as a whole to scale and process more requests concurrently. It doesn't magically make those slow network calls to the RSS feeds any faster, so be prepared to think of other ways to improve your user interface to indicate to your users that something is happening and that they are not needlessly waiting.

There's more...

When it comes to ASP.NET MVC-based applications, things are even easier. Your controller still inherits from the `AsyncController` class; however, instead of having to write method pairs for the beginning and ending of an asynchronous operation, you simply have to create a controller method that returns a `Task<T>`. Take a look at the following example:

```
public async Task<ActionResult> Index()
{
  await LongRunningMethod();
  return View();
}
```

This is much better than how asynchronous controllers worked in previous versions of ASP. NET MVC; it is now much easier.

See also

▸   The *Making your code asynchronous* recipe at the beginning of this chapter

Working with actors and the TPL Dataflow Library

With Visual Studio 2010 and .NET 4.0, we were given the **Task Parallel Library** (**TPL**), which allowed us to process a known set of data or operations over multiple threads using constructs such as the `Parallel.For` loop.

Coinciding with the release of Visual Studio 2012, Microsoft has now given us the ability to take any data we like and process it in chunks through a series of steps, where each step can be processed independent of the others. This library is called the **TPL Dataflow Library**.

An interesting thing to note about this library is that it was originally included as part of .NET Framework in the pre-release versions, but the team moved it to a NuGet distribution model so that changes and updates to the package could be made outside of the normal .NET life cycle. A similar approach has been taken with the **Managed Extensibility Framework** (**MEF**) for web and Windows Store apps. This change to the distribution model shows a willingness from Microsoft to change their practices so that they can be more responsive to the developer's needs.

From a terminology perspective, the processing steps are called **Actors** because they "act" on the data they are presented with and the series of steps performed are typically referred to as a pipeline.

A fairly common example of this is in image processing where a set of images needs to be converted in some way, such as adding sepia tones, ensuring all images are in portrait mode, or doing facial recognition. Another scenario might be taking streaming data, such as sensor feeds, and processing that to determine actions to take.

This recipe will show you how the library works. However, to keep things simple, we won't do any fancy image processing. Instead, we'll just take some keyboard input and display it back on the screen after having converted it to uppercase and encoded it using Base64. If you would like to explore further after completing this recipe, you will find some references to more information listed later in this recipe.

In order to do this, we will use an `ActionBlock` object and a `TransformBlock` object. An `ActionBlock` object is a target block that calls a user-provided delegate when it receives data, while a `TransformBlock` object can be both a source and a target. In this recipe, you will use a `TransformBlock` object to convert characters to uppercase and encode them before passing them to an `ActionBlock` object to display them on screen.

Getting ready

Simply start a premium edition of VS2013 or use VS Express for Windows Desktop and you're ready to go.

How to do it...

Create a DataFlow powered application using the following steps:

1. Create a new application targeting .NET Framework 4.5 by navigating to **Visual C# | Console Application** and name it `DataFlow`.

2. Using NuGet, add the `TPL Dataflow` library to the project. The package name to use for installation when using the **Package Manager Console** is `Microsoft.Tpl.Datalfow`; otherwise, search for `TPL` on the **Manage NuGet Packages for Solution** dialog. (Refer to the *Managing packages with NuGet* recipe in *Chapter 4, .NET Framework 4.5.1 Development*, if you need a refresher on how to do this.)

3. Open `Program.cs` and at the top of the file, add the following using statements:

```
using System.Threading;
using System.Threading.Tasks;
using System.Threading.Tasks.Dataflow;
```

4. In the `Main()` method of `Program.cs`, add the following code to define the `ActionBlock`. The method in the `ActionBlock` object displays a `String` on the console and has a `Sleep` method call in it to simulate long running work. This gives you a way to slow down processing and force data to be queued between steps in the pipeline.

```
var slowDisplay = new ActionBlock<string>(async s =>
    {
        await Task.Run(() => Thread.Sleep(1000));
        Console.WriteLine(s);
    }
    , new ExecutionDataflowBlockOptions { MaxDegreeOfParallelism =
4 }
);
```

5. In the `Main()` method, continue to add the code for `TransformBlock`. The `TransformBlock` object will take a char as input and return an uppercase Base64 encoded string. The `TransformBlock` object is also linked to the `ActionBlock` object to create a two-step pipeline as follows:

```
var transformer = new TransformBlock<char, string>(c =>
{
    var upper = c.ToString().ToUpperInvariant();
    var bytes = ASCIIEncoding.ASCII.GetBytes(upper);
    var output = Convert.ToBase64String(bytes);
    return output;
});
transformer.LinkTo(slowDisplay);
```

6. Now add the following code to take input from the console and pass it to the first step of the pipeline (the `TransformBlock` object in this case). You also need to close and flush the pipeline when you hit *Enter* so that you can exit the program:

```
while (true)
{
    var key = Console.ReadKey();
    if (key.Key == ConsoleKey.Enter)
```

```
    {
        transformer.Complete();
        Console.WriteLine("waiting for the queue to flush");
        transformer.Completion.Wait();
        slowDisplay.Complete();
        slowDisplay.Completion.Wait();
        Console.WriteLine("press any key");
        Console.ReadKey();
        break;
    }
    transformer.Post(key.KeyChar);
}
```

7. Run the program. When the console window appears, just randomly press characters, and when you are done hit *Enter*. You should see an output similar to the following screenshot. Note how the encoded strings appear in batches up to four, though this may be one or two if you have a CPU with less than four cores.

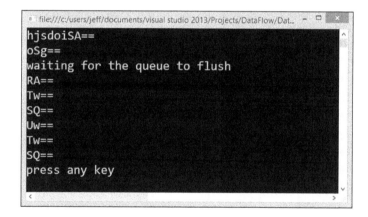

How it works...

Let's look at what just happened. First, you defined two actors. The first being the `ActionBlock` object that takes a string and displays it on screen and a second, the `TransformBlock`, that takes a character as input and returns an encoded string as the output. You then linked the `TransformBlock` object to the `ActionBlock` object to create the pipeline for the data to flow through.

Next, you took data that was being streamed to you (the console key presses) and passed each key press to the pipeline as soon as it arrived. This continued until the user hit *Enter*, at which point the `Complete()` method is used to tell the actors that they should expect no more data. Once the queues have been flushed, the user is prompted to hit a key to close the program. (If you don't flush the queues, you will lose the data that is still in them when the program completes—never a good thing.)

> You can watch the queue flushing process by entering a bunch of characters and then immediately pressing *Enter*. Depending on the speed of your machine, you will see the **waiting for the queue to flush** message scroll past followed by the remaining characters.

Now, when you ran the program, the `TransformBlock` object did its work very quickly and passed its output to the `ActionBlock`. The interesting thing to note is that even though the data was queuing up to be processed by the `ActionBlock` object, the amount of code you had to write to do that was zero. The TPL Dataflow Library takes care of all the difficult plumbing code, thread management, and the communication of data between actors, as well as determining how many actors it can run at once.

There's more...

You may also be wondering what happens in less straightforward scenarios, such as when you want to conditionally pass data or messages to the next actor. Fortunately, the TPL Dataflow Library is quite powerful and this recipe is just an introduction to what it offers. For example, the `LinkTo()` method has a predicate parameter that you can use to filter the messages and decide which actors should do what.

You could also batch up data for processing in the later steps by adding data to a buffer using the `BufferBlock` object and only passing buffered data to subsequent pipeline steps when the buffer is full. There are a lot of possibilities, so feel free to go and explore what the library has to offer.

The eagle-eyed among you may also have noticed that the lambda function used by the `ActionBlock` object featured the `async` keyword. This was done so that the action block doesn't itself block execution of the program when performing the long-running task and prevent any more input from being processed.

See also

▸ For more information about *Task Parallel Library (TPL)*, visit
`http://msdn.microsoft.com/en-us/library/dd460717(v=vs.110).aspx`

▸ For more information on *Dataflow*, visit
`http://msdn.microsoft.com/en-us/library/hh228603(v=vs.110).aspx`

▸ The *Making your code asynchronous* recipe

▸ The *Debugging parallel code with IntelliTrace* recipe in *Chapter 5, Debugging Your .NET Application*.

7
Unwrapping C++ Development

In this chapter, we will cover:

- ▶ Using XAML with C++
- ▶ Unit testing C++ applications
- ▶ Analyzing your C++ code
- ▶ Using a custom rule set
- ▶ Working with DirectX in Visual Studio 2013
- ▶ Creating a shader using DGSL
- ▶ Creating and displaying a 3D model
- ▶ Using the Visual Studio Graphics Diagnostics

Introduction

Before the rise of .NET, Java, and newer languages, C++ occupied a dominant position as the go-to choice for development of Windows applications. As the 21st century progressed, the use and popularity of these other languages grew, while C++ seemed to suffer somewhat without a vocal champion. As a result, this led to C++ becoming more of a specialist language, to the point where it is now commonly seen as the language for writing operating systems, device drivers, game engines, and similar applications where speed is of the essence.

In recent years, this decline has somewhat moderated due to a renewed push in C++ support by Microsoft, as well as renewed interest by developers who find that so-called "bare-metal" programming may provide better performance for applications running on portable devices. Without ignoring .NET or JavaScript, Microsoft has been improving C++ support. VS2013 demonstrates this as it includes several components of the C++11 language standard and some long-requested pieces of the C99 standard.

As a C++ developer or someone interested in C++ with Visual Studio 2013, you will find improved support for modern C++ through both support for language standards as well as improved tooling in Visual Studio itself.

This chapter will cover a variety of areas to show how VS2013 can make your C++ development more productive. We will start by looking at XAML, we'll then spend some time on some useful diagnostic tools, and then conclude with a look at some DirectX-based features.

Using XAML with C++

User interface development with C++ for Windows applications can be a challenging experience. When Visual Basic first appeared all those years ago, developers flocked to it because building a user interface in it was so much more productive than building the equivalent UI using C++, and C++ has never really caught up since.

Over recent years, with Microsoft moving away from WinForms, and the rise of declarative interface design with XAML, building a flexible yet powerful user interface has never been easier. The functionality offered by XAML-based UI technologies is impressive, with data binding in particular being a genuine productivity enhancement.

Meanwhile, C++ developers have seemingly been left further and further behind. The most common source of user interface development is typically found in game studios. Starting with Visual Studio 2012, the power and flexibility of the XAML-based user interface design is now available for C++ developers, making C++ a legitimate choice for business applications.

 C++ can only use XAML when creating WinRT applications. You cannot use this combination together to create traditional Windows desktop applications.

It's not just business applications that benefit though. Developers of DirectX applications can use XAML to render interface elements and composite them with their application's DirectX output. For game developers, this might be things such as application menus, score displays, and so on. Alternatively, you can have XAML-based applications with islands of DirectX in them, allowing developers of applications with a need for 3D imaging (such as medical or geospatial systems) to mix and match DirectX and XAML as required.

The choice and flexibility is up to you. For this recipe, you'll create a simple XAML-based interface with data binding to see how it all fits together.

Getting ready

Ensure that you are on a Windows 8.1 machine. Windows Store app development is not supported on prior versions of Windows.

Start a premium version of Visual Studio 2013 or use VS Express 2013 for Windows and you will be ready to go.

How to do it...

Create the app by following these steps:

1. Create a new **Blank App (XAML)** project by navigating to **Visual C++ | Windows Store** and name it `CppDataBinding`.

2. Open the `MainPage.xaml` file and add the following code inside the `<Grid>` element:

```
<Border BorderBrush="LightBlue" BorderThickness="4"
  CornerRadius="20" Margin="5">
  <StackPanel Margin="5">
    <TextBlock Text="Red level" Margin="5" />
    <Slider x:Name="redLevelSlider" Minimum="0"
      Maximum="255" Value="{Binding Path=RedValue,
      Mode=TwoWay}"
      Margin="5" Width="255" HorizontalAlignment="Left" />
    <TextBlock Text="Numeric value:" Margin="5"/>
    <TextBox x:Name="tbValueConverterDataBound"
      Text="{Binding Path=RedValue, Mode=TwoWay}"
      Margin="5" Width="150" HorizontalAlignment="Left"/>
  </StackPanel>
</Border>
```

3. For the data binding to work, you will need an object to bind to. Add a new header file to your project and call it `MyColor.h`. As a note, hold off on compiling the code until you get to step 9. Compiling it before will result in compiler errors.

4. Enter the following code as the content of the `MyColor.h` source file:

```
#pragma once
#include "pch.h"

using namespace Platform;
using namespace Windows::UI::Xaml::Data;

namespace CppDataBinding
{
```

```
[Bindable]
public ref class MyColor sealed : INotifyPropertyChanged
{
public:
  MyColor(void);
  virtual ~MyColor(void);

  virtual event PropertyChangedEventHandler^
    PropertyChanged;
  property String^ RedValue
  {
    String^ get() { return _redValue; }
    void set(String^ value)
    {
      _redValue = value;
      RaisePropertyChanged("RedValue");
    }
  }
protected:
  void RaisePropertyChanged(String^ name);

private:
  String^ _redValue;
};
}
```

5. Add a new C++ file named `MyColor.cpp` and enter the following code as its content:

```
#include "pch.h"
#include "MyColor.h"

using namespace CppDataBinding;
using namespace Windows::UI::Xaml::Data;

MyColor::MyColor(void) {}
MyColor::~MyColor(void) {}

void MyColor::RaisePropertyChanged(String^ name)
{
  PropertyChanged(this, ref new
    PropertyChangedEventArgs(name));
}
```

6. Now go to the `MainPage.xaml.h` file and add the `MyColor.h` file to the `#include` list.

7. Still in the `MainPage.xaml.h` file, go to the public members of the `MainPage` class and add the following line of code that is highlighted:

```
public:
    MainPage();
    property MyColor^ _myColor;
```

8. Next, navigate to the code-behind file for the `MainPage` class (`MainPage.xaml.cpp`) and add the following highlighted lines of code to the constructor:

```
MainPage::MainPage()
{
    InitializeComponent();
    _myColor = ref new MyColor();
    this->DataContext = _myColor;
}
```

9. Compile and run the application. You should see a screen similar to the following screenshot. As you enter values in the text field or move the slider, the two fields should remain in sync, as shown in the following screenshot:

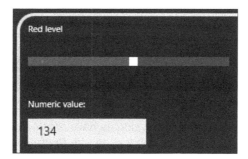

How it works...

The C++ code you have been writing is C++/CX, an extension of normal C++. You can still use normal C++ (without extensions) if you prefer, but it will mean dealing with the `IInspectable` interface and writing more COM code than would otherwise be the case.

The `ref` keyword you used for creating an instance of the `MyColor` class tells the compiler that you are using a Windows runtime object. The carat (^) symbol on variable declarations is a reference-counting smart pointer to a Windows runtime object. It is similar to a normal pointer but performs reference counting and automatic cleanup of resources when the last reference is cleared.

Data binding in C++ kicks into action when you insert the `[Bindable]` attribute on a class. When the compiler sees this, it will automatically generate code in a file called `xamltypeinfo.g.cpp` that implements the appropriate binding behaviors for interacting with the XAML markup.

In your code, you implemented the `INotifyPropertyChanged` interface. This was done so that you could use the two-way binding between the data class and the UI elements on the screen. The implementation of the interface should look familiar to anyone who has worked with the `INotifyPropertyChanged` interface in either WPF or Silverlight.

There's more...

If you were compiling the code after each step of the recipe, you may have seen a few compiler errors, some of which might have not made much sense.

If you compiled the application after step 5, you may have seen a number of errors in the `XamlTypeInfo.g.cpp` file.

This occurs because of the way the compiler handles the `[Bindable]` attribute and the generation of the code. The generated code not only includes the `.h` files from the XAML pages in the application, but also includes generated code for any types that are bindable. This means that if you have a bindable type but no references to it in any of the `.xaml.h` files, you will have undeclared identifier errors. Adding the `#include` statement for the bindable class' header file as you did in step 6 fixes this compiler error.

Unit testing C++ applications

Previously, we saw the .NET-based *Unit testing .NET applications* recipe in *Chapter 4, .NET Framework 4.5.1 Development*, but C++ developers have not been forgotten, and Visual Studio 2013 includes built-in support for unit testing with CppUnit.

C++ developers can choose from several types of unit test projects such as the **Native Unit Test Project**, the **Unit Test Library (Windows Store apps)** project, and the **Windows Phone Unit Test App** project. The first applies exclusively to desktop C++ development, the second applies exclusively to Windows Store apps, and the third is for Windows Phone-based apps.

In this recipe, we'll create a simple piece of code and add some unit tests to it that take advantage of the **Native Unit Test Project**.

Getting ready

Simply start Visual Studio 2013 (Express for Windows Desktop or a premium version) and you're ready to go. You can do this in any version of modern Windows since you're going to be creating a **Native Unit Test Project**.

How to do it...

To unit test your code, perform the following steps:

1. Create a new **Native Unit Test Project** by navigating to **Visual C++ | Test** and accepting the default project name.

2. In the **Solution Explorer** window, right-click on the project and select **Class Wizard...** from the menu to create a new class.

3. Click on the **Add Class...** button in the dialog box to add a new class to the project. Use the class name `BankVault` and click on the **Finish** button, as shown in the following screenshot:

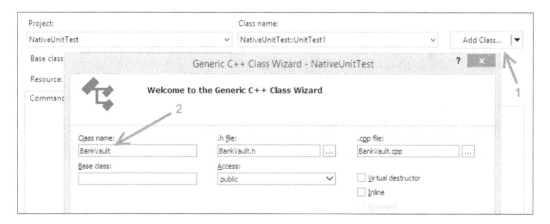

4. The **Class Wizard** will update its context to the newly-added `BankVault` class. Click on the **Methods** tab and then click on the **Add Method...** button within that tab.

5. In the **Add Member Function Wizard**, set **Function name** to AddFunds and add a parameter named amount of type int (yes, this bank vault only accepts whole units of currency). Don't forget to click on the **Add** button to add the parameter. This is shown in the following screenshot:

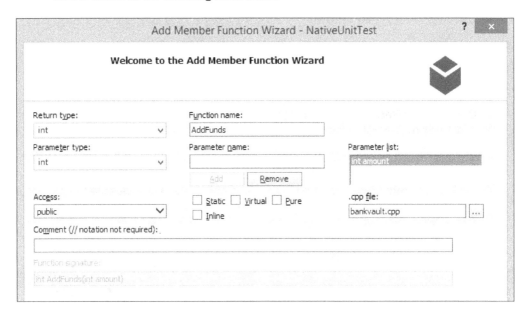

6. Click on **Finish** in the **Add Member Function Wizard** and then click on **OK** in the **Class Wizard** window.

7. Open the unittest1.cpp file under the **Source Files** folder from **Solution Explorer**, and at the top of the file, add a #include statement for the BankVault.h file:

    ```cpp
    #include "BankVault.h"
    ```

8. Update the body of the TestMethod1 method as follows:

    ```cpp
    TEST_METHOD(TestMethod1)
    {
      // TODO: Your test code here
      auto vault = new BankVault();
      auto totalFunds = vault->AddFunds(100);
      Assert::AreEqual(100, totalFunds);
    }
    ```

9. From the Visual Studio menu, select **Test** | **Run** | **All Tests** (or press *Ctrl + R, A*).

10. The code will compile. The **Test Explorer** screen will then appear and show the results of running the test, as shown in the following screenshot:

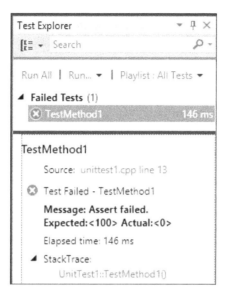

 If you are using Visual Studio Premium or Ultimate, **Test Explorer** can be configured to automatically run after each build. To do this, select **Test** | **Test Settings** | **Run Tests After Build**, so that the unit tests will run automatically each time the solution is built.

11. Switch back to the `BankVault.cpp` file and navigate to the `BankVault` destructor. Update the code as follows:

```
int total = 0;

int BankVault::AddFunds(int amount)
{
  total += amount;
  return total;
}
```

12. Build the solution and wait for a few moments. As soon as the build completes, **Test Explorer** should refresh and show the results of the unit test (if so configured on Visual Studio Premium or Ultimate). Assuming you made the correct changes, the code should now look like the following screenshot:

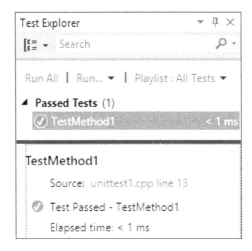

13. Let's add a few new methods. In the `BankVault.h` file, add the following lines of code that are highlighted:

```cpp
class BankVault
{
public:
  BankVault();
  ~BankVault();
  int AddFunds(int amount);
  void StageHeist();
  int CurrentFunds();
};
```

14. In the `BankVault.cpp` file, add the implementation for these two methods as follows:

```cpp
void BankVault::StageHeist()
{
  total = 0;
}

int BankVault::CurrentFunds()
{
  return total;
}
```

15. Now, add another test in the `unittest1.cpp` file just after the `TestMethod1` parameter for these new methods by adding the following code:

```
TEST_METHOD(RobTheBank)
{
  auto vault = new BankVault();
  auto totalFunds = vault->AddFunds(200);
  Assert::AreEqual(200, totalFunds);
  vault->StageHeist();
  totalFunds = vault->CurrentFunds();
  Assert::AreEqual(0, totalFunds);
}
```

16. Compile the solution and wait for **Test Explorer** to rerun the tests. You should now see one failing test result and one passing result, as shown in the following screenshot:

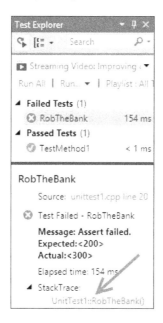

17. There's a small mistake in your code, and clicking on the first line of the stack trace in the error detail (indicated by the arrow in the prior screenshot) should help you isolate the problem (the initial funds aren't as expected). Start to fix the problem by navigating to the `BankVault.h` file and adding a private `int` variable named `total`:

```
class BankVault
{
public:
  BankVault();
  ~BankVault();
```

```
      int AddFunds(int amount);
      void StageHeist();
      int CurrentFunds();
    private:
      int total;
    };
```

18. In the `BankVault.cpp` file, remove the `int total = 0;` declaration and change the class constructor to initialize `total` to zero.

19. Compile the code one last time. The tests will be rerun and **Test Explorer** will show all tests working as expected.

How it works...

The test project you created already includes a reference to the CppUnit test framework as well as the necessary header files to define the various `Assert` methods available and the macros for creating the test methods.

You could build all of this by hand, but there's really no need to do so when the project template has defined it for you up front.

There are a few slight differences when creating a unit test library project for a Windows Store app. You will be referencing the WinRT libraries instead of normal libraries. You will be using the C++/CX extensions, and you can only add references to other WinRT-based libraries.

There's more...

The option to run unit tests with code coverage is available within **Test Explorer**. However, for unit test library projects of a Windows Store app, you will get no results as the diagnostic data adapters are not supported for unit tests of Windows Store app libraries.

Coverage information is only supported for native unit test projects, and coverage analysis will be displayed in the **Code Coverage Results** window.

Running a unit test in debug mode

In the .NET languages, you can right-click inside a test method in the code window and select the option to run and debug a unit test. This isn't available for C++ unit tests.

To debug C++ unit tests, you must select them from **Test Explorer** and either right-click on them and choose the **Debug Selected Tests** context menu option or select **Test | Debug | Selected Tests** from the Visual Studio menu.

See also

▸ The *Unit testing .NET applications* recipe in *Chapter 4, .NET Framework 4.5.1 Development*

Analyzing your C++ code

Static analysis of C++ code is a feature offered by VS Express and the premium editions of Visual Studio. Static analysis is a useful way to locate potential problems in your code and provides a way to catch a wide range of problems early in the development cycle.

In this recipe, we will show you how to use Visual Studio's built-in static analysis tools.

Getting ready

Start Visual Studio and create a new **Empty Project** under Visual C++, giving it a name of your choice.

How to do it...

For this project, perform the following steps:

1. Right-click on the project and select **Properties**.
2. Navigate to **Configuration Properties | General**, change **Configuration Type** to **Static Library (.lib)**, and click on **OK**.
3. Add a new **Header File** to the project and name it `AnalyzeThis.h`.
4. Enter the following code in the body of the header file:

```
class AnalyzeThis {

public:
  int LookHere(int param);
};
```

5. Add a new **C++ File** to the project and name it `AnalyzeThis.cpp`.
6. Enter the following code in the body of the file:

```
# include "AnalyzeThis.h"

int AnalyzeThis::LookHere(int param)
{
  int x;
  int y;
```

```
        if (param > 0) x = param;
        if (param < 0) y = param;
        return x + y;
    }
```

7. Compile the project. There should be no errors or warnings.

8. Right-click on the project and select **Properties** again. Select the **Code Analysis** group and ensure that **Enable Code Analysis on Build** is checked. Click on **OK** to close the window.

9. Right-click on the solution in the **Solution Explorer** window and select **Run Code Analysis on Solution** (*Alt + F11*). This option is also available in the menu by navigating to **Build | Run Code Analysis on Solution**.

10. The **Code Analysis** tool window will be displayed, and it will show a single warning about the use of uninitialized memory, as shown in the following screenshot:

11. Click on the entry to expand it. The reasons for the analysis warning will be shown, and the code where the warning occurs will be highlighted, as shown in the following screenshot:

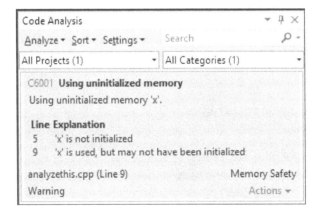

12. Change the code so that both x and y are initialized correctly with zero values.

13. Rerun the analysis. No messages should be displayed.

How it works...

Visual Studio uses a set of predefined rules to examine your code for common mistakes and poorly written code. In our example, the code may have compiled cleanly, but it would cause problems in operation as the x and y variables are not initialized. Static code analysis seeks to find these types of mistakes earlier in the development cycle rather than waiting and hoping for them to be caught later by unit tests or the QA department.

There's more...

This recipe works with both VS Express and the premium editions. However, with the paid editions, there is a bit more customization available. The rule set used by the analyzer can be modified to suit your preferences. The **Rule Set** setting, which can be accessed by going to **Settings** on the **Code Analysis** window (shown in the following screenshot), offers several choices based on the level of details required or the type of application being developed:

See also

▸ The *Using a custom rule set* recipe

Using a custom rule set

The built-in rule sets that come with Visual Studio cover a variety of usage scenarios and provide a way to use the **Code Analysis** tool in your projects immediately. Of course, depending on the complexity and needs of your project, the default rules may need to be customized and combined, as this recipe will demonstrate.

Getting ready

We are going to continue with the project we created in the *Analyzing your C++ code* recipe. You will need Visual Studio Professional or higher in order to modify rule sets.

How to do it...

To use a custom rule set, perform the following steps:

1. Open the project created in the previous recipe.

2. Open the `AnalyzeThis.cpp` file and add the following highlighted code:

    ```
    # include "AnalyzeThis.h"

    int x = 0;
    ```

3. Right-click on the project (not solution) in Solution Explorer and select **Properties**. The following screenshot will appear:

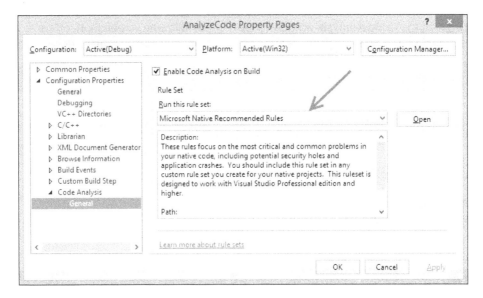

4. In the drop-down list indicated in the preceding screenshot, you may select a different individual rule set or pick and choose a combination of rule sets to apply to your project.

> By convention, rule sets have the `.ruleset` extension and are stored in the following location:
>
> ```
> C:\Program Files (x86)\Microsoft Visual Studio 12.0\
> Team Tools\Static Analysis Tools\Rule Sets
> ```

5. For our purposes, ensure that the **Microsoft Native Recommended Rules** tab is selected, and then click on **Open**.

6. The rule set editor will open. Go to **Microsoft.VC.AmbiguousIntent** or enter C6244 in the search box. The rule we will enable is **C6244**: **Local declaration hides global**, which is shown in the following screenshot:

7. After enabling the rule, let's rename the rule set to reflect that we have customized it. Open the **Properties** window by pressing *F4* or selecting **View | Properties**. Change the name of the rule set to the one of your choice, as shown in the following screenshot:

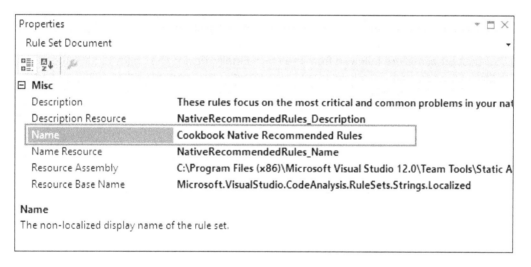

8. Once changed, save your changes (*Ctrl + S* or by right-clicking on the filename and selecting **Save**). Visual Studio will prompt for a new file name, as the built-in rule sets are write-protected.

9. Verify that your new rules are being used by right-clicking on the project, choosing **Properties**, and selecting your newly created rule set under **Configuration Properties | Code Analysis | General** (the same process as in step 3).

10. Rebuild the solution (*Ctrl* + *Shift* + *B*) and then rerun the Code Analyzer (*Alt* + *F11*). With our new rule activated, our second variable's declaration was detected, as shown in the following screenshot:

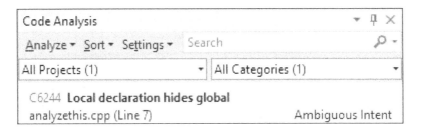

How it works...

This recipe has shown how the existing rule sets can be combined and/or modified to suit the needs of your project. If you are inheriting a legacy code base, this analysis can provide a great starting point for where improvements can be made. The customization allows you to focus on items of a particular importance or, just as easily, minimize the clutter from rules that don't concern you. If you are starting a new project, you may opt for a rigorous approach so that best practices are followed from the start. Finally, having the ability to save these changes into an external file allows them to be stored with a project so that all developers can follow the same practices.

There's more...

There are two rule sets provided for native code in Visual Studio 2013:

▶ The **Microsoft Native Minimum Rules** rule set contains rules for basic correctness, such as potential security holes and application crashes (invalid memory access, buffer overruns, and so on).

▶ The **Microsoft Native Recommended Rules** rule set is a superset of the minimum rules and provides a more in-depth set of rules to evaluate. It also includes rule checks for lock problems, race conditions, and other concurrency-related issues.

To get an understanding of what rules each rule set uses, go to the project's properties and select the **Code Analysis** settings. Clicking on the **Open** button will display the rules that are enabled for the rule set. In order to see all available rules, click on the red down arrow in the toolbar. For Microsoft's official definitions of all available rule sets, consult the article, *Code analysis rule set reference* at `http://msdn.microsoft.com/en-us/library/dd264925.aspx`.

Working with DirectX in Visual Studio 2013

C++ and DirectX are being promoted by Microsoft as the primary way to build high-performance games in Windows 8.x with XNA left out in the cold. XNA developers can still use XNA in Windows 8.x but only for desktop applications, and not for creating Windows Store apps.

 Developers looking for the spiritual (if not outright) successor to XNA are encouraged to check out MonoGame, an open source implementation of the XNA Framework at http://www.monogame.net/.

As a DirectX developer, you will be pleased to know that there is no longer a separate DirectX download required for Windows 8.1. The DirectX SDK is now incorporated into the Windows SDK, and the DirectX 11.2 runtime is built into the Windows 8.1 operating system. For older versions of Windows, the current requirement to download a separate SDK and runtime remains in place.

If you have used previous versions of DirectX and C++, then you will find Visual Studio 2013 somewhat different as you will be using C++/CX. Many of the DirectX calls have differences in them, not only due to the use of `ref` pointers, but also in the way displays are referenced and how restrictions are enforced by the Windows Store app sandbox. It will most likely require some tweaking to the approaches you may have used in the past.

For this recipe, we'll use the default application template to display a rotating cube on the screen and then alter the code to stop and start the rotation when we touch the screen, click the mouse, or press a key.

Getting ready

Start Visual Studio 2013 in Windows 8.1 and you're ready to go. You will want to use VS Express for Windows or one of the premium editions as we are creating a Windows Store app.

How to do it...

Create the app by performing the following steps:

1. Create a new **DirectX App** project by navigating to **Visual C++ | Windows Store** and name it `RotatingCube`.

2. The default project template includes all of the code to display a cube, apply shaders to it, and then rotate it. Before you go any further, ensure that the application works by compiling and running it. You should see a screen similar to the following screenshot:

3. Stop the application by pressing *Alt + F4* and then switch back to Visual Studio. Before editing, ensure debugging has stopped by pressing *Shift + F5* or clicking on the stop button on the toolbar. In the `App.h` file, add the following code block to the protected event handler declarations:

```
void OnPointerReleased(Windows::UI::Core::CoreWindow^
  sender, Windows::UI::Core::PointerEventArgs^ args);
void OnKeyDown(Windows::UI::Core::CoreWindow^ sender,
  Windows::UI::Core::KeyEventArgs^ args);
```

4. To the private variables in that same header file, add the `bool m_isRotating;` statement.

5. In the `App.cpp` file, locate the `App::SetWindow` method and add the following highlighted code to register the event handlers for the user input events and to set the `m_isRotating` flag:

```
// Start recieving touch/mouse events and keyboard events
window->PointerReleased +=
  ref new TypedEventHandler<CoreWindow^,
  PointerEventArgs^>(this, &App::OnPointerReleased);
window->KeyDown +=
  ref new TypedEventHandler<CoreWindow^,
  KeyEventArgs^>(this, &App::OnKeyDown);
m_isRotating = true;

DisplayInformation^ currentDisplayInformation =
  DisplayInformation::GetForCurrentView();
```

6. Now add the following code for the event handlers at the end of the `App.cpp` file. The handlers simply toggle the `m_isRotating` flag to indicate whether to rotate the cube or not:

```
void App::OnPointerReleased(Windows::UI::Core::CoreWindow^
  sender, Windows::UI::Core::PointerEventArgs^ args)
{
  m_isRotating = !m_isRotating;
}
```

```
void App::OnKeyDown(Windows::UI::Core::CoreWindow^ sender,
  Windows::UI::Core::KeyEventArgs^ args)
{
  m_isRotating = !m_isRotating;
}
```

7. Locate the `App::Run()` method and wrap the `m_main->Update();` call in an `if` statement that checks the `m_isRotating` flag, as shown in the following code snippet:

```
if (m_isRotating) {
  m_main->Update();
}
```

8. Run the application and notice that you can start and stop the rotation by pressing any key, clicking with the mouse, or tapping on the screen.

9. Stop the application when you have finished testing.

10. The colors on the cube are determined by a combination of a vertex shader and a pixel shader. The vertex shader uses the color assigned to each vertex in the cube's definition, in the `Sample3DSceneRenderer::CreateDeviceDependentResources()` method, and each pixel shader is shaded based on blending the colors of the vertices nearest to it. Open the `SamplePixelShader.hlsl` file to look at the pixel shader.

11. At the moment, the shader simply takes the color passed to it and sets the alpha channel to `1.0f`, making it opaque. Alter the shader to remove all traces of red from the cube by changing the body of the `main()` method to the following code snippet:

```
float4 main(PixelShaderInput input) : SV_TARGET
{
  float3 removedRed;
  removedRed = float3(0.0f, input.color.g, input.color.b);
  return float4(removedRed, 1.0f);
}
```

12. Rebuild and run the application. The cube should now look similar to the following screenshot, with no red color visible:

How it works...

The key areas to focus on in this application involve creating the drawing surface and the handling of the user input. You saw how the user input can be handled via the event listeners and that the `PointerEventArgs` class is used for both touch- and mouse-based input.

Most of the work done while creating the rendering surface is encapsulated in the `Direct3DBase` class (`DeviceResources`). It is in here that the call to the `D3D11CreateDevice` method is made, as is the call to the `CreateSwapChainForCoreWindow` method, which is needed in order to get DirectX up and running correctly.

It is also useful to note that an application manifest is included in the project, and that the linker has prepopulated references to the required DirectX libraries so that you don't need to remember to add them yourself.

There's more...

The pixel and vertex shaders used in the application are written using **High-Level Shading Language** (**HLSL**), a C++ style **Domain Specific Language** (**DSL**) for describing how the color should be calculated for each rendered pixel in an object.

When the compiler sees an HLSL file, it compiles it into a `.cso` file that you can then use in your application. You can see this in the `Sample3DSceneRenderer::CreateDeviceDependentResources()` method where the `.cso` files of the two shaders are read into memory and then passed to the DirectX calls to create shader instances. The shaders are then used later in the `Sample3DSceneRenderer::Render()` method, with the vertex shader called before the pixel shader to ensure that the cube renders correctly.

Is managed DirectX supported?

With Windows Runtime and the improvements in how .NET languages interoperate with COM in Windows 8, you may be wondering if DirectX development using managed languages such as C# is possible. The answer is yes, but not without using third-party libraries. If you are interested in using DirectX in a managed language, you may want to keep an eye on open source projects such as SharpDX (`http://sharpdx.org/`). Just keep in mind that this approach is not supported by Microsoft and that DirectX applications written in .NET will run a little slower than native C++ applications. Regardless of this, applications built using third-party libraries should still be able to pass the verification process and be listed in the store.

See also

- ▸ The *Creating a Windows Store app* recipe in *Chapter 2, Getting Started with Windows Store Applications*
- ▸ The *Creating a shader using DGSL* recipe
- ▸ The *Using the Visual Studio Graphics Diagnostics* recipe

Creating a shader using DGSL

Starting with Visual Studio 2012, Microsoft has added a new mechanism for building shaders, using a language called **Directed Graph Shader Language** (**DGSL**). This language can be used to create very complex shaders that are still easily understandable at a high level and are therefore more maintainable than shaders written in pure HLSL.

In this recipe, we'll create a shader that applies a texture to an object and colors it.

Getting ready

Ensure that you are running Windows 8.1 and start Visual Studio 2013, either one of the premium versions or Express version for Windows.

How to do it...

Create a shader by performing the following steps:

1. Create a new **DirectX App** project by navigating to **Visual C++ | Windows Store** and give it a name of your choice.

2. Right-click on the project, select **Add | New Item**, and then choose **Graphics | Visual Shader Graph (.dgsl)**. Leave the name as the default one, `Shader.dgsl`, and click on **Add**.

3. The shader will be added to the project and the design surface will be displayed. Open the toolbox (located on the left-hand side of the screen, or use *Ctrl + W, X*) to see all of the nodes that can be used in your shader. Click on the black background of the design surface to see the properties of the shader. In the following screenshot, the toolbox is marked on the left (red box), and the property window is marked on the right (red arrow):

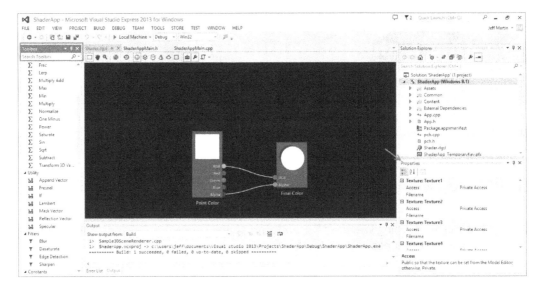

4. From the **Toolbox** window, drag a **Texture Sample** node onto the design surface.

If you have trouble finding the **Texture Sample** node in the toolbox, use the search box at the top of the toolbox to filter the items displayed.

5. In the properties for the **Texture Sample** node you just added, set the **Filename** property to the full path (not relative path) of the `SmallLogo.png` file in the `Assets` folder. You can do this fairly easily by selecting the image file in **Solution Explorer**, copying the full path from the **Properties** window for the file, and then pasting that value into the **Filename** property of the **Texture Sample** node.

6. Drag a **Texture Coordinate** node from the **Toolbox** window onto the design surface.

7. On the side of each of the shader nodes are connectors, the small circles that represent the input and output variables for each node. Drag the **Output** connector of the **Texture Coordinate** node to the **UV** input connector of the **Texture Sample** node to link the two nodes together, as shown in the following screenshot:

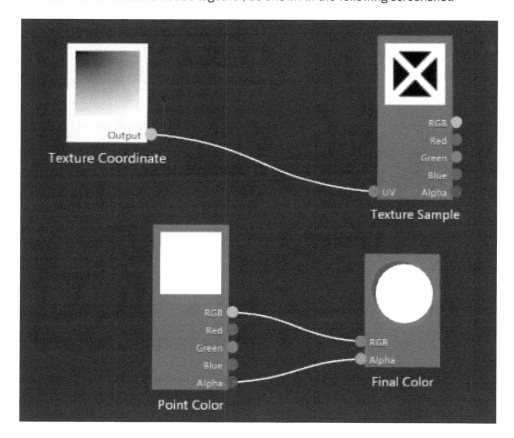

8. Next, you should color the texture based on the color of the point at which it will be applied. To do this, drag a **Multiply** node onto the designer and connect the **RGB** output of both the **Point Color** and **Texture Sample** nodes to the **X** and **Y** inputs of the **Multiply** node.

9. Then, drag the output of the **Multiply** node to the **RGB** input of the **Final Color** node. In doing so, the **RGB** link from the **Point Color** node to the **Final Color** node will be removed as inputs can only have one source, as shown in the following screenshot:

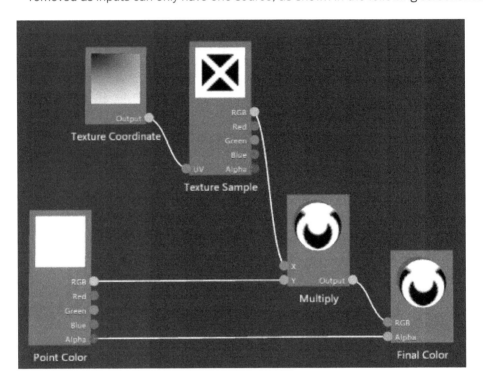

10. In the document toolbar, click on the **Preview with teapot** button (shown in the following screenshot) so that we can see the results using the classic object in 3D rendering demos:

11. In the shader designer, select the **Final Color** node and then hold down the *Ctrl* key while you move the mouse scroll wheel forward to zoom in on the element until you can zoom no further. You will now see a better 3D representation of what the shader will do to a model, as shown in the following screenshot:

12. Press and hold *Alt* and then click-and-drag on the teapot to rotate it so that you have a better idea of how the texture will be applied to the various surfaces of the teapot.

13. Save the `Shader.dgml` file by pressing *Ctrl + S*.

14. On the left side of the designer toolbar, click on the **Advanced** icon. It will display a menu where you can choose to export the shader as HLSL, a compiled pixel shader (`.cso`), or as a C++ header file (`.h`). Select the HLSL file option and save the shader into your `Documents` folder. The following screenshot shows where the **Export As...** command is located:

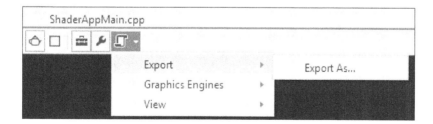

15. From the Visual Studio menu, select **File** | **Open** | **File** or press *Ctrl + O*, and then open the file you just saved. You can now see the HLSL version of the shader you created.

How it works...

Shaders are effectively a pipeline of instructions that affect the rendering of an object on the screen. They can be applied to vertices, pixels, and geometries to produce varying effects. The key to all shaders is to try and do as few operations as possible. The higher the number of nodes in a shader, the more computationally expensive they will be, and the slower your overall frame rate in the application will be.

In this particular recipe, the shader we built was fairly rudimentary since the intent was to show how a shader can be built in Visual Studio. For complex shaders, such as flame or smoke, there are parameter nodes for **Time** and **Normalized Time** that you will want to use. For geometry shaders, you will want to consider using nodes such as **World Position** and **Mask Vector**.

See also

> ▸ The *Creating and displaying a 3D model* recipe
> ▸ The *Working with DirectX in Visual Studio 2013* recipe

Creating and displaying a 3D model

In the previous *Creating a shader using DGSL* recipe, you created a shader for applying a texture to a model. It would be great if there was an easy way to create your own 3D models, and Visual Studio provides a mechanism for doing just that. Visual Studio offers a fairly basic 3D modeling tool, and while it's nowhere near as fully featured as Maya or other specialist modeling tools, it does come in the box. It meets the needs of the homebrew developer or those simply wanting to "rough in" some models or tweak some properties of a model supplied by a designer.

Getting ready

This recipe uses the shader from the previous *Creating a shader using DGSL* recipe. So, if you haven't already completed that, go ahead and do so now. If you have completed it, then open up the solution you created as you're ready to get started.

How to do it...

Create a 3D model using the following steps:

1. Right-click on the project and select **Add** | **New Item**.
2. In the dialog box, choose **Graphics** | **3D Scene (.fbx)**, and leave the name as Scene. fbx before clicking on **Add**.

3. Visual Studio will open the scene editor where you can create your model. Ensure that the **Toolbox** and **Properties** panes are visible, and then add a cylinder to the scene by double-clicking on the **Cylinder** node in the **Toolbox** window.

4. Select the cylinder in the designer by clicking on it. In the scene editor toolbar at the left of the design surface, click on the scale icon. The cylinder will be overlaid with x, y, and z drag handles (the red, green, and blue boxes) which you can use to resize the object in any single direction, and a central drag handle (a white box) for scaling the object evenly in all directions. Resize the cylinder to make it larger by clicking on the central white handle and dragging it to the right, as shown in the following screenshot:

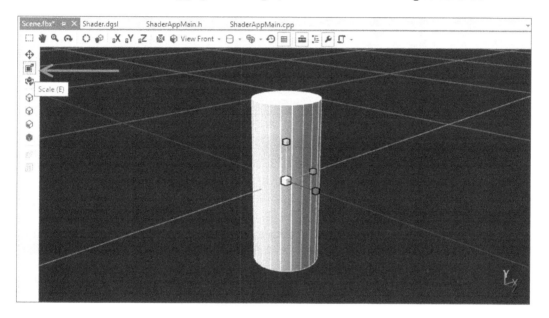

5. In the **Properties** window, locate the **Effect** property:

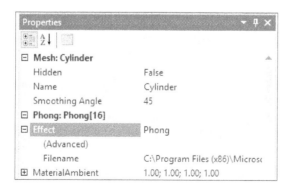

6. Click on the plus next to the **Effect** property to expand its details, as shown in the preceding screenshot, and click on the ellipsis (**...**) on the **Filename** property to open the file selection dialog box.

7. Browse to the `Shader.dgsl` file you created in the previous recipe and click on **OK**.

8. Change the value of the **Name** property in the shader's property group to `MyShader`.

9. In some cases, the change will not take place immediately, but it will refresh the next time the **Properties** window is asked to display properties for the cylinder. You can force this by clicking on a file in **Solution Explorer** and then clicking on the cylinder again. You should also see that the scene has been updated to show the effects of the shader on the cylinder.

10. A common way of looking at 3D models is to look at the wireframe. To view the scene in wireframe mode, click on the wireframe icon on the main toolbar (not the embedded toolbar). It's the last icon in the list, as shown in the following screenshot:

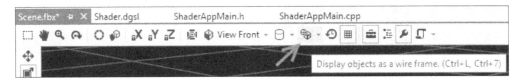

How it works...

At this point, you now have a model that is ready to be used. As mentioned in the introduction, the modeling tool is not meant to compete with full-featured 3D modeling tools and is instead offered only as an entry-level modeling toolkit.

Given that the packaging of models is typically application-specific, Visual Studio provides neither an inbuilt method for packing models into a data file nor a method to load them. The choice of how you package models depends on your application, its performance characteristics, and any of the restrictions you need to work within. Because of this diversity, Visual Studio provides a single, simple method for editing a model and for everything else, it's up to you.

There's more...

There are many more features available in the model viewer than were covered in this recipe. Most of these features are self-explanatory and deal with the basics of moving and rotating objects within the scene, changing selection modes, and changing view modes. Advanced functionality, such as merging objects, is contained under the **Advanced** menu on the left side of the designer's toolbar.

- ▸ The *Creating a shader using DGSL* recipe

Using the Visual Studio Graphics Diagnostics

One of the hard things to do in DirectX applications is determine the cause of a visual glitch or bug on the screen. Despite the best efforts of developers to avoid bugs, there are many websites featuring screenshots taken by gamers of weird things happening in a game.

Visual Studio addresses some of the debugging issues for DirectX applications by including a new **Graphics Diagnostics** toolset that lets you look at pixel history to determine just how a specific pixel came to be rendered on the screen. Let's see how it works.

Getting ready

Simply start a premium version of Visual Studio 2013 on Windows 8.1 and you're ready to go.

How to do it...

For this recipe, perform the following steps:

1. Create a new **DirectX App** project by navigating to **Visual C++** | **Windows Store** and leave the default name as it is.

2. The project template includes code to display a spinning cube, so build the application to ensure it compiles.

3. Start the diagnostics by pressing *Alt + F5* or by choosing **Debug** | **Graphics** | **Start Diagnostics** from the Visual Studio menu.

4. When the application starts, you should see the debugger's HUD displayed in the top-left corner of the application.

5. While the application is running, press *Print Screen* a few times to capture some frames from the application. The debugger HUD should update to display the captured frame, indicating that the capture was successful.

6. Stop debugging when you are ready, and in Visual Studio, you should see something similar to the following screenshot:

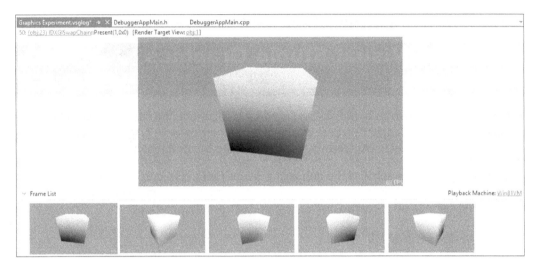

7. Select one of the frames you captured from the **Frame List** window, and in the frame view, click on one of the pixels in the cube. If you can't see the entire frame, you can hold *Ctrl* and drag with the left mouse button to pan around the frame.

8. The **Graphics Pixel History** window should have appeared when you clicked on the pixel. If it isn't showing, in the graphics toolbar, click on the pixel history icon, as shown in the following screenshot:

9. The history of that selected pixel will be shown on the screen:

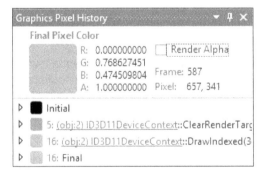

10. In the preceding screenshot, this selected pixel was initially blue (the background was black), and was eventually rendered as green. Your color will most likely be different. Click on the expansion arrow for the event when the color changes to expand it.

11. Expand the triangle further to show all of its component's details, as shown in the following screenshot:

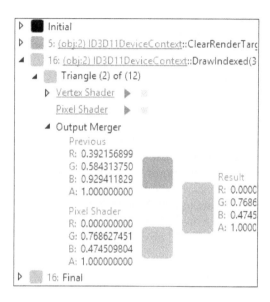

12. Clicking either on the **Vertex Shader** or **Pixel Shader** links will take you to the HLSL source for the shader so that you can see the shader calculation.

13. You can examine how the shader values were calculated even after normal debugging has concluded. Click on the debug icon (the play button) for one of the vertices in the **Vertex Shader** link or for the **Pixel Shader** link to debug it using the captured values. Step through the shader code until the debugger finishes, as shown in the following screenshot:

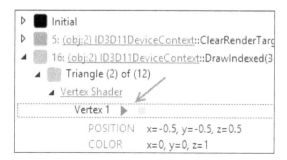

14. From the Visual Studio menu, select **Debug | Graphics | Event Call Stack** or click on the **Event Call Stack** button in the **Graphics** toolbar. The **Graphics Event Call Stack** window will be displayed, similar to the following screenshot:

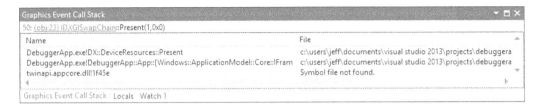

15. This is a normal call stack, so double-click on one of the method calls from your application to jump to that line of code.

16. From the Visual Studio menu, select **Debug | Graphics | Event List**, or click on the event list icon on the **Graphics** toolbar. A list of all DirectX operations that occurred in rendering the frame will be shown. Clicking on any of the events will show the operation details in the document area, allowing you to delve further into what occurred. It will also update the **Graphics Event Call Stack** window to show call stack information, when available, and the frame preview window, to show what the frame looked like at that specific point in time, which can be very helpful in locating overdraw problems.

How it works...

The Graphics Diagnostics toolset is the result of the work that was put into the PIX debugging tool that shipped with the DirectX SDK. With it now being built directly into Visual Studio, the user experience is much better for developers.

The level of detail presented by these tools is extensive and should help you track down the root cause of many of your rendering problems.

There's more...

One thing that wasn't touched on in the recipe was the rendering pipeline. If you want to look at the way a frame was built up, then understanding how the object meshes were used can be very useful.

If you select a DirectX Draw event from the **Graphics Events List** window, and then select **Debug | Graphics | Pipeline Stages** from the menu, you will see how the frame was put together. Clicking on one of the stages in the **Graphics Pipeline Stages** window will show you the details of that stage in a document preview tab, as shown in the following screenshot:

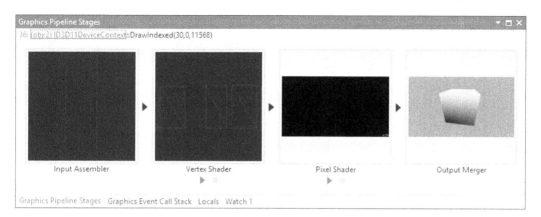

8

Working with Team Foundation Server 2013

In this chapter, we will cover:

- ► Creating a new TFS project
- ► Managing your work
- ► Using local workspaces for source control
- ► Performing code reviews
- ► Getting feedback from your users
- ► Using Git for source control

Introduction

Team Foundation Server (**TFS**) is a popular companion for users of Visual Studio that provides Microsoft's approach to source control and project management. Developers working in traditional corporate software development will frequently use TFS as a way to coordinate their activity with that of product owners, quality assurance, and release engineers.

TFS is a separate product from VS2013, and exists in both paid and free (TFS Express) versions. The primary difference between the two is that TFS Express is designed for smaller developer teams and thus supports five users, while the full version has no such restrictions. Day-to-day usage will typically involve connecting to TFS via Visual Studio or the TFS web browser interface.

With the advent of VS2013, Microsoft has created **Visual Studio Online** (**VSO**). One aspect of VSO is that it provides Microsoft-hosted TFS service, which provides developers with an area to create and store their projects without needing to take on the additional task of administrating a server.

Regardless of the approach you take, this chapter will look at the major features and concepts of TFS and how they can support your work in Visual Studio. The recipes in this chapter will walk you through using these new improvements and features, so let's get started.

Creating a new TFS project

Visual Studio Online represents Microsoft's rebranding of what used to be Team Foundation Service combined with new abilities to write code directly on the web. We are going to use VSO to host a new development project that we can connect to via any version of VS2013. Using VSO will let us focus on the project setup, while Microsoft can then run the server for us.

The concepts to create a new project are similar, whether you are using VSO or standalone TFS. Since in many cases corporate users merely access a previously configured TFS environment, this example will let all readers follow along.

Getting ready

You will want to have a Microsoft account ID available, and you can either create a new ID for this chapter or use one of your existing IDs. You will also want to have a copy of VS2013. We will be using Visual Studio Express for Windows Desktop, but the concepts are applicable to all versions.

How to do it...

Perform the following steps:

1. Connect to Visual Studio Online (`http://www.visualstudio.com/`) and create a VSO account (if you already have a Microsoft account, you will be adding VSO capabilities).

2. The account URL is something you will be using as the access point to your projects, so pick something meaningful (or at least something you won't mind reading everyday). Your URL will ultimately have a form similar to `https://teamname.visualstudio.com`.

 Multiple projects can be housed at the same URL, so you may want to avoid using a name that is project specific.

3. After account creation, you can create a new project and enter the details for the new project. Enter a project name of your choice. For the purpose of the recipe, we are going to select **Team Foundation Version Control** and the **Microsoft Visual Studio Scrum 2013.2** process template, and click on **Create project**, as shown in the following screenshot:

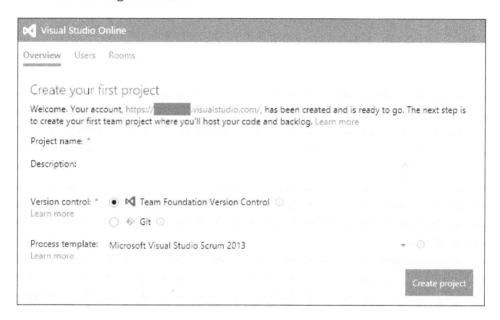

4. Once created, you will be able to connect to this project with Visual Studio. For easy access, you can have VSO open your copy of VS2013 directly via the link at the lower right of the project page, as shown in the following screenshot. However, this recipe will continue by showing you how to connect to a TFS/VSO project from within VS2013.

5. Open your copy of VS2013. The **Team Explorer** window should be on the right, but if it is not, you can open it through **View | Team Explorer** or *Ctrl + \, Ctrl + M*. Once visible, click on **Select Team Projects...**, as shown in the following screenshot:

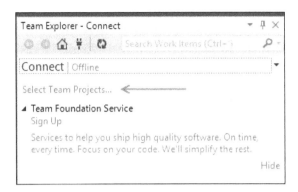

6. The ensuing dialog box will offer several choices. Looking at the following screenshot, the dropdown marked with **1** indicates which TFS you are browsing. For this recipe, if it doesn't show your VSO-based Team Foundation Server, then click on the **Servers...** button (marked with **2**) so that it can be added.

   (This would also be where an existing self-hosted TFS address could be entered if you are not using VSO.) Returning to the following screenshot, once a server is selected, you will have the option to select one or more projects to access. Here, the **VSCookbook** project is selected. Click on **Connect** once you have chosen the appropriate server and project(s).

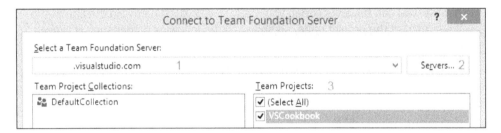

7. On a brand new TFS project, such as the one in this example, VS2013 will then prompt you to configure your workspace. Click on the **Configure your workspace** link shown in the notice area, as in the following screenshot:

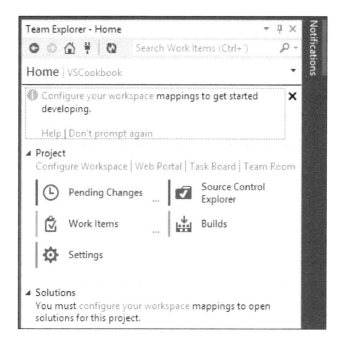

8. The **Configure Workspace** dialog area will then open. To complete the process, click on the **Map & Get** button, as shown in the following screenshot:

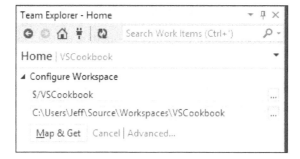

How it works...

Visual Studio Online provides all of the functionalities of TFS with the added benefit of server management details being handled by Microsoft. In our example, a new site and project were created to hold your project's source code and work items. By using version control, you will benefit from the ability to track changes to your source code and simplify maintenance. Working with other developers on a common project is easier as everyone involved can always obtain the most current version of the source code from a centralized location that doesn't require e-mailing zip files around. Better still, the details of your project will not be lost if your local developer's machine crashes.

There's more...

The preceding recipe establishes a brand new, but empty workspace. To add a new or existing solution, use the appropriate link in the **Team Explorer** window, as shown in the following screenshot:

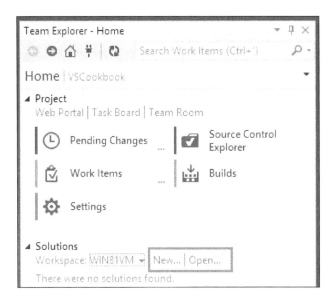

If you click on **New...**, your project will be part of your newly established VSO workspace. If you click on **Open...**, you will have the extra step of opening an existing project, and then right-clicking on that project in **Solution Explorer** to add it to source control.

Managing your work

Whether you work in a team or as an independent developer, the odds will be high that you will have a list of requirements describing what you need to build. Scrum teams use product backlogs, traditional teams use functional specifications, and other teams will have their own variations of these. Even as an independent developer, you probably maintain at minimum a to-do list of features to add and bugs to fix. Using TFS, this information can be stored as the various work item types in the team project.

In this recipe, we'll show you how to manage your work using Visual Studio 2013 and TFS.

Getting ready

You will need to have access to a TFS project, like the sample one created in the *Creating a new TFS project* recipe, or another one that you have access to.

The recipe also requires that your team project be based on the **Microsoft Visual Studio Scrum 2013** process template. If your project uses a different process template, the work item types may be different from those in the recipe.

Start Visual Studio 2013 and you're ready to go.

How to do it...

Perform the following steps:

1. When you first connect to TFS, you will need to set up the connection if you have not already done so. From the Visual Studio menu, navigate to **Team | Connect to Team Foundation Server....** Use the **Servers** button in the connection dialog to add a new connection for the TFS you want to connect to, and then connect to the project collection and the specific team project you wish to use for this recipe.

2. If the **Team Explorer** tool window isn't visible, open it by navigating to **View | Team Explorer** from the menu by pressing *Ctrl + \\, Ctrl + M*, or by using the **Quick Launch** tool.

3. When it is open, ensure you are connected to TFS by confirming that the **Home** hub is displaying the correct team project name, as shown in the following screenshot:

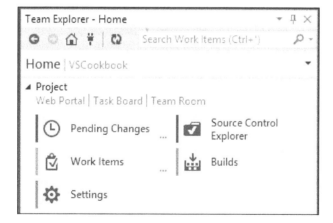

 Your **Home** hub may look slightly different if your team project has a team portal or reporting is enabled.

4. This recipe needs some work for you to track, so start out by creating a new work item. Click on the **Work Items** entry in **Team Explorer** to navigate to the **Work Items** hub.

5. Click on the **New Work Item** dropdown from the **Work Items** hub and click on **Product Backlog Item** from the list, as shown in the following screenshot:

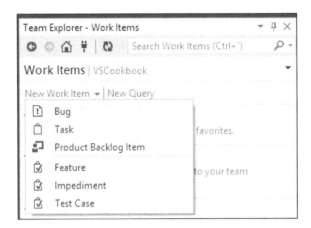

6. A new **Work Item** form will be displayed in the Visual Studio document area. Enter a title of your choice and set the **Assigned To** user as yourself. You can set the value of any of the other fields as you wish. When you are ready, click on the **Save Work Item** button in the form's toolbar or press *Ctrl + S* to save the work item.

7. Right-click on the background of the **Product Backlog Item** form (that is, right-click on the white space) and select the **New Linked Work Item...** option (*Shift + Alt + L*).

8. In **Work Item Type**, select **Task** from the list and enter a **Title** for the item before clicking on **OK**.

9. The linked work item will have automatically set you to be the **Assigned To** person, so just hit *Ctrl + S* to save the work item, or click on the **Save Work Item** button.

10. In **Team Explorer**, double-click on **Unfinished Work** under **Queries | Shared Queries | Current Spring**, which will now display the outstanding work items, as shown in the following screenshot:

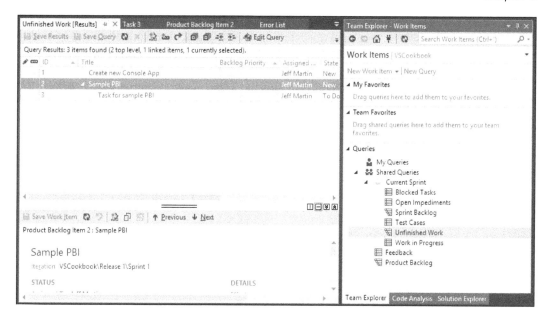

11. To start work, click on the **Task** that you created in step 9. Then change the state to **In Progress** and then click on **Save Work Item**.

Something to remember about the states under TFS

Depending on the configuration, states are typically changed in sequence. This means a newly created item cannot be changed directly to **Done**. Saving a work item after each state change will usually allow you to advance the choices for the state available.

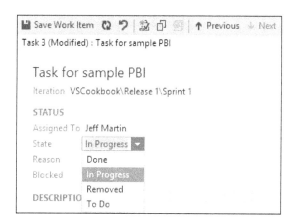

12. If you look at the **Work in Progress** query, this task will now show in the results.

13. Behind the scenes, the task will be moved to **In Progress**. Let's assume you did some useful work (simply making a quick edit to an existing source file, and so on) so that we can commit our changes to TFS.

14. Navigate to **Pending Changes** by clicking on the **Home** icon on the **Team Explorer** tab and clicking on the **Pending Changes** tile. (Also available under **View | Other Windows | Pending Changes**.)

15. To include this task with your commit, you can either drag it onto **Team Explorer** or you can add it by **ID** (both methods are highlighted in the following screenshot). Once a work item and changed source file(s) are associated, you will be able to enter a **Comment** and click on **Check In**:

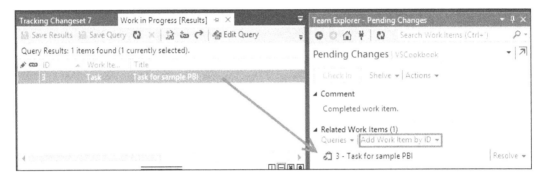

16. Visual Studio will prompt you when you click on **Check In**, as shown in the following screenshot of the dialog box, just click on **Yes**:

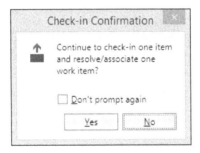

17. You can verify that the item is complete by refreshing your query. You will notice that your **Task** item is no longer seen, as it has been marked **Done** by TFS for you.

How it works...

The **Team Explorer** window provides an overview of the common tasks available for working with projects stored in TFS (whether it is locally hosted or part of VSO). **Pending Changes** keeps track of outstanding modifications made since the last commit. **Work Items** keeps track of the work items available in TFS with those marked **In Progress** appearing in the **Work in Progress** query.

You can check the details of a query by selecting the query, right-clicking on it, and selecting **Edit Query**. The task category doesn't need to be limited to just the **Task** work item type, but can also incorporate any custom work item types you include in the task category.

If you double-click on a work item in **Team Explorer** that isn't already opened, it is opened by default in the preview pane in Visual Studio to prevent window clutter.

There's more...

A couple more areas of Team Explorer are available for use to increase the effectiveness of the tool for your development work.

Using favorites

A key part to effectiveness using **Team Explorer** is creating and using queries. Making a copy of an existing query and editing it to suit your needs is a quick way to customize the tool. Whether you use custom queries or the standard ones, drag your frequently used queries into **My Favorites** or **Team Favorites**, as shown in the following screenshot. In the screenshot, the **Work in Progress** query has already been dragged to **My Favorites**, but the same customization is available for **Team Favorites** too.

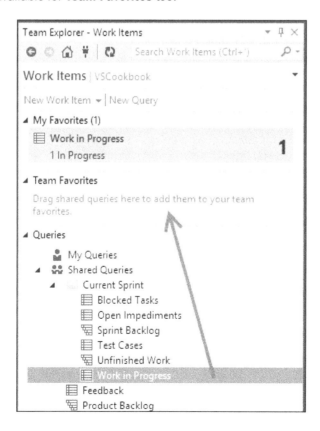

Shelving active work

Team Explorer generally encourages you to have only one logical task in progress at a time. This can help you limit the amount of work in progress you have and push you towards finishing a task completely before starting the next one. If you want to improve your personal productivity and work smarter, not harder, then this is a good practice to follow.

Unfortunately, if you plan to only work on one task at a time, then what happens when you need to pause what you are doing and deal with an emergency issue? If you have used previous versions of TFS, you may be familiar with the concept of shelving and unshelving code. Shelving takes a copy of the changes you have made, stores them on the server, and then optionally resets your local workspace. Unshelving is just the reverse of that. Shelving is available in all editions of VS2013. The Shelve menu is located on **Pending Changes** as shown in the following screenshot:

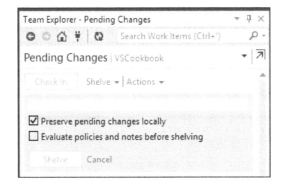

With Visual Studio Premium or higher, you also have the added ability to suspend work. This automatically shelves your current changes and the current state of your Visual Studio windows when you hit the button. It then resets your workspace, clears the work items that were in progress, and puts you back in a state ready to start another work item. To access this, click on **My Work**, expand **In Progress Work**, and then click on the **Suspend** button, as shown in the following screenshot:

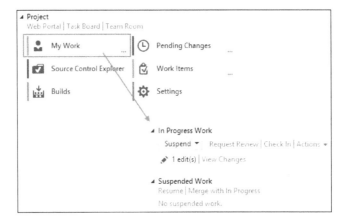

See also

- The *Using local workspaces for source control* recipe
- The *Performing code reviews* recipe

Using local workspaces for source control

One of the biggest complaints users have had with previous versions of TFS is the source control management system and the server-based workspace approach. With this approach, the server keeps track of what files it thinks you have on your development machine, and all of the check-in and check-out operations require communication with the server.

It makes offline work very difficult, and if ever there are changes on your development machine that the server isn't aware of, you may face problems during check-ins and "get latest" operations. To prevent this from happening, TFS sets the read-only flag on all files that are under source control, but this only frustrates developers more since they can't easily edit files unless they use a tool that knows how to communicate with TFS.

While there can be valid reasons to use the historical approach, it would be best if the tools fit your work patterns rather than adjusting your behavior to fit the tools. Local workspaces provide that exact flexibility. TFS is still the source of truth for source control, and it is the only place where check-ins can occur. However, the decision over which files have been changed now occurs on your development machine, not TFS. Further, Visual Studio no longer needs to ask TFS if it can open a file for editing or not. Also, you can use any program you want to edit files because the read-only flag is no longer applied to files. This change also improves the offline editing scenario and you no longer need to mess around with the "go offline" and "go online" operations.

In this recipe, we'll make some changes to the source code so that you can see how this newer approach to source control works.

Getting ready

As before, you will need to have access to TFS in order to follow this recipe. It would be best if you also had a sandbox team project—a project where you can try things and change data without worrying about it affecting your normal work.

Start Visual Studio 2013, connect to your team project, and you're ready to go.

How to do it...

Perform the following steps:

1. Create a new Visual Basic-based **Class Library** using the default name. Ensure that the **Add to source control** option is checked.

2. You may be prompted to choose a source control system; if so, select **Team Foundation Version Control**.

3. If you choose a local path for your project that is not already mapped to a folder in source control, you will be prompted for a location in TFS where it should be stored. Select a folder in your source control tree where you want to store the project and click on **OK**.

4. In **Team Explorer**, navigate to the **Pending Changes** tile. The files that will be added to source control are shown in the **Included Changes** section. Since this is a brand new project, all of the files are scheduled to be added. The following screenshot shows the list of files that will be part of our check in:

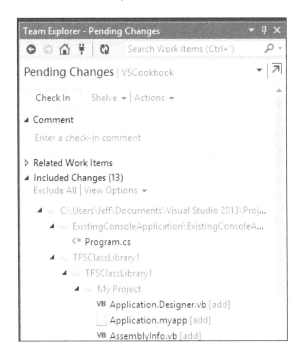

5. Enter a check-in **Comment** to describe what you are doing and then click on **Check In** to submit the changes to TFS, as shown in the following screenshot. If you are asked to confirm your check-in, click on **Yes**.

6. The files will be checked-in and a confirmation of the changes will be displayed in **Team Explorer**. If you wish to look at the contents of the changeset, you can click on the changeset number displayed in the notification, as shown in the following screenshot:

7. In **Solution Explorer**, right-click on the class library project and select **Open Folder in File Explorer**.

8. Right-click on `Class1.vb` and open the file with Notepad.

9. Add some comments to the body of the class (as shown below), save your changes, and then close Notepad.

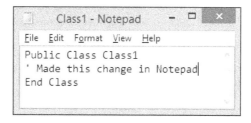

10. Switch back to Visual Studio and, if prompted to reload any files, select **Yes to All**.

11. In **Solution Explorer**, you should now see that `Class1.vb` has been modified (it will have a checkmark next to it). Navigate to **Team Explorer** and within that, go to the **Pending Changes** tile. You should now see that `Class1.vb` is listed as a pending change, as shown in the following screenshot:

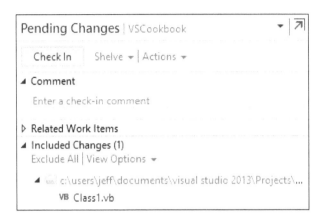

12. Switch back to **File Explorer** (formerly **Windows Explorer** in Windows 7) and make a copy of `Class1.vb`. Edit the file in Notepad and change the class name to `Class2`. Alter the comments in the body of the class to differentiate it further from the original before saving it and closing Notepad. Rename the copy to `Class2.vb`.

13. Switch back to Visual Studio and navigate to the **Team Explorer | Pending Changes** tile. The new file you just added won't be listed as an included change, but it has been detected as a change. Since it's not part of the solution, you will only see it by looking at the **Excluded Changes** section and clicking on the **Detected** link.

    Instead of including the file into source control directly, you'll want to add it to the solution properly. To do so, navigate to **Solution Explorer** and click on the **Show All Files** button on the toolbar.

14. Right-click on `Class2.vb` and click on **Include in Project**, as shown in the following screenshot:

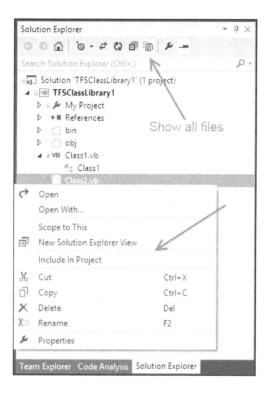

15. Navigate to **Team Explorer** and the **Pending Changes** tile again and confirm that the file is now included as a pending change. Add a check-in **Comment** and then click on **Check In** to reflect the changes. As you can see in the following screenshot, the file **Class2.vb** was detected and marked with **[add]** by Visual Studio:

16. In the preceding steps, we renamed the file before we committed it. Let's look at what happens if you use **Windows** (**File**) **Explorer** to rename a file outside of Visual Studio. Rename Class2.vb to a name of your choosing (our example will use FirstClass.vb).

17. Switch back to Visual Studio and navigate to the **Pending Changes** tile in **Team Explorer**. The rename isn't detected automatically since it wasn't made in Visual Studio. However, you may notice that there are two changes in the **Detected Changes** section (1 add, 1 delete), as shown in the following screenshot:

18. Click on the **Detected** link and you will see that the rename is detected as a **delete** of the old filename and an **add** of the new filename. You can let Visual Studio know that this change is actually a rename by selecting both changes (*Ctrl* click on each item) in the add/delete pair, right-clicking one and choosing the **Promote as Rename** option. If prompted to rename all instances of Class2, click on **Yes**. When this is done, just click on the **Cancel** button to close the **Promote Candidate Changes** window. The following is the screenshot of the **Promote Candidate Changes** window:

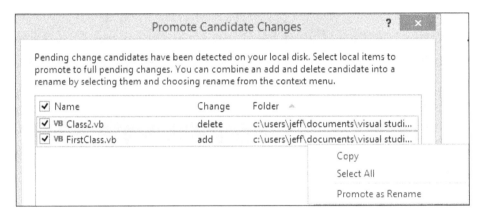

19. Not only is the rename now listed in the **Included Changes** section, but the solution file has also been updated to reflect the change and is also included as a pending change. The **Pending Changes** tile should now look similar to the following screenshot:

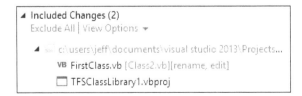

20. Check-in your changes when you are ready.

How it works...

When using a local workspace, Visual Studio creates a hidden local folder named $tf and stores zipped copies of the workspace version of your source files within it. Visual Studio detects changes by comparing the contents of your local files and folders to the contents of the $tf folder and adds any differences as pending changes.

 It might be an obvious warning, but don't delete the $tf folder or any of its contents, not even if you are short on disk space. Doing so will cause significant problems.

You might have noticed that at no time during the recipe did you need to change the read-only flag on any of the files, nor did you need to check-out any files for edit. In fact, the only time Visual Studio communicated with TFS was during the check-in process. All other changes were managed and tracked locally.

This should alleviate a lot of pain for people who have been used to older versions of TFS and the way server-tracked workspaces operated.

 You cannot check in when offline. Check-in operations are still server based and require that you be online and connected to TFS.

The detected changes list can grow quite large over time and you may want to ignore certain folders or files (for example, the /obj and /bin folders). You can either create .tfignore files to specify what files and paths to ignore, or in **Team Explorer**, you can open the list of detected changes and exclude files either individually, by extension, or by the folder path. Doing so will create or alter .tfignore files for you and add them to the pending changes list so that they can be checked-in and shared with all of the other developers on the team.

There's more...

Be aware that when using a local workspace, you will no longer have any real visibility on the server about who has checked-out a file. The exception to this is locking files. If you lock a file, the server is notified and can report that you have locked it.

Unshelving a shelveset now merges any shelveset changes with your local edits. Any conflicts between the shelveset and your local version will cause a merge conflict and you will need to resolve it in the normal manner.

See also

▸ The *Managing your work* recipe

Performing code reviews

When developing in a team, one of the more widely recommended practices for improving code quality and overall consistency is to conduct code reviews. Visual Studio 2013 combines with TFS to support the code review process and make it as efficient as possible.

In this recipe, you'll see just how this works.

Getting ready

You will need to have access to TFS in order to follow this recipe. It would be best if you use a sandbox team project. This is a project where you can try things and change data without worrying about it affecting your normal work.

You will also need to have two accounts you can use, one for the submitter of the code review and one for the reviewer. If you don't personally have two accounts, that's ok. Create a test account or get a colleague to act as your reviewer. Note that you should create this second account before beginning the recipe.

Start Visual Studio 2013 Premium or higher and connect to your team project using the submitter's account.

How to do it...

Perform a code review using the following steps:

1. Start a new C# **ASP.NET Web Application** project using the **MVC** template and add the solution to the source control (**Team Foundation**). Refer to the *Using local workspaces for source control* recipe if you're not sure how to do this.

2. Go to the **Pending Changes** tile in **Team Explorer** and check-in the code.

3. Open the `HomeController.cs` file under the `Controllers` folder, change the contents of the message text for `About()` and `Contact()`, and change the name of the `About` method to `AboutUs`.

4. Open the `Index.cshtml` view under the `Views\Home` folder and alter the text of the page to something you like. The **Pending Changes** tile should now look similar to the following screenshot:

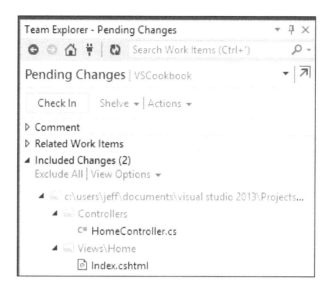

5. Click on the **Actions** drop-down menu and select **Request Review**, as shown in the following screenshot:

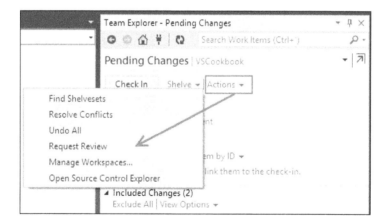

6. In the **New Code Review** pane, enter the name of your reviewer and press *Enter*. The reviewer should be the second user account you are using in this recipe, as mentioned in the *Getting ready* section. Add a subject for the code review and then click on **Submit Request**, as shown in the following screenshot:

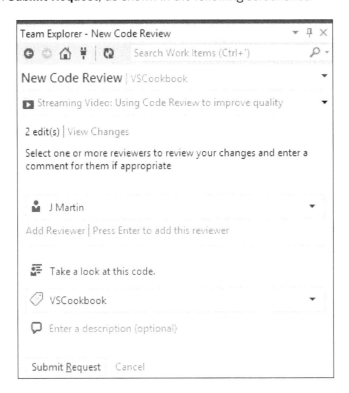

Team Explorer will then switch to the **My Work** display and show the code review request as an outgoing request, as shown in the following screenshot:

7. Switching to your reviewer user account, open Visual Studio and connect to Team Foundation Server.

8. In **Team Explorer**, open the **My Work** tile. You should see a code review request displayed. Note the arrow next to the review, indicating it is an incoming request for you to look at, as shown in the following screenshot:

9. Double-click on the code review task to begin the review process. **Team Explorer** will switch to the **Code Review** pane and display the details of the review and information on the files that have been modified, as shown in the following screenshot:

10. Click on **Accept** in the top section of the **Code Review** window to start the review process and dismiss the accept/reject message.

11. Click on the `HomeController.cs` file in the code review. You will see both the original and modified versions of the file displayed using Visual Studio's **diff** viewer, as shown in the following screenshot:

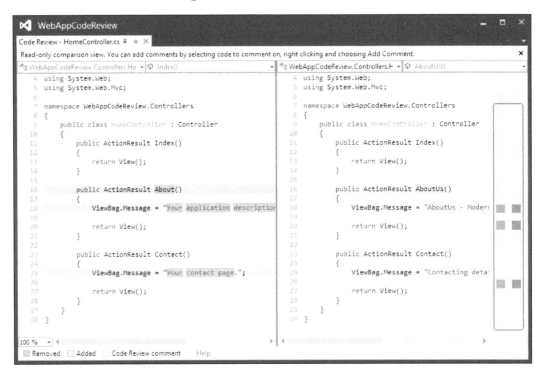

12. Select the entire **AboutUs** method from the right-hand pane, right-click on the selection, and then choose **Add Comment** from the context menu, as shown in the following screenshot:

13. The focus switches to the comment box in the **Code Review** pane. Enter a comment, as shown in the following screenshot, and then click on **Save** (*Ctrl + Enter*):

14. Click on the checkbox next to the `HomeController.cs` file in the **Code Review** pane to indicate that there are no further comments to make on that file.

15. Click on the **Add Overall Comment** link and supply a general comment on the code review, and then click on **Save** (*Ctrl + Enter*), as shown in the following screenshot:

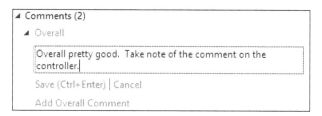

16. Make further comments on the review as you wish, and when you are done, click on the checkbox next to `Index.cshtml`. When you have entered all of the comments that you wish to make, click on the **Send & Finish** link, choosing the **With Comments** option from the dropdown that appears.

17. Switch back to the submitter's user account. In **Team Explorer**, go to the **My Work** tile and click on the refresh button (assuming you left Visual Studio running). Click on the arrow next to the review request to see the status of the review, and if the review is complete, double-click on it to display the **Code Review** hub.

18. Click on the `HomeController.cs` file in the **Code Review** hub and the diff viewer will be displayed, including highlights of where comments have been made by the reviewer.

19. As the submitter, you would then take action on the review comments as appropriate. For the purpose of this recipe, you're just going to close the code review. Click on the **Close Review** drop-down link and select **Complete** from the list of options to close the entire code review request.

How it works...

If you noticed, the code review occurred on code that wasn't even checked-in to the source control. Behind the scenes, asking for a code review automatically creates a shelveset for the reviewer to look at. Unlike the **Suspend & Shelve** operation, requesting a code review doesn't reset your workspace or clear any of the work items you have marked as **In Progress**.

You can also request reviews for changesets that have already been checked-in and other shelvesets that have been manually created.

See also

- The *Managing your work* recipe
- The *Using local workspaces for source control* recipe

Getting feedback from your users

When working on a product, one of the most valuable things you can do is get feedback from your users as to whether the software you have built meets their requirements or not, and what their opinions of it are. You will notice that in TFS terminology, the word "stakeholder" is used over "user"—representing the diverse sources of feedback that exist. Besides traditional users, several groups want their voice heard—including design, QA, and the product owner's funding development.

Even if you have a process that defines clear acceptance criteria for requirements, and you have a clear definition of what it means to be "done" with a piece of work, you still want feedback from these stakeholders to determine whether there are any other points that may have been missed when the requirement was first discussed, or if new ideas have occurred now that they have seen the software running.

A normal feedback process involves telling your users that the software is available and asking them to please go and try it and let you know what they think. The feedback you get can often be patchy, verbally reported, and hard to turn into actionable items for improving the software.

Let's take a look at how gathering feedback can be streamlined by using TFS.

Getting ready

Just make sure you have access to TFS and a team project. As before, we will be using Visual Studio Online for our demonstration screenshots.

How to do it...

Gather feedback from people by following these steps:

1. Go to the **Web Portal** site for your team project, and in the **Other Links** section of the home page, you should see a **Request feedback** link. Click on the link to start the feedback-gathering process, as shown in the following screenshot:

2. A dialog will appear asking you to fill in the information in three distinct sections. Section 1 is named **Select Stakeholders**, and you must enter the details of the people you want feedback from. They must be valid TFS users in order to be selected. For this recipe, enter your own account here, as shown in the following screenshot:

3. In section 2, supply the details of how users should access the application. This would typically be the details of a test site or application to install and run. For example, enter www.packtpub.com as the address of the web application/site.

4. In section 3, add details for the specific feedback you want from your users. Note that the **Add feedback item** link is available to add extra items for feedback, as shown in the following screenshot:

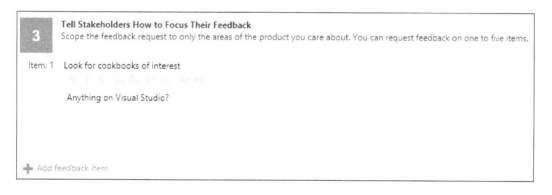

5. Click on the **Send** button to send the e-mail. You will receive a message similar to the one shown in the following screenshot:

VisualStudioOnline@microsoft.com   Sun, Dec 15 11:06 PM
to Jeff Martin
cc Jeff Martin

Jeff Martin is inviting you to provide feedback on team project VSCookbook

We want your feedback for the following items:

1. Look for cookbooks of interest

Start your feedback session

If the feedback tool is not already installed on your machine, install the feedback tool.

Thanks,
Jeff Martin

If clicking the "Start your feedback session" link fails to launch the feedback session, copy the following URL (mfbclients://███*.visualstudio.com/DefaultCollection/p:VSCookbook?rid=7) and paste it into a browser address bar to start the session.*

6. Because Visual Studio automatically installs the feedback client, you can just click on the **Start your feedback session** link in the e-mail. The **Feedback** client will then launch.

7. Click on the application link to launch the website and then click on the **Next** button in the feedback client.

8. The feedback client is now ready to accept feedback from the users, and the specific instructions you entered for the feedback session are shown to the recipient. The following screenshot shows our sample question to the reviewer, and provides a rich text editor. This allows the reviewer to clearly document their work and provide screenshots or other options:

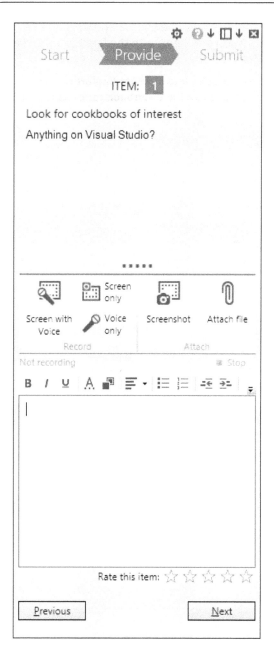

9. In the comment section, enter some text and then click on the **Screenshot** button. Select a section of the screen for your snapshot by dragging the mouse to create a rectangle. Notice that the screenshot you take is inserted wherever the cursor is in the comments box. Click on the **Next** button to continue.

10. A summary of the feedback will be shown, and you can rate each item using a five-star approach. If you are happy with the feedback you have provided, click on **Submit and Close** to complete the feedback session.

11. Switch back to Visual Studio, and in **Team Explorer**, navigate to the **Work Items** tile and double-click on the **Feedback** query to run it, as shown in the following screenshot:

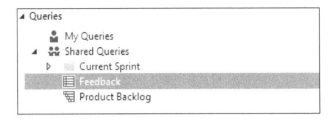

12. The query results will display all of the feedback responses received from your users. Select one of the items in the list to view the specific details of the feedback along with any images and attachments that may have been created by the feedback tool.

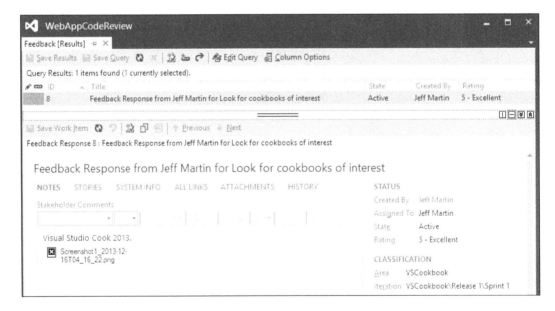

13. At this point, you can create new work items based on the feedback or close the items, just as you would for any other work item.

How it works...

Under the hood, all feedback requests are stored as work items in TFS. The feedback client adds all responses as child work items that are linked to the feedback request. If your users record feedback using audio or video, then that data will be included as an attachment to the work item so that you can replay it when you review the responses.

Using Git for source control

Git has become a popular choice for source control as an alternative to the classical centralized source control approach. Originating in the open source world for use in development of the Linux kernel, it has since spread in the software development world to be used on a variety of platforms.

While Git has been available for Windows as a standalone tool for several years, shortly after the release of Visual Studio 2012, Microsoft formally supported Git via the second update to VS2012. With Visual Studio 2013, Git support is built-in and readily available for use with your projects.

The basic concept of Git is that it takes the approach of decentralized source control. Rather than having a central server that serves as the sole repository, Git facilitates distributed repositories. In practice, this means that each developer can have a full copy of the repository on their local developer machine. Developers can perform their normal workflow of code editing, compiling, and debugging, all while committing code to their local repository. This promotes experimentation and makes it easier to roll back undesired changes.

When a developer considers their work to be complete for a particular feature or milestone, they can then, at this point, upload their code and associated development history to a remote Git repository as needed. This repository can be anything from a fellow developer to a designated corporate source control server. It also facilitates multi-platform development, as Git clients exist for Mac and Linux, so you can easily interact with developers on those platforms who will be using your familiar Visual Studio tools.

This recipe will show how Git can be used with your projects and be a useful tool even if you are a solo developer.

Getting ready

For this recipe, we will be using VS Express 2013 for Windows Desktop, but any of the premium editions may also be used. The concepts are applicable to any version of Visual Studio from Version 2012.2 or later.

How to do it...

Activate Git with the following steps:

1. We will begin by creating a new C#-based **Console Application**. The default name may be used, but before closing the New Project dialog box, be sure that the checkbox for **Add to source control** has been checked, as shown in the following screenshot:

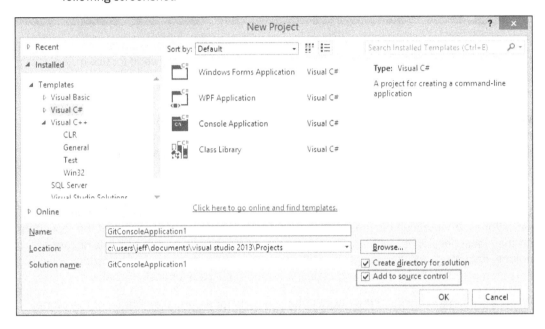

2. After clicking on **OK** on the **New Project** dialog box, Visual Studio will then prompt you to choose a source control system. Pick **Git**, as shown in the following screenshot, and click on the **OK** button:

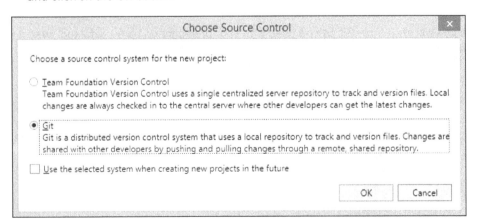

3. Visual Studio will now present you with the familiar main editing screen. If it is not already open, click on the **Team Explorer** tab. Alternatively, you may open it via **View | Team Explorer**.

4. Once **Team Explorer** is open, click on the **Settings** tile, as shown in the following screenshot:

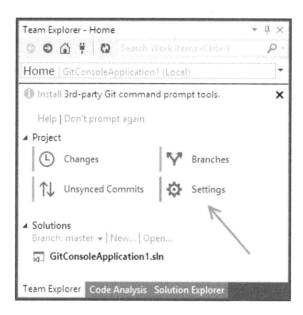

5. On the next screen that appears, click on the **Git Settings** link, as shown in the following screenshot:

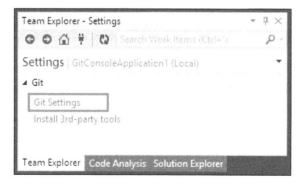

6. At this point, you will see the master settings page. Under **Global Settings**, you will need to enter a username and e-mail address. This information will identify your work and activities in every Git repository that you interact with. Complete these fields now in order to proceed with the recipe, and note that you can always change them later. Once they are entered, click on the **Update** button. The following screenshot illustrates all of these fields:

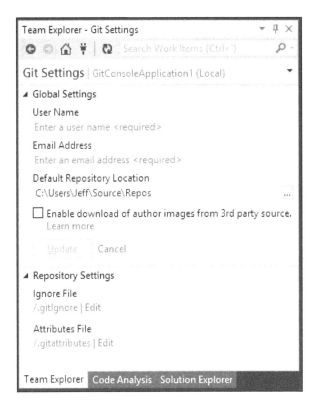

 Global Settings apply to every repository that you interact with. Besides the name and e-mail address, you will see that you can set the default location for where your Git repositories are stored on your machine.

Repository settings are specific to each repository and can be changed to suit specific needs. We won't change them now, but for future references, observe that this is where your .gitignore and .gitattributes files can be edited.

7. After entering your name and e-mail, you will return to the previous Git settings screen. Navigate back to the main **Team Explorer** page by clicking on the back arrow or home icon on the toolbar.

8. Now that the required settings have been configured, let's commit our initial project file. "Commit" is the term used in Git to describe the action of your recording changes to the repository. On the **Team Explorer** page, click on the **Changes** tile, which will open a screen, as shown in the following screenshot:

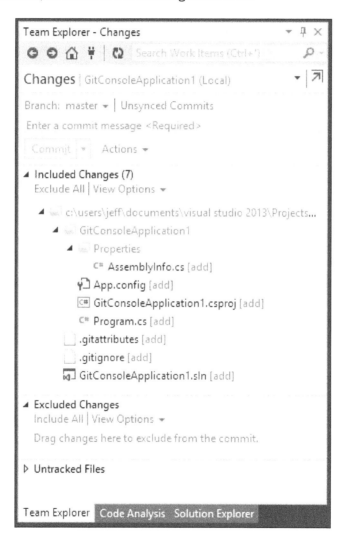

9. There is a lot of information being displayed, so let's look at each grouping. Starting from the top, you will see a text field requiring a description of what is about to be committed. Git convention is that the first line in the description is a summary of the commit, while any additional lines are used for greater detail about what is being commited.

   Included Changes is a list of all the files that will be committed. Since this is a brand new repository, all of the files are considered new to Git. The files' status is denoted with the text label **[add]** after each filename.

   Excluded Changes is a list of files that Git recognizes as having changed since the last commit, yet you do not want them to be entered into the repository.

   Untracked Files are files that Git recognizes as new since your last commit. Since we are about to make our first commit, there are no previous commits available for comparison.

10. Since the current defaults are desired, enter a commit message and click on the **Commit** button.

11. Visual Studio will indicate when the commit is complete with a brief notice and a portion of the commit ID. Every commit made to a Git repository is assigned a unique ID string generated by an SHA-1 hash. Rather than showing the full ID, Visual Studio displays a portion for easy reference. Click on the **Commit** link to see the details of our first commit, as shown in the following screenshot:

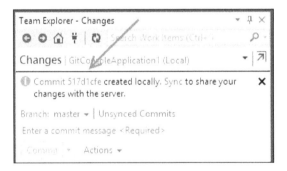

12. The **Commit Details** screen shows the pertinent information of the selected commit. As you will see in the following screenshot, it lists several details about the commit selected, such as the name and e-mail of the committer, date/timestamp, commit message, and the files added or modified:

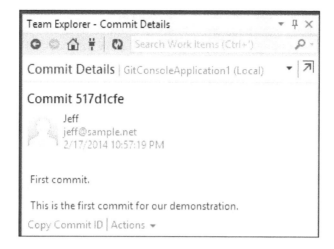

 Easy access to the full commit ID is provided by clicking on the **Copy Commit ID** link, which will copy the full SHA-1 hash to your system's clipboard.

13. The whole point of using source control is to track and manage changes to your source code, so let's make some. First, enter text of your choice into the `Main()` method of your project's C# file. Then, right-click on the project's name in **Solution Explorer** and add a new **Class**. The default name is fine.

14. As you make these changes, you may notice that Solution Explorer is updating to reflect the change in the file status. A green plus icon is appended to the `Class1.cs` file to indicate the status of pending add. Since we have created this new class in step 13 and after our first commit, Git realizes that it is new. A red checkmark is placed in front of `Program.cs` to indicate a pending edit, reflecting the text you added in step 13, as shown in the following screenshot:

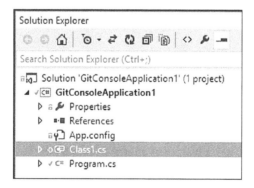

15. Let's now commit these changes to the repository. Click on **Team Explorer**. If it is still visible, click on the back arrow to enter a new commit. Notice in the following screenshot that **Changes** has updated to only show the modified files, a much shorter list than what we saw in step 8:

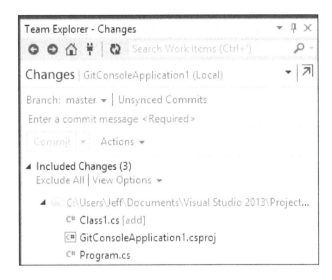

16. Enter a commit message and click on **Commit**.

17. After Visual Studio finishes the commit, click on the **Actions** drop-down menu and select **View History...**, as shown in the following screenshot:

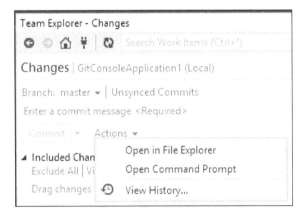

18. Visual Studio will show a history of all the commits that have been made to your project's repository. Notice that the first line of the commit message is shown along with the name of the developer who made the commit. The date/timestamp is displayed on the right-hand side. The red master icon indicates that this is the head for the branch named master as shown in the following screenshot:

 Head is a term used in Git to refer to the most recent commit that was made. In our simple repository, the changes have been linear. But in many production environments, commit history can get a bit more complex and this can be helpful in describing what's changed and how things have changed.

19. Double-clicking on either of these commit messages will provide more details about what the commit included. When the project is fresh in your mind, the details are easy to remember and the changes are obvious. When working with multiple contributors or when dealing with long-term projects, Git's organized recording of changes can make new development much easier.

How it works...

Git is an advanced piece of software that provides many powerful features in exchange for its complexity. It uses the SHA-1 algorithm to provide a checksum of the data header being committed. Using this algorithm provides accurate tracking while continuously ensuring the integrity of your repositories since discrepancies in checksums will alert you to inconsistencies. They also provide a unique way to identify each commit made.

There's more...

We have only scratched the surface of what Git can do and the value it can provide in your software development efforts. You can use these tools to clone (make a local copy) of a remote repository into your local development environment. For example, the Bootstrap framework described in *Chapter 3, Web Development – ASP.NET, HTML5, CSS, and JavaScript,* maintains its project files in a Git repository at `https://github.com/twbs/bootstrap`. This project is hosted on GitHub, which offers an alternative to TFS for code-sharing and team collaboration.

Git also has a multitude of features for branching and merging. Branching has many uses and is almost a necessity when supporting existing software. For example, you can create a development branch that lets you work on the next version of your application. Meanwhile, a release branch can be created, which represents the copy of your code that is in production. Exploring new concepts or making risky changes can be done in the development branch, allowing the release branch to remain in a bug-free, buildable state.

Since the Git tools in Visual Studio do not yet offer the full functionality of the command-line tools, an option has been provided to easily add them. As you may have noticed in steps 4 or 5, Visual Studio offers the ability to install third-party Git command prompt tools. These provide the full range of Git functionality on your local Windows machine. More information on the benefits of installing these tools is available in the article, *Work from the Git command prompt*, at `http://msdn.microsoft.com/en-us/library/dd286572(v=vs.120).aspx`.

See also

- Git has an extensive online manual available at `http://git-scm.com/`
- If you would like to use Git on your development machine, but still need to interact with external TFS severs, consider visiting `http://gittf.codeplex.com/` or `https://github.com/git-tfs/git-tfs`

9
Languages

In this chapter, we will cover:

- ▸ Fortifying JavaScript applications with TypeScript
- ▸ Integrating Python into Visual Studio
- ▸ Integrating Python with .NET

Introduction

Historically, Visual Studio focused on specific Microsoft-centric languages including C++, C#, and Visual Basic. Between the Internet, mobile devices, and the ever-increasingly rapid pace of change, new computer languages are being created in an effort to ease development and present new solutions to problems.

In this chapter, we will look at TypeScript, Python, and IronPython, a few languages that offer some unique capabilities when compared to the "traditional" languages offered in Visual Studio.

Fortifying JavaScript applications with TypeScript

JavaScript's role in web development has gone from being considered a starter language for hobbyist programmers to being regarded as a serious tool for building both client and server modern web applications. This change means that the size and scope of JavaScript applications has grown tremendously, and with that growth, the costs to manage the complexity have also increased. To address this, Microsoft has developed the open source project TypeScript, which is a superset of JavaScript that adds static type checking.

As of this writing, the TypeScript project has not released version 1.0. However, it is considered stable enough that Microsoft is using it for portions of Visual Studio Online and the Xbox Music service.

Visual Studio 2013 adds integrated support for TypeScript projects, and users of Visual Studio 2012 can add support with a free plugin (see `http://www.typescriptlang.org/`). Let's take a look at how TypeScript can benefit your web application.

Getting ready

For this specific example, we will be using Visual Studio 2013, but you should be able to follow along with Visual Studio 2012 if you install TypeScript support.

How to do it...

Let's perform the following steps to see how TypeScript can fortify your JavaScript applications:

1. Open Visual Studio 2013 and create a **HTML Application with TypeScript** type of project, as shown in the following screenshot:

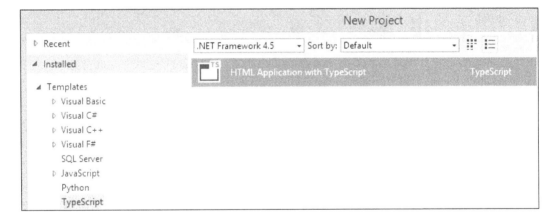

2. Accept the default project name and create the project.

3. The default project will open with a small sample that, when executed, will produce a web page that shows a simple clock. When you look at the source, it is pretty sparse, as shown in the following screenshot:

```
┌─────────────────────────────────────────────────────────────┐
│ ⟨e⟩        http://localhost:2161/ - Original Source  ─ □  ✕  │
├─────────────────────────────────────────────────────────────┤
│ File  Edit  Format                                          │
│  1  <!DOCTYPE html>                                          │
│  2                                                          │
│  3  <html lang="en">                                        │
│  4  <head>                                                  │
│  5      <meta charset="utf-8" />                            │
│  6      <title>TypeScript HTML App</title>                  │
│  7      <link rel="stylesheet" href="app.css" type="text/css" />│
│  8      <script src="app.js"></script>                     │
│  9  </head>                                                 │
│ 10  <body>                                                  │
│ 11      <h1>TypeScript HTML App</h1>                        │
│ 12                                                          │
│ 13      <div id="content"></div>                           │
│ 14  </body>                                                 │
│ 15  </html>                                                 │
└─────────────────────────────────────────────────────────────┘
```

4. If you notice, beyond some HTML, there is not much except for a reference to a file called `app.js`. Returning to Visual Studio, the most closely-related source file is `app.ts`. So where did the `app.js` file come from? Going back to our original explanation of TypeScript, remember that it is a superset of the JavaScript language. This means all valid JavaScript code is also valid TypeScript code. When TypeScript is compiled, JavaScript is generated. In this case, our file `app.ts` is compiled by Visual Studio to `app.js`. You can find the `app.js` file if you look inside your project folder. It is at the same location as your project's web config files.

How it works...

Since TypeScript ultimately compiles down to JavaScript, you may be wondering what the advantages of using it are. First, using TypeScript allows meaningful IntelliSense support. For example, examine the `app.ts` file that is part of our project. The following screenshot shows one of the available IntelliSense menus that can appear while editing:

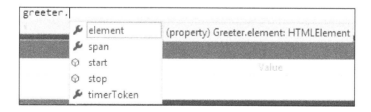

Second, TypeScript (as its name suggests) allows type checking. Consider the `greeter` class and how Visual Studio is able to help by comparing the differences, as shown in the following screenshot:

```
var greeter = new Greeter(el);
greeter.element = 10.00;

   Cannot convert 'number' to 'HTMLElement':
     Type 'Number' is missing property 'onmouseleave' from type 'HTMLElement'.
```

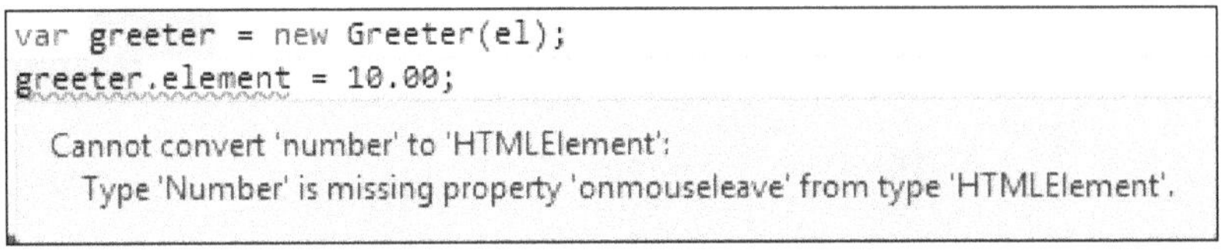

Since TypeScript is being used, Visual Studio detects an error with the assignment, as shown in the preceding screenshot. Conversely, in the JavaScript code (shown in the following screenshot), Visual Studio did not detect the error:

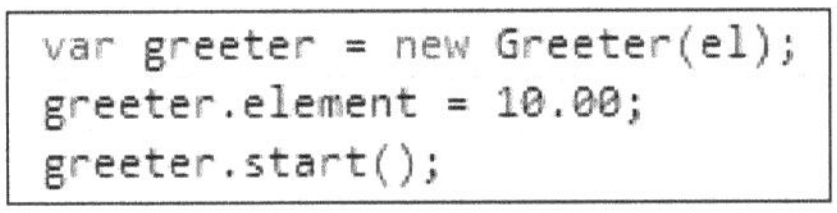

```
var greeter = new Greeter(el);
greeter.element = 10.00;
greeter.start();
```

This creates a bug that is easy to overlook. In smaller applications, the lack of type checking can usually be managed by the programmer. However, with larger applications, or unfamiliar code bases, it becomes much more difficult. Catching the error immediately saves debugging time later.

Visual Studio works with the TypeScript compiler (`tsc.exe`) to produce valid JavaScript that works on any browser or platform that supports JavaScript. This compatibility means you can use TypeScript in your projects without requiring your users to install something new. Since the nature of the TypeScript language is more specific than JavaScript, you can catch errors sooner and increase the power of IntelliSense. This allows you to keep the good parts of JavaScript (fast and powerful design capabilities) while increasing its safety and usability in large projects.

There's more...

You don't need to create a brand new project just to take advantage of TypeScript. It can be easily added to your existing web projects. From within an existing web project, add a new item (*Ctrl + Shift + A*), or right-click on your project name or directory within the **Solution Explorer** window, and select **TypeScript File**, as shown in the following screenshot:

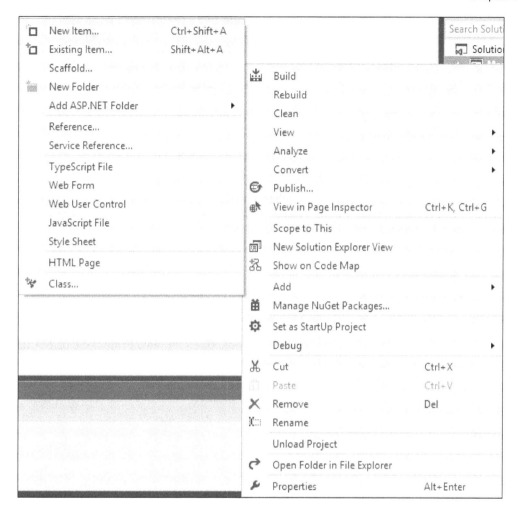

If you would like to try TypeScript but are wondering about all of the existing JavaScript code that would need to be converted, don't worry. Library types for many popular JavaScript projects, including Backbone.js, Node.js, and jQuery, are available at DefinitelyTyped (`https://github.com/borisyankov/DefinitelyTyped`).

Integrating Python into Visual Studio

Python was created by Guido van Rossum in the early 1990s and quickly developed a following among developers across the world. Python is a dynamic, general-purpose language well suited for all types of projects. Among its many features are support for multiple paradigms (object-oriented, functional, and so on.), a rapid development cycle (thanks to its interpretive nature), and its structured approach to syntax.

Microsoft has released **Python Tools for Visual Studio 2013** (**PTVS**) so that those of us on the Microsoft platform can easily try and use Python within Visual Studio. Whether you would like to just sample Python, or create a new application from the ground up, you will be able to do so while using the tools with which you are already familiar. In this recipe, we will see how Visual Studio can become a highly-tuned Python development environment.

Getting ready

For this recipe, you will want to download and install PTVS, which is located at `http://pytools.codeplex.com/`.

Next, you will want to install a version of Python for PTVS to work with. You can find the latest versions of Python at `http://python.org`. There, you will find the two main releases (as of this writing), 2.7.6 and 3.3.3. For this recipe, choose 3.3.3. The Python home page provides a good description of the difference between the two versions.

How to do it...

Once you have installed PTVS and Python, open Visual Studio and perform the following steps:

1. Let's take a look at the available project types. Open the **New Project** dialog box (*Ctrl + Shift + N*). Under **Templates** | **Python**, you will see several Python-based options, as shown in the following screenshot:

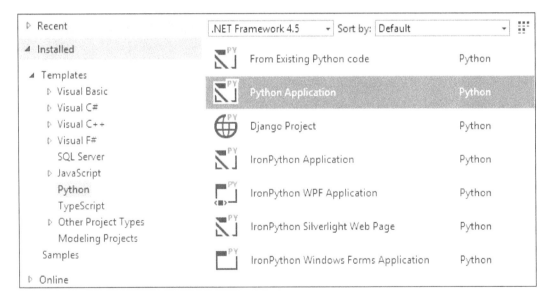

2. Create a new **Python Application**, as highlighted in the preceding screenshot, using the default name.

3. Once the project opens, you will see a friendly `Hello World` Python program. This can be executed the same way as any other Visual Studio project.

4. The first new IDE addition we will look at is the **Python Environments** window. This can be accessed through **View | Other Windows | Python Environments**.

5. This window is used to view the currently selected Python interpreter (in this case, **Python 3.3** is installed) and make changes to your overall Python environment. If you have multiple versions installed, you can set the default one, as shown in the following screenshot:

6. Another very helpful window is the interactive prompt. One of Python's strengths is **REPL (Read-Evaluate-Print-Loop)**. PTVS provides an easy way to access this from within Visual Studio. Activate this by navigating to **VIEW | Other Windows | Python 3.3 Interactive**.

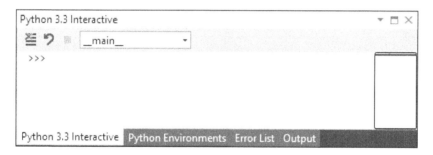

7. This window lets you enter the Python code directly, for immediate execution, as shown in the preceding screenshot. If you need to test a command or run a quick experiment, you can do so from within your editor. Also, because you are in VS2013, you get the navigation scroll bar, IntelliSense, and the ability to easily cut and paste results.

8. Add the following code to your original Python file:

```python
print('Hello World')
a=20
b=80
print("Results: " + (b+a))
```

9. Then, run the program. You will get a `TypeError`. One way to solve this is through the use of the **Interactive Window**. Highlight the added lines of code, right-click on them, and choose **Send to Interactive**, as shown in the following screenshot:

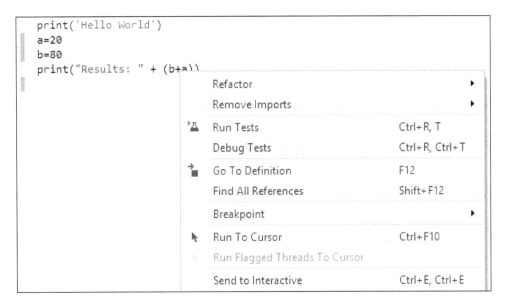

10. Once sent, the **Interactive Window** will rerun the code, and you will see the same error again. We can use this window to quickly work through solutions. With your cursor at the **>>>** prompt, just press the up arrow key to cycle through the program's lines. Edit the `print` line as follows:

```
print("Results: " + str(b+a))
```

 When you add the `str` type, your cursor will still be in the middle of the line, so be sure to get to the end of the statement before pressing *Enter*.

11. The correction will produce the following code:

```
>>> print("Results: " + str(b+a))
Results: 100
```

12. This solved the problem, so we can now add the `str` type to our file and continue with development.

How it works...

PTVS turns Visual Studio into a real, full-fledged, developing environment for Python. In conjunction with the Python interpreter, PTVS allows you to use Python in a familiar setting without needing to learn new tools.

There's more...

Since PTVS integrates the full Python language, covering all of the benefits it provides cannot be accomplished in a single recipe, or even in a single book. Some of the additional features that PTVS supports include integration with the test runner, profiling, and remote debugging. The previously mentioned Python Tools for Visual Studio's home page (`http://pytools.codeplex.com/`) is a great source of information.

Integrating Python with .NET

We've just explored how PTVS can easily integrate Python into VS2013. Now, Will now look at IronPython, which integrates Python with the .NET and Mono platforms.

IronPython provides the ability to write applications that use WPF and WinForms as well as easily call the .NET code from within your Python program. Whether you want to do some rapid prototyping or build a full application, IronPython can be a useful addition to your developer toolbox.

Getting ready

IronPython is available for download at `http://ironpython.codeplex.com/`. This recipe assumes you have installed PTVS as described in the *Integrating Python into Visual Studio* recipe.

How to do it...

Once you have installed IronPython, open Visual Studio 2013 and perform the following steps:

1. We are going to create new project using the **IronPython Windows Forms Application** template under **Python**.

2. The project will open with a Python listing in the editor window. This gives us an application skeleton that we can easily extend. Press *F5* to see what it looks like in its starting form.

3. We are now going to add some code to show a little bit more interactivity. Edit the `MyForm` class so that it matches with the following code:

```python
class MyForm(Form):
    def __init__(self):
        # Create child controls and initialize form
        self.Text="Iron Python"
        goButton = Button()
        goButton.Text = "Go"
        goButton.Click += self.goButtonPressed
        self.label = Label()
        self.label.Text = "Ready to go!"
        self.label.Location = Point(40,40)
        self.label.Height = 25
        self.label.Width = 200
        self.Controls.Add(goButton)
        self.Controls.Add(self.label)
        pass

    def goButtonPressed(self, sender, args):
        self.label.Text = "Go button pressed"
```

4. Once entered, view the results by running the application again (press *F5*). The result is shown in the following screenshot:

5. As mentioned in the introduction to this recipe, one of the advantages of this integration is the ability to rapidly prototype the .NET code. We will continue this recipe by showing how this can work with a C# DLL.

6. Right-click on the same project and create a new project by using the **Class Library** template under **Visual C#**. Keep the default name as `ClassLibrary1`.

7. Add the following method to your new class library:

```
public static int generate(int a, int b)
{
   Random rand = new Random((int)DateTime.Now.Ticks);
   return (rand.Next(a)+b);
}
```

8. Build the library through **Build | Build ClassLibrary1**. This will produce a class with a pseudo random number for our use. Now, we will update our Python to make use of it.

9. In the Python file, add the following highlighted line:

```
clr.AddReference('System.Drawing')
clr.AddReference('System.Windows.Forms')
clr.AddReferenceToFileAndPath(r"..\ClassLibrary1\bin\Debug\
    ClassLibrary1.dll")
```

10. Similarly, add the following highlighted `import` statement:

```
from System.Drawing import *
from System.Windows.Forms import *
from ClassLibrary1 import *
```

11. Change the method for the button press action, as shown in the following code:

```
def goButtonPressed(self, sender, args):
    classy = Class1()
    self.label.Text = "Random number received: " +
        str(classy.generate(10,4))
```

12. Run the application and click on the **Go** button. You should see something similar to the following screenshot:

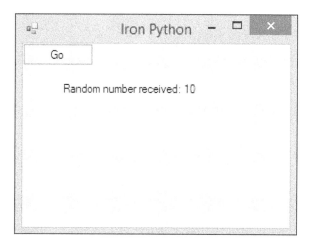

How it works...

By directly targeting the .NET and Mono runtimes, IronPython offers a different way to take advantage of Python. IronPython is able to do this as it runs on a **Dynamic Language Runtime** (**DLR**) that in turn runs on the CLR used by .NET languages. The conventional CPython interpreter (the Python environment that is the most widely used) is written in C and typically runs stand-alone.

In our example, we first demonstrated how IronPython lets you easily build a WinForms application. Then, we created a proof-on-concept C# library to show how the resulting DLL can be accessed from Python with very little cost. This gives you a lot of freedom, whether you want to add more functionalities to your Python-based programs or test the .NET code without needing to spend a lot of time writing routine setup code.

Visual Studio Medley

In this appendix, we will cover:

- Creating installer packages
- Submitting apps to the Windows Store
- Creating Visual Studio add-ins and extensions
- Creating your own snippets

Introduction

There are many little details that contribute to the success of a program. In this appendix, we will look at several different topics that don't fit into a specific category but remain useful and could be the missing ingredient your project needs. The first two recipes deal with some ways of getting your application ready for distribution to your end-users. The remaining two provide some ways to improve your productivity with the Visual Studio IDE.

Creating installer packages

The release of Visual Studio 2012 marked the removal of the popular **Visual Studio Installer** project type. Just like 2012, Visual Studio 2013 offers a version of the third-party **InstallShield**. In this case: **InstallShield Limited Edition**.

The need for an installer depends on the type of application you are working on. If you are creating a Windows Store app, then you don't need an installer, as the new deployment model makes installers obsolete. If you are creating a web application, then Microsoft would suggest you to either use the **XCopy** or the **MSDeploy** web deployment technology. When it comes to traditional desktop applications, you may want to use InstallShield. You can always fall back to using the **WiX** (**Windows Installer XML**) toolset (http://wixtoolset.org/) for creating projects.

In this recipe, we will use InstallShield to create an installer package for a simple application.

Getting ready

The recipe assumes you haven't yet installed InstallShield Limited Edition. If you have, then some of the early steps in this recipe will be different.

Simply start Visual Studio 2013 (Professional or higher), and you're ready to go.

How to do it...

Create an installer using the following steps:

1. Create a new **Visual C# | WPF Application** project and name it `Simple WPF Application`.

2. Go to the project properties page by right-clicking on the project in **Solution Explorer** and selecting **Properties**. In the **Application** tab, set the icon for the application to either an icon of your choice or the icon located at `C:\Program Files (x86)\Microsoft Visual Studio 12.0\Common7\IDE\ItemTemplates\CSharp\General\1033\Icon\Icon.ico`.

3. Build the solution to make sure it compiles properly. If you have already installed InstallShield Limited Edition, you can jump down to step 7.

4. Right-click on the solution and add a new project using the **Other Project Types | Setup and Deployment | Enable InstallShield Limited Edition** template.

5. A browser window will appear with instructions on how to enable InstallShield in Visual Studio 2013. Click on the link to redirect to the InstallShield website, register your details, and download the file as directed. When the download completes, save your solution, close Visual Studio 2013, and then run the InstallShield setup executable.

6. Restart Visual Studio 2013 and open the solution you created in Step 1.

7. Right-click on the solution in **Solution Explorer** and choose **Add | New Project...** from the context menu. In the **Add New Project** dialog, choose **Other Project Types | Setup and Deployment | InstallShield Limited Edition Project**, give it the default name, and then click on **OK**.

8. If this is the first time you have used InstallShield after installation, you will be asked whether you wish to evaluate the software or register it. Choose to register and activate the product using the serial number you should have received in your e-mail.

9. The InstallShield **project assistant** will appear in the document window, as shown in the following screenshot:

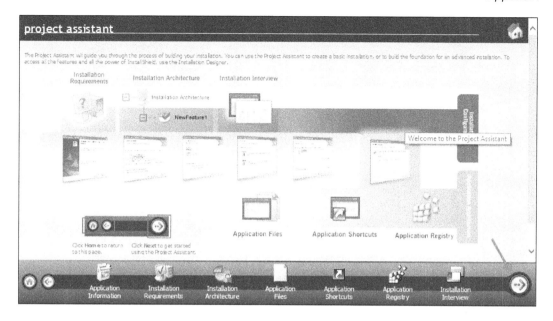

10. Click on the right arrow (the "next" button) at the bottom of the **project assistant** window to advance to the **Application Information** page. Enter a company web address, such as www.company.com.

11. Advance through the project assistant until you get to the **Application Files** page. Select the **My Product Name** node from the tree and then click on **Add Project Outputs**, as shown in the following screenshot:

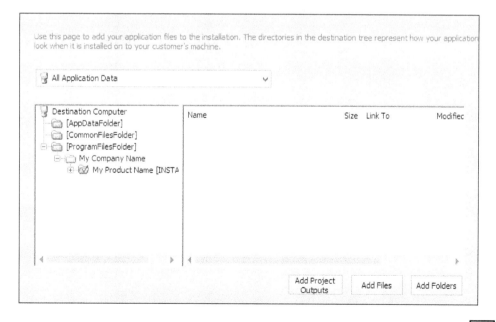

12. In the **Visual Studio Output Selector** dialog, select the **Primary output** item and click on **OK**.

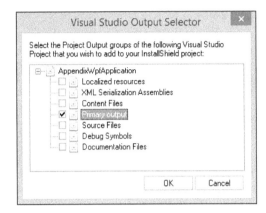

13. Click on the next button to go to the **Application Shortcuts** page. Click on the **New...** button to add a shortcut to your application. Choose **[Program FilesFolder] | My Company Name | My Product Name | Simple WPF Application.Primary output** from the dialog and click on **Open**.

14. The shortcut is named **Built** by default. That's not very useful, so click on the shortcut name to edit it and rename it to `Simple WPF Application`.

15. Right-click on the **Setup1** project in **Solution Explorer** and select **Install** from the menu. If prompted to build out-of-date projects, click on **Yes**.

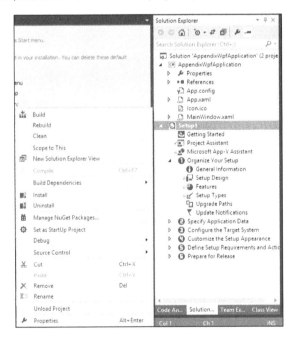

16. Follow the steps through the setup wizard to install the program. Verify that the program is installed correctly by looking for the application in your Start menu or Start page, as shown in the following screenshot:

17. Remove the program from your system by right-clicking on the **Setup1** project (from within Visual Studio) and selecting **Uninstall**.

How it works...

InstallShield reduces the complexity of creating installers by providing a set of sensible default configuration options and an easy-to-use user interface. It also understands exactly how the Windows installer system works and warns when there are problems in how you have configured the installation process. For example, if you recall the warning outputs from the *Creating installer packages* recipe when the package was built, you would have seen a warning about the .NET Framework and how it would be a good idea if this framework was included with the setup kit to ensure people who don't have .NET already installed won't have extra setup dependencies.

A license for the limited edition is provided free of charge with Visual Studio 2013 and will be sufficient for basic installation purposes. If you need a heavily-customized installation process, then you should investigate the more advanced versions of InstallShield, or competing offerings such as **Nullsoft Scriptable Install System** (**NSIS**), or the previously mentioned WiX.

See also

▸ Microsoft has developed **ClickOnce**, which can also be used to deploy Windows-based applications. More information is available at `http://msdn.microsoft.com/en-us/library/t71a733d.aspx`.

▸ Developers writing applications in C++ should also review the ClickOnce information at `http://msdn.microsoft.com/en-us/library/ms235287.aspx`.

▸ Nullsoft Scriptable Install System (NSIS): `http://nsis.sourceforge.net/Main_Page`.

Submitting apps to the Windows Store

While existing legacy desktop style applications can be distributed using the traditional methods (as described in the *Creating installer packages* recipe), the only way to distribute Windows Store apps will be via the Windows Store, and they must pass a certification process for that to happen.

Certification is the process by which Microsoft ensures that apps available in the Windows Store will meet certain performance and quality standards. As a developer, the Store makes it easy for customers to obtain and install your app. In this recipe, we'll look at how the certification process works. Since apps for Windows 8 can only be maintained at this point, we'll focus on creating a new app for Windows 8.1.

Getting ready

To start, you will need either VS Express for Windows or one of the premium editions of Visual Studio 2013 and Windows 8.1.

How to do it...

Perform the following steps:

1. Start a new project by navigating to **Visual C# | Windows Store | Blank App (XAML)**.

2. From the menu, navigate to **Project | Store** and select **Open Developer Account...**.

> A **Developer Account** is different from a **Developer License**. The account is used to publish apps to the Windows Store. The license is used on your local computer for testing and developing apps. Microsoft has recently modified the Developer Account so that the same account can be used for both Windows Store apps and Windows Phone development.

3. A browser window will open and you can apply for a developer account using the process as outlined on the page. Windows Store accounts may require a payment of a small license fee, so have a credit card handy when you perform this step.

4. Once you have an account, switch back to Visual Studio, and from the menu, choose **Project | Store | Reserve app name...**.

5. Again, a browser window will open, and you will be directed to the Windows Store to register the name for your application. Follow the process as described on that page.

6. From the Visual Studio menu, select **Project | Store | Edit App Manifest** and use the information from the app name reservation to populate the appropriate fields. Take particular note of the fields on the packaging tab.

7. Alternatively, you can select the **Project | Store | Associate App with the Store...** menu entry and follow the steps of the wizard to automatically populate the packaging tab with the appropriate values. This option will let you choose from a reserved app name as well as reserve a new name if needed.

8. At this point, you are ready to write your application.

 Current Microsoft guidelines will allow an app name to be reserved for a year. If your app is not submitted by this deadline, the reservation will expire.

9. Verify your application using the **Windows App Certification Kit**. Refer to the *Validating your Windows Store app* recipe in *Chapter 2, Getting Started with Windows Store Applications*, to do this.

10. Package your application for uploading to the Store by choosing **Project | Store | Create App Packages...**.

11. Next, upload the resulting package to the store by selecting **Project | Store | Upload App Packages...** from the menu and following the steps presented in the ensuing upload wizard.

12. Once the upload completes, you can monitor the progress of your package through the approval process using the tools provided by the Store.

How it works...

The Store submenu is only available when running Visual Studio in Windows 8 and when you have opened the solution for a Windows Store app. When you upload a package to the store, there are a number of basic sanity checks to verify if your package is acceptable and meets the requirements of the Windows Store. These checks include running the certification toolkit on your app and verifying the manifest information against the information you supplied when you registered the app name. Using Visual Studio's Associate app with the Store wizard is an easy way to make sure you don't have any typographical errors in your manifest. It also improves the chances of a successful first-time submission.

There's more...

Earning money with Windows Store apps is not limited solely to upfront purchase revenues. You may also distribute your app using a trial mode that encourages a try-before-you-buy approach. Apps may include the ability to support in-app purchases and in-app advertising using your choice of ad platforms, and it may implement a custom transaction system if you so desire.

 For in-app purchases and trial versions of your product, Microsoft bundles supporting functionality in the `Windows.ApplicationModel.Store` namespace to make it easier for you to build applications with these features. A sample app is available using these features here: `http://code.msdn.microsoft.com/windowsapps/Licensing-API-Sample-19712f1a`

If you want to confirm what the requirements are for App certification, refer to the Microsoft documentation on the subject at `http://msdn.microsoft.com/en-us/library/windows/apps/hh694083.aspx`.

Sideloading

The Windows Store makes public distribution of applications very easy, but certain line-of-business or custom apps will not want to take this approach. **Sideloading** is the process by which developers can bypass Store restrictions and avoid public distribution for the corporate/enterprise market. For information on this approach, refer to `http://technet.microsoft.com/en-us/library/hh852635.aspx`.

See also

▶ The *Packaging your Windows Store app* recipe in *Chapter 2, Getting Started with Windows Store Applications*

▶ The *Validating your Windows Store app* recipe in *Chapter 2, Getting Started with Windows Store Applications*

Creating Visual Studio add-ins and extensions

When Microsoft released Visual Studio 2010, they changed the approach to extensibility by introducing the VSIX format. The number of extensions in the Visual Studio gallery is a testament to how successful this change has been.

So, what do you do if you want to make your own add-ins and extensions in Visual Studio? This recipe will walk you through that process, though the magic that happens inside the add-in or extension is up to you.

Getting ready

To create extensions, you will need the Visual Studio 2013 SDK (`http://www.microsoft.com/en-us/download/details.aspx?id=40758`) and the Professional or higher version of Visual Studio, which you can download from Microsoft.

Once the SDK is installed, start Visual Studio 2013 and you're ready to go.

How to do it...

Perform the following steps:

1. Start a new project by navigating to **Other Project Types | Extensibility | Visual Studio Add-in** and the default name.

2. The **Add-in Wizard** will be launched. Click on **Next** on the first page.

3. Choose the language you want to develop in. For the recipe, choose **Create an Add-in using Visual C#** and click on **Next**.

4. Click on **Next** to choose the default **Application Host** (which will default to **Microsoft Visual Studio 2013**).

5. Provide a name and description for the add-in if you are feeling creative, otherwise just click on **Next**.

6. Click on **Next** to use the defaults for the add-in options, click on **Next** again to skip **'Help About' Information**, and finally click on **Finish**. The wizard will generate an application skeleton including all of the references necessary for building Visual Studio 2013 add-ins. At this point, you can add the details of your add-in, but for this recipe, we will continue without it.

7. Pressing *F5* will start a new instance of Visual Studio in the debug mode (it may take a while to start) where you can use the add-in manager (**Tools | Add-in Manager...**) to enable your add-in and check its functionality. For this recipe, leave the add-in as it is.

8. Add a new project to your solution by right-clicking on the solution in the **Solution Explorer** and add a new project using the **Editor Viewport Adornment** template by navigating to **Visual C# | Extensibility**, leaving the name as the default. If this option isn't available, check if you have installed the Visual Studio SDK correctly.

 The VSIX file is not in the same location as the template used in step 1. You will find the VSIX in `AppendixVSAddin1\ViewportAdornment1\source.extension.vsixmanifest`, while the add-in project file is located in `AppendixVSAddin1\AppendixVSAddin1\` if you are using the default names.

9. Open the `source.extension.vsixmanifest` file and populate the **Author** field with your name.

10. Set the new extension project as the default startup project (by right-clicking on the project in the **Solution Explorer** and clicking on **Set as StartUp Project**) and press *F5* to start debugging. A new instance of Visual Studio will be launched using the experimental hive. The experimental hive is a separate set of Visual Studio settings you can use when testing extensions that won't affect your normal development settings. (You will notice that you are prompted to set your settings, just as you did the first time you launched Visual Studio 2013 after installing it.)

 Because a debugger is attached, starting the experimental instance of Visual Studio may take longer than you are used to. It will have **Experimental Instance** in the title bar to help distinguish it from your regular instance of Visual Studio.

11. When Visual Studio has finished loading, it will automatically instantiate the extension, making it active and available. From the Visual Studio menu, select **File | New | File…**, then select **General | Text File** and click on **Open**. You should see a purple box at the top-right corner of the editor surface, as shown in the following screenshot, proving that the extension is working as expected.

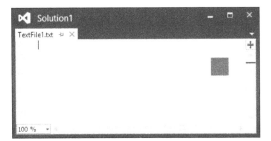

12. Close the experimental instance of Visual Studio.

How it works...

There's a big difference between add-ins and extensions in Visual Studio. Add-ins are the old way of extending Visual Studio and are fairly complex to build, whereas **Extensions** are the preferred approach from Visual Studio 2010 onwards and are much easier to implement.

An add-in needs to implement an extensibility interface, and while this means your add-in can work with Visual Studio versions prior to 2010, it is limited to functionality exposed by the DTE interfaces, and as a developer you need to deal with a number of COM interfaces. An extension, on the other hand, needs to implement a **Managed Extensibility Framework** (**MEF**) contract and is not restricted in the API's it can access or in the way it is implemented.

There's more...

There is a lot more flexibility in building extensions over add-ins and this also applies to the update and distribution mechanism. However, if you really need to get to the internals of Visual Studio, or if you need to support Visual Studio 2008 or earlier, then you will need to look at the add-in approach.

The **Extension Manager** complements the NuGet package system described in the *Managing packages with NuGet* recipe in *Chapter 4, .NET Framework 4.5.1 Development*. The difference is that Extension Manager focuses on enhancements to Visual Studio, while NuGet is used to obtain libraries that you will be distributing with your application.

 When you complete the recipe, if you want to remove every trace of your add-in from Visual Studio remove the `.addin` file from `Documents\Visual Studio 2013\Addins`.

Creating your own snippets

Visual Studio snippets are a great way to quickly write repetitive chunks of code using the same basic structure and can save you a lot of time and typing. Snippets have been extended to work on more than just standard code files, and should be considered whenever you find yourself writing similar code over and over. Using snippets can save time and reduce the possibility of bugs: write the code correctly once and then re-use.

For example, you may want to generate a class signature that inherits from a specific base class you use in your application, or you may have a certain attribute that needs to be placed above method calls to enable logging, or you may have specific IDs you want to use in HTML elements to ensure CSS styles can be consistently applied to your web pages. Unfortunately, out of the box Visual Studio still doesn't have a built-in way of authoring snippets. Therefore, you will need to write some XML. Fortunately, it only takes a few minutes to create a snippet, and the time you can save once it exists makes it worth doing.

This recipe will show you how to create your own snippets and make them available inside Visual Studio.

Getting ready

Simply start Visual Studio 2013 and you're ready to go.

How to do it...

Create your own snippet using the following steps:

1. From the menu, choose **File** | **New** | **File...**, select **XML File**, and click on **Open**.

2. Populate the file using the following XML code:

```xml
<?xml version="1.0" encoding="utf-8"?>
<CodeSnippets
xmlns="http://schemas.microsoft.com/VisualStudio/2005/
CodeSnippet">
  <CodeSnippet Format="1.0.0.">
    <Header>
      <Title>Wrap text in a span</Title>
      <Shortcut>spanned</Shortcut>
      <SnippetTypes>
        <SnippetType>Expansion</SnippetType>
        <SnippetType>SurroundsWith</SnippetType>
      </SnippetTypes>
    </Header>
    <Snippet>
      <Declarations>
        <Literal>
          <ID>id</ID>
          <Default>elementId</Default>
```

```
      </Literal>
    </Declarations>
    <Code Language="HTML">
      <![CDATA[<span id="$id$">$selected$</span> is now in a
span!]]>
    </Code>
  </Snippet>
 </CodeSnippet>
</CodeSnippets>
```

3. Save the file as `spanned text.snippet` in your `Documents` folder.

4. From the menu, select **Tools | Code Snippets Manager...**. The shortcut is *Ctrl + K*, *Ctrl + B*.

 If you are using Virtual Studio Express for Windows and cannot locate the **Code Snippets Manager...** on your menu, enable **Expert Settings** via **Tools | Settings | Expert Settings**.

5. Click on the **Import...** button. Select the file you saved in step 3 and click on **OK**.

6. Leave the location as **My HTML Snippets**, as suggested, and click on **Finish**. The snippet file will automatically be copied to the appropriate location in `Documents\Visual Studio 2013\Code Snippets`.

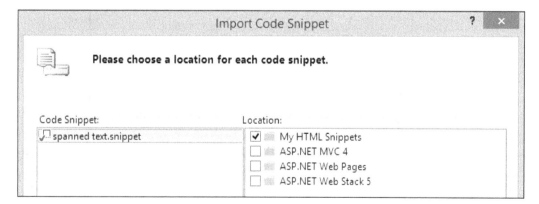

7. In the **Code Snippets Manager**, change the **Language** to **HTML** and expand the **My HTML Snippets** location, as seen in the following screenshot, to confirm your snippet has been loaded. After confirming this, click on **OK** to close the dialog.

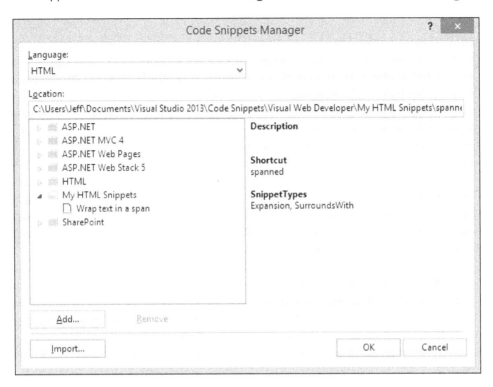

8. From the menu, select **File | New | File...**, then select **General | HTML Page**, and click on **Open**.

9. In the content of the `body` tag, enter `<p>this is some text</p>`.

10. Select the words `is some`, right-click on the selection, choose **Surround With...**, then **My HTML Snippets | Wrap text in a span**, and hit *Enter*.

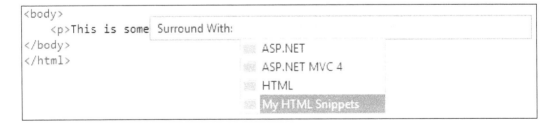

11. The snippet will be expanded and the contents of the `id` attribute for the span will be selected. Enter the text `myId` to replace the highlighted `elementId` placeholder and hit *Enter*. The cursor will move to the end of the closing `span` tag.

How it works...

The `Header` section is where the display title of the snippet is given, a shortcut name (in this case `spanned`), a human-friendly description, and what type of snippet is being defined. Our example is in the `Expansion` and `SurroundsWith` categories. This means our snippet can be used with the selected text (`SurroundsWith`) or at the cursor's current position in the editor (`Expansion`).

The `Snippet` section is where the bulk of the work is done. Visual Studio automatically scanned the code body of the snippet for an identifier placeholder of `$id$` so that it could populate it with the default value and prompt you for your own value.

By declaring the snippet as a `SurroundsWith` snippet, the selected text is passed to the `$selected$` placeholder in the body. Since `Expansion` is also supported, if you enter the snippet on a blank line, Visual Studio will still just generate the following text:

```
<span id="elementId"></span> is now in a span!
```

There's more...

There is a **Snippet Designer** project on CodePlex (`http://snippetdesigner.codeplex.com/`) that offers a GUI tool to make creating snippets much easier. It also enables you to select a section of code and export that as a snippet so that you have an easy starting point for making your own custom snippets.

Remember that snippets are more than just a simple text entry/replacement mechanism, and it's worth spending a little time looking through the full schema reference for snippets on MSDN at `http://msdn.microsoft.com/en-us/library/ms171418(v=vs.120).aspx` to get a better idea of what they can do for you.

Index

Thank you for buying
Visual Studio 2013 Cookbook

About Packt Publishing

Packt, pronounced 'packed', published its first book "*Mastering phpMyAdmin for Effective MySQL Management*" in April 2004 and subsequently continued to specialize in publishing highly focused books on specific technologies and solutions.

Our books and publications share the experiences of your fellow IT professionals in adapting and customizing today's systems, applications, and frameworks. Our solution-based books give you the knowledge and power to customize the software and technologies you're using to get the job done. Packt books are more specific and less general than the IT books you have seen in the past. Our unique business model allows us to bring you more focused information, giving you more of what you need to know, and less of what you don't.

Packt is a modern, yet unique publishing company, which focuses on producing quality, cutting-edge books for communities of developers, administrators, and newbies alike. For more information, please visit our website: www.PacktPub.com.

About Packt Enterprise

In 2010, Packt launched two new brands, Packt Enterprise and Packt Open Source, in order to continue its focus on specialization. This book is part of the Packt Enterprise brand, home to books published on enterprise software – software created by major vendors, including (but not limited to) IBM, Microsoft and Oracle, often for use in other corporations. Its titles will offer information relevant to a range of users of this software, including administrators, developers, architects, and end users.

Writing for Packt

We welcome all inquiries from people who are interested in authoring. Book proposals should be sent to author@packtpub.com. If your book idea is still at an early stage and you would like to discuss it first before writing a formal book proposal, contact us; one of our commissioning editors will get in touch with you.

We're not just looking for published authors; if you have strong technical skills but no writing experience, our experienced editors can help you develop a writing career, or simply get some additional reward for your expertise.

Visual Studio 2012 Cookbook

ISBN: 978-1-84968-652-5   Paperback: 272 pages

50 simple but incredibly effective recipes to immediately get you working with the exciting features of Visual Studio 2012

1. Take advantage of all of the new features of Visual Studio 2012, no matter what your programming language specialty is!

2. Get to grips with Windows 8 Store App development, .NET 4.5, asynchronous coding and new team development changes.

3. A concise and practical First Look Cookbook to immediately get you coding with Visual Studio 2012.

Visual Studio 2013 and .NET 4.5 Expert Cookbook

ISBN: 978-1-84968-972-4   Paperback: 400 pages

Over 40 recipes for successfully mixing the powerful capabilities of Visual Studio 2013 with .NET 4.5

1. Provides step-by-step instructions, helping you to learn the various components and technologies of .NET development with Visual Studio 2013.

2. Filled with examples that clearly illustrate how to integrate with the technologies and frameworks of your choice.

3. Helps you keep pace with the fast growing IT industry and gain expertise on upcoming technologies, common forms of debugging and software testing.

Please check **www.PacktPub.com** for information on our titles

**Software Testing using
Visual Studio 2012**

Software Testing using Visual Studio 2012

ISBN: 978-1-84968-954-0   Paperback: 444 pages

Learn different testing techniques and features of Visual Studio 2012 with detailed explanations and real-time samples

1. Using Test Manager and managing test cases and test scenarios.

2. Exploratory testing using Visual Studio 2012.

3. Learn unit testing features and coded user interface testing.

4. Advancement in web performance testing and recording of user scenarios.

**Reporting with Visual Studio
and Crystal Reports**

Reporting with Visual Studio and Crystal Reports

ISBN: 978-1-78217-802-6   Paperback: 148 pages

Create a reporting application from scratch using Visual Studio and Crystal Reports

1. A step-by-step guide that goes beyond theory, letting you get hands-on experience.

2. Utilize a dataset and table adapter as data sources for your report.

3. Learn how to add reports to forms and pass parameters dynamically.

Please check **www.PacktPub.com** for information on our titles

www.ingramcontent.com/pod-product-compliance
Lightning Source LLC
Chambersburg PA
CBHW062102050326
40690CB00016B/3173